10.00

TRAILS OF THE TROUBADOURS

Lo, the Sweet Troubadour

TRAILS OF THE TROUBADOURS

BY

RAIMON DE LOI

ILLUSTRATED BY

GIOVANNI PETRINA

KENNIKAT PRESS
Port Washington, N. Y./London

TRAILS OF THE TROUBADOURS   1 - 21 - 75

First published in 1927
Reissued in 1970 by Kennikat Press
Library of Congress Catalog Card No: 78-102837
SBN 8046-0752-4

Manufactured by Taylor Publishing Company   Dallas, Texas

CONTENTS

[v]

CONTENTS

[vi]

ILLUSTRATIONS

Chapter I

Lo, the Sweet Troubadour

Chapter I

1

I⊤ is a heavy white road that leads to Carpentras, a road blanketed with the rich odor of newly pressed grapes, the acrid smell of dust, of sun-baked tomatoes, of dried grass, and, in spots, with the tonic perfume of cooling cedars. As noon passes, the heaps of tomatoes piled outside the doors of sheds take on a richer red, the dark green of the cedars turns black, and the road becomes cadaverous.

As we toiled up this road we were suddenly arrested by the square Tour d'Orange which, silhouetted against a green sky, towered above the city walls like the upraised arm of a policeman. A startled wind rustled the leaves of a neighboring fig-tree. An over-ripe fruit splashed to the ground. The Lady-Who-Married-Me took my arm and whispered

"Let's wait a bit . . . I'm afraid I'm tired . . . I'm afraid . . ."

We leaned on our sticks in the dusty road and waited.

A gust of wind blew through the Porte d'Orange and down the white road, raising the dust in our faces. The inhospitable spirits were leaving. Then the arched mouth of the tower lighted up, and in that casual fashion which indicates that one housewife after the other is thinking about supper for her husband, small lights began laughing in the windows above the city walls.

We proceeded up the hill.

This was the land of the troubadours, and along the trails we were following had passed many a prince and poet, and poet-prince, and princely poet who was frequently more powerful than the master he nominally served. It stretched south to the Mediterranean, west to the Atlantic, and northwest to the sometime seat of many an English king—Tours and Le Mans.

We had read of the troubadours in the volumes of German scholars who thought they were contributing to that poor thing called human knowledge, and we had read the songs of the troubadours—the first love-songs in western Europe—buried now in gaily illuminated manuscripts; and we had said:

"Where they wandered, let us wander; where they loved, let us love; where they sang, let us sing. Let us get into direct contact with the mystic earth that bore them. Let us feel with our hands the rough stones of the towers from which they threatened to throw themselves and penetrate the secret portals which still open inward on lovely gardens where they entered to find happiness or, in some cases, death."

We trod trails in southern France that few tourists have ever trod, and we saw cities that few tourists have ever seen. "Ah, yes," said our host in one village, "we have frequent tourists. Two weeks ago a party from Marseilles stopped for lunch; a month ago some students came through on foot."

The records of the troubadours' lives have been preserved, not only in the songs they made about themselves —they were surprisingly lacking in reticence for men as desperate as they pretended to be—but also in the gossip about them, doubtless elaborated by the fertile brains of their rivals and enemies.

From these records we know which castles the troubadours liked to visit, and by translating the names of the castles into their modern equivalents it is possible to reconstruct with reasonable accuracy the itineraries they followed northward to London and Paris and eastward to Rome and Jerusalem.

The cities they visited were not suburban villages but were built for eternity, and until eternity they will stand unless torn down to make way for modern factories. This, however, is improbable. Modern industry has turned away from most of these cities whose battlements still stand resisting now the attacks of time as they resisted then the attacks of armies. Streets that were once so thronged with courtiers and men-at-arms "that you would have thought the walls would have burst with the crush" are now traversed at infrequent intervals by the turgid ox bearing a burden of fire-wood. The large and spacious chambers of gracious ladies whose beauty was perhaps greater than their discretion are now populated by a cock and his harem of peaceful hens. The audience-chamber of a proud prince is now the home of a meditative ass.

For those of us who get a cynical satisfaction in comparing our civilization with the civilizations of others this is fortunate. The ass and the hens are far less destructive than their more passionate predecessors, and so long as the ruins of Les Baux—now fortunately protected from demolition by the government—and Bollène and many another village we shall pass presently are occupied by these, they will be preserved. Nor is it entirely a matter for regret that perfect automobile roads have replaced the ancient trails. The ancient roads, though interesting enough to us, were for the people who used them very bad roads. Indeed one cannot regret the passing at a ripe old age of a civilization like that of the troubadours. It did its share for us and left more than one mark on our habits of thought. The only thing one can regret is that its monuments are so slightly known to the modern world which passes through the troubadour country year after year on its way to the Riviera.

Most of these tourists are peacefully asleep when they reach the land of the troubadours in the London-Nice Express. They will breakfast in Marseilles and take dinner on the Boulevard des Anglais in Nice. Some of these tourists are happier asleep and happier leading an English life among English people in a blessedly un-English climate than they would be awake and wandering with the poets. Others, however, are cheated of many a pleasant side-trip by guide-books which, attempting to present all the information about a country, present no information because the essential facts are buried in a mass of details.

To segregate some of these essential facts about the Middle Ages and to arrange them as a series of trips through central France by car, on foot, by cycle, or with a donkey, to follow, in these trips, the footsteps of famous men who made them almost a thousand years ago, is the purpose of these chapters.

I shall not trouble the reader with large blocks of historical information or descriptions of churches or works of art. Information and description of this kind are available elsewhere. I shall rather go with him as he follows the trail of this or that poet or prince, gossiping with him as the poet or prince would have gossiped. But because he may want to know what kind of people these troubadours were, I shall attempt a very brief reconstruction of the spirit of the people we shall meet. Then I shall follow the portions of the trail that were made most vivid by Bernard de Ventadour, Richard the Lion-Heart, Bertrand de Born, Jaufre Rudel, and Raimon de Miravel, by Petrarch and Peire Vidal. Many of the cities they passed were already a thousand years old when they first entered them. These greater antiquities will not distract, for they may be found listed elsewhere for the use of the conscientious tourist.

All of these trails were the roads of the Middle Ages and lead as all roads led then, to Marseilles, the last important stop on the way to Rome, the center of the medieval world.

2

The color of life in the Middle Ages was a deep, glaring, and unmitigated red. Life was fast; life was hard; life was for youth and lived with such energy and enthusiasm that whatever was done of good or bad was done with an

[7]

absolute intensity. Richard the Lion-Heart, a writer of indifferent poems but a great patron of poets—particularly those who wrote poems in his honor—was dead when he was forty-one; before he was eighteen he had conquered a kingdom. At an age when our modern youth are being persuaded that virtue is its own reward, the medieval youth were proving that the essence of virtue is a strong arm, agile wit, and a cynically realistic conviction that the battle is, after all, to the swift, the strong, the sure. When they were not making war or playing at politics, they were playing at love or making poems; and they made love and poetry with the same ardor and ruthlessness that they displayed in the taking of cities and the killing of enemies.

Most of the evil they did has died with them, but the fruits of their slight leisure, their poetry, and their philosophy—both a kind of game picturing a make-believe world—have survived.

We of modern times frequently confuse the game with the candle. Because medieval wars were conducted on a small scale, we think they were of small importance to the men who were killed in them; because medieval poetry was very brilliant, we use it to cast a false light on medieval manners. Galahad is a literary myth created by a popular novelist of the thirteenth century writing for medieval flappers. But because love and poetry were games, do not assume that they were frivolous pastimes. Time in those golden days was money and was created to be spent to good advantage. The troubadours worked hard at their play; they played hard at their work.

A particular group of fashionable young men who frequented the courts in and about Marseilles, Toulouse, and Tours were called troubadours. They fashioned for us two arts: the art of lyric poetry and the art of love, which they referred to as the "gay science." Although there had been lyric poetry before the troubadours, it had never been raised to the perfection to which they raised it. Although there had been arts of love before the troubadours, they metamorphosed those arts and gave them the forms in which love is practised to-day.

In modern times the art of love has fallen into a decay. Women are, I suppose, still beautiful, and passion is still a fluid force in the spirits of men; but in the affectation of a scientific interest in emotions we are apt to affect a superiority to the emotions we are analyzing. Whereas men in the twelfth century affected to be more moved by love than they could possibly have been, men of the twentieth century affect to be less moved than we know in fact that they actually are.

But despite our ingenuous affectation of dispassionateness, the medieval theory of love has become a real part of our being. It is on record that men, even in modern times, have compared the women they loved to all the flowers of the botanical dictionary, that they have insisted that these women were superior in wisdom to the wise women of the past, present, and future. Many of us still believe that the maiden should be coy and the lover despairing, although we know that lovers are more often despairing because maidens are not coy enough. The lover's humility which makes him the slave of the beloved, and his arrogance which makes him her defender, which we now consider the instinctive equipment of every civilized man, were formulated by the troubadours of the tenth to the thirteenth centuries.

These precepts are contained in exquisite poems, in lengthy philosophical dissertations on love, and in allegories. The philosophical dissertation on love has, in modern times, become a psychological monograph on immorality; for the allegory we no longer have sufficient intellectual industry; but the lyric poem remains now as it was then, a source of delight. For the troubadours sang of love in the springtime, of the passions and despairs of lovers, of the beauty and cruelty of women, themes which still retain for us an enduring interest.

The strangely artificial relation which existed between the despairing lover and the charming lady, and between the charming lady and her heavy husband to whom she had been married for reasons of state, was soon regulated by a legal code. What this code was has been reported in many documents, but with particular charm in one called "The Art of Honest Loving" by Andreas, a chaplain. In general, the lover must be true to the king and queen of love; he must fast for love every other day; and he must stir up others to love.

In particular he must be discreet and secret, for true love is always clandestine. When the poet writes to his mistress he must refer to her under an assumed name. This name ultimately became an open secret in the court, yet it was considered bad form to address a lady with absolute frankness.

The lover must be constant to one lady; he must be

patient with her moods; he must be meek and afraid of being over-bold; he must be conscious of his inferiority to his mistress; he must think of nothing unpleasant for her sake; he must be thoughtful to please her; he must think no evil of her; he must keep his person and his dress neat and clean for her sake; and finally, he must defend her honor and reputation at all costs. The observance of this rule led to innumerable difficulties. Frequently the ladies had no honor, which, as in the case of Loba de Perrautier, led to tragedy.

To these may be added several other customs. The lover was supposed to wander alone musing on his lady; he was supposed to be sleepless when she was cruel, to dream of enjoying her love, to be wretched in her absence, to be a master of the language of love and the signs of lovers, and to maintain his interest in love even when he had grown old.

Only knights, clerks, and ladies of gentle birth were citizens of the kingdom of love. These citizens were urged to love one another but, with peculiar naïveté, were prohibited from marrying each other. The authors are unanimous that love between husband and wife is impossible. "Though husband and wife be both citizens of the kingdom of love, they are citizens of different counties, and between these counties there is constant strife, and each must be faithful to serve the lord and mistress of his particular county who are also the vassals of the Lord of Love."

One of the subtleties of the gay science is illustrated in a story about Lancelot. Lancelot was on his way to rescue Guinevere. Guinevere was a lady of questionable reputation who had the habit of getting kidnapped and always wanted rescuers. One biographer suspects her of being a shape-shifter who appeared during the day as a lady but could also assume the form of a snake. At a ford, Lancelot became engaged with an evil knight of the region (all knights who were your enemies were then, as they are to-day, evil knights) and lost his horse. He faced the problem of transporting himself for some distance clad in several tons of armor. A peasant with a cart gave him a lift, but when he appeared before his lady in this ignoble position she refused to receive him. This adventure was, for the Middle Ages, as much a social problem as the "Doll's House" is for us. What is a lady to do when her knight presents himself in that way? How can one accept the love of a knight who does things as impossible as riding in a peasant's cart? Indeed could a modern lady love a man who eats with his knife, who is seen with vulgar companions, who is for good reason or bad transported to her house in a butcher's cart?

But these were refinements.

Thus, my friends, if you should ask seriously, why the trails of the troubadours, I should answer you just as seriously, therefore the trails of the troubadours: because these men were sophisticated, subtle, and perverse, because the color of their life was red, and, above all, because they had a youth and a love of living which they imparted to the songs they sang and the trails they followed.

These trails led, as you shall see if you turn the next page, through the land of a virile race, a race which was destroyed by a great international war.

3

If you will step over to the moon and look up to see the earth, a huge globe swinging above your head, you may be able to distinguish that part occupied by nations which, ten years ago, engaged in a great military struggle. They will seem remarkably small and close together. You may wonder why nations whose domains were separated only by imaginary lines should have found it necessary to murder each other.

When we look back through a distance of a thousand years to southern France we see a similar picture. Southern France was divided into duchies, kingdoms, and principalities as Europe is divided into kingdoms and republics; then as now the countries were separated by imaginary lines and divided by jealousy. It was ruled by a large number of barons, each baron surrounded by a gay and warlike court whose business it was to protect the baron's land and to kill the baron's enemies. Days of peace were treasured because they were infrequent. The arts of peace were treasured both because they were exquisite and because they were in pleasant contrast to the usual business of life. A society which is engaged in affairs as grim as the affairs of the Middle Ages devotes its playtime to intense relaxation. The fever in the blood of these men effervesced in difficult, charming, and complicated poetry.

The barons and their courts lived in fortified castles on hills surrounded by moats and capped by towers so arranged as to afford protection against attack. Knighthood was, at the beginning of the period we are wandering through, in

[13]

high flower, although a very different flower from the picture of it presented in the stories of the Round Table and the Holy Grail. The knights were not really sensitive courteous gentlemen who devoted their lives to the rescue of kidnapped maidens or the defense of a lady's honor. Too frequently they were responsible for the kidnapping of the maidens whom they robbed of all honor. The work of the troubadours has overcast the morals of the knights of old with a glamour which they do not in any sense deserve.

The ladies of the castle had their first taste of marriage while very young. They were frequently betrothed at the mature age of two, married in the ripe middle age of eight or nine, and expected to undertake the administration of a castle when senile decay had set in—at the age of fourteen. The husband was very heavy and exercised absolute rights. He could confine his wife to her room for years; he could chastise her with a rod, starve her, humiliate her in a thousand ways, even make her a servant to his mistress. He could dispose of her whenever he pleased. As the fathers of the church had not yet decided whether women had souls, the rights of women were somewhat hypothetical; and although they were probably accorded greater freedom in fact than they could claim by law, they were, in a very real sense, the vassals of their husbands. Under these conditions it is not surprising that the dreams of adolescent girls should have turned to young squires of the court who said exquisite things exquisitely; or that they should have been delighted to hear poems addressed to themselves in which they, rather than their husbands, were represented as all powerful. Nor is it surprising that these girls should have found means to betray their husbands, who were after all busy men engaged in the administration of a kingdom.

A reading of the work of the earliest troubadours shows that the poems were written not for the men of the Middle Ages but for the women; and the society described by the troubadours when they were serious is not society as it was but society as they wished it might be. The tradition of the self-sacrificing melancholy lover which has dominated lyric poetry for the last thousand years is an effeminate tradition based on the aspirations of unhappily married medieval ladies.

The troubadours were a comparatively small corporation of very fashionable young men. They were, for the most part, men of gentle birth. If of low birth, they were awarded, after they had attained position as a troubadour, the rights and privileges of gentlemen. Richard the Lion-Heart was king of England. His grandfather, William IX of Poitiers—said to have been the earliest troubadour—was both a poet and duke. And the hundred others, William de Foix, Bernard de Ventadour, Raymond V of Toulouse, and the rest, were all men of great power.

But the social position of the troubadour is not entirely explained by the statement that he is a man of gentle birth with the talent for writing poetry who chooses love as his theme and writes to please the ladies of the court. He performed another service which made him very valuable to the society which he graced.

The troubadour was the publicity agent for the court in which he lived. Please remember that there were in those days no newspapers for the dissemination of scandal and gossip and no political paragraphers who celebrated the virtues of politicians. Yet as commerce and industry began to flourish and life became more and more complicated the shrewd barons of the south of France found it necessary to devise means whereby they could attract to their courts a better kind of fighting-man, make alliances with more powerful neighbors, and tell the world of the power of their swords as well as of the beauty of their wives. They found the troubadours useful in solving this problem.

A lady distinguished a troubadour from among many other more powerful courtiers because she realized that his songs about her beauty would attract to her court many powerful nobles. Her husband, being a medieval gentleman, suffered from the old-fashioned vice of jealousy but was complaisant because he realized that the presence at his court of many powerful nobles made him formidable to his enemies. Further he kept a sharp eye on the activities of his wife, and if she betrayed him he had the right to kill both her and her lover. This sometimes happened. Occasionally the troubadour mistook the passion he feigned for a passion which he really felt; and in one instance, he actually attempted to marry the lady who was the subject of his verse.

This was very wrong. For in the polite society of those days it was well enough for gentlemen to write songs praising the beauty of women above all other things; but a gentleman should realize that the writing of poetry to a lady was very different from making that lady his wife. He might make her either his real or his ideal mistress; but if she were his wife their positions would be reversed and she would be by law and custom his slave.

The people of the Middle Ages have been misrepresented by romantic critics. Because we knew little about them, we were led to assume that they knew little about anything; because most of them could not write, we have been led to assume that they could not think or that their thought was simple and childish. Because they lived in manor-houses we have been convinced that they had what we would call good manners. Because some of them loved God, we have assumed that they hated the flesh and the devil.

As a matter of fact these assumptions are all erroneous. The people of the Middle Ages were wise beyond their years and ours, and because their thinking was frequently as direct as a child's it had moments of shattering lucidity. Although they lived in manor-houses, were the lords of the universe, and had their own rigid system of etiquette, that system was not our system. They blew their noses on their sleeves, ate with their knives and fingers, spat on the floor, slept without pajamas, spoke in loud voices, killed without mercy, were lacking in what we like to call a sense of proper decency, and in general behaved in a manner which would shock a Billingsgate fishwife. Some of them did fear God; most of them loved beautiful women.

4

The troubadours were, as I have pointed out, a special group in the social organization of the Middle Ages. During the two hundred years through which they flourished

(1050–1250) they founded and developed a tradition of writing and loving which when taken over by Dante and Petrarch became part of the literary code of all succeeding generations. This tradition has influenced the work of all writers of love poems, even the writers of popular ballads in the music-halls of the present time.

Their home was the south of France, which at that time was the center of elegance. They wandered from court to court praising the ladies, disseminating gossip, and carrying out the complicated work of free-lance journalist, advertising agent, ambassador, and warrior. Most of them became acquainted at some time in their careers with the English kings whose residences were in the cities of Aquitania now known as Touraine. From here the trails led in two directions. The great military highway went southeast to Lyons and south along the Rhone to Marseilles. The poets' road went south to Toulouse and thence east to Marseilles. The two routes inclosed a large part of France which when fully explored should yield treasure. But for the present I shall confine myself to the highways and shall follow particularly those portions which were made vital by Bernard de Ventadour, Richard the Lion-Heart, and others of the gilded youth.

Chapter II

The Trail of a Troubadour Queen

PARIS TO POITIERS

Chapter II

1

THERE are trails and trails. When one sits in the café in the *place* after a long hike, with the tiredness slipping sweetly down into one's feet, watching a well groomed woman trying by subtle wiles to keep her son's attention from the much rouged *petite femme* who is on the make, one says, "To-morrow, it may be, I shall walk through the fields beside the river, and I shall arrive, in the afternoon, when the sun is right, at the clean little city of Blois." One says it calmly, with peace in one's heart, knowing that by all the laws of probability one *will* arrive and that the sun *will* be right. But there is another kind of a trail, equally sweet. It is the trail one follows when one says: "By St. Anthony of Padua, I shall leave this town of Tours. It is filled with *jeunes filles anglaises* and *vieilles filles américaines*, and char-à-bancs, and guides, and nobody here does as his ancestors did, and the Tourainians make of their great past a monkey on a string which they exhibit to ignorant strangers. By St. Anthony, the patron of honest tramps, I shall leave this place; I like not the laughter of the English, nor the voices of the Americans, nor the stench of the char-à-bancs, nor the itching palms of the guides, nor the meretricious inhabitants of this city. I shall leave tonight, and to-morrow I shall watch the lizards crawling over the wall at Poitiers, and I shall talk with the patron of my café in the evening about those strange people who, having a home, leave it to wander over the face of the earth, for, 'Think you, monsieur, one is never comfortable save *chez soi.*' ". And realizing that the impossible *place* at Poitiers is made tolerable only because night has thrown over it a blanket which hides its glaring and rather cheap modernity, one will agree. The trail of anger and the trail of contentment are normal and natural, and one can understand them. But who can understand or justify the trip taken by Eleanor, queen of the troubadours, when, big with the child of her lover, she fled, after a hurried divorce, the court of her husband, King Louis VII of France, by night marches and in disguise to reach the capital of her own kingdom, Poitiers the proud, there to meet that lover, Henry, duke of Anjou, the only man in Europe strong enough to hold her?

In her career Eleanor had two husbands, and both had infirmities: the first, King Louis of France, had an ingrowing conscience; the second, King Henry of England—he was Henry of Anjou when she married him—had an ingrowing toe-nail. The man with the conscience was beyond his age and never quite understood it; the man of the toe-nail was of his time, he reveled in it, he rode on the wave of it; he was, by all standards of all ages, a strong man. For years he never knew defeat, in war, in intrigue, or in passion. His lands were the broadest and his scepter the most powerful that Europe had seen in five hundred years. Yet Eleanor broke him in the end as she had broken Louis of France in the beginning. She lived to see him robbed of his lands and his power, robbed even of his clothes and his jewels, lowered into a grave at Fontevrault, his huge body covered inadequately by the petticoat of a charitable prostitute.

2

In the year of grace 1926 thousands of people traveled from Paris to Poitiers via Orleans, Blois, and Tours and looked with more or less indifferent eye on a country which is now much the same as it was a thousand years ago. If these people thought at all, one knows well what they thought. They thought that nature was wonderful, or the reverse; and they thought that the hotels, the roads, the sky, the food, were good or bad or dirty; and they placed a good Anglo-Saxon curse or benediction upon each of these in turn. Whatever they thought was fairly obvious, and what Eleanor of Aquitaine, their illustrious precursor, thought, was probably just as obvious but very different. The trails which Eleanor, the queen of the troubadours, followed over the face of the green earth are devious, and the trails which her mind followed are more devious still; wherever she went there were loud laughter and song and intrigue and heartbreak; wherever she went there was a crowd of exquisites, of poets, of gentlemen, of knights, of strong men, of hangers-on. She was a whirlwind, and no man now can tell what she thought when she traveled from

Paris to Poitiers in 1152 or why she thought it; but of this you shall hear more in a moment.

Her grandfather, William IX, puissant duke of Aquitaine and first of the troubadours, arranged that on the day Eleanor married Louis, the young heir apparent to the throne of France, she should bring him a dowry of lands twice as large as his kingdom; William arranged further that the control of these lands should remain forever in her hands and in the hands of the issue of her body; and God arranged that on her marriage day her father-in-law should die so that this the first of the husbands of Eleanor might seem to be favored above all other men. When Eleanor's grandfather had arranged these things to his satisfaction and had seen that the marriage ceremony was properly performed—Eleanor was a chit of a thing fifteen years old and her husband a youngster of eighteen—he formally abdicated in her favor: and when she had received homage from the lords of a country stretching between Tours and Toulouse, he slipped into a pilgrim's coat and followed the trail to Compostella, where he died in a rocky cave.

Who knows of what that young thing was thinking when she was married in great state in the cathedral of St.-André at Bordeaux or to whom she was speaking when she was caught in the crush at the great door of the cathedral? The priests chanted and Louis followed the service with pious and contrite heart while Eleanor gazed boldly over the company. Thibaut the poet, count of Blois, was there, and the count of Champagne. Suger, the cleric and her husband's best friend, acted as the official representative of the king of France. Who else? Ebles II of Ventadour was, no doubt, of the company, with, perhaps, Bernard, the poet, in his train; and all the poets and troubadours between Bordeaux and Béziers must have participated in the festivals, the courts of love, and the gossip for which this great company was the occasion.

She is a gifted youngster, that Eleanor who will be your companion from Paris to Poitiers. She is supposed to have been beautiful, but no one can tell at this distance of time. The testimony of poets is worthless, for poets are notoriously liars, and besides, Eleanor was generous and understood the value of a good poet or two in her train. She was a poet herself; and by right of inheritance—her grandfather William of Aquitaine was the earliest of the troubadours— and by right of a bitter tongue, a passionate temperament, and a shrewd intelligence she was recognized as the critic and arbiter of the poetry of her time. Her good word was worth a fortune, and her epigram could ruin a career. The testimony of her lovers means nothing; for he who loved Eleanor could gain by her favor the right to hold any land he had been strong enough to win; and if he won her hand . . . remember she was a great heiress. And those other lovers, those whom she had no intention of marrying, what of them? But none could resist her. What she wanted she took. Yet in the end Louis preferred dishonorable poverty to her gay company, and Henry finally shut her up in a tower for safe-keeping. But this testimony cannot be denied, the universal testimony that she could both read and write. This was an accomplishment possessed by few people, either men or women, of that age. A few of the poets were able to read poetry and to compose it but were unable to write it down in black and white. Many of the great ones, the self-made men who had begun as poor but honest inferiors and had left their poverty, honesty, and inferiority—even as men of another time—far behind them, regarded higher education as somewhat effeminate. They knew what was what and when need arose could hire a learned clerk for a few pounds a year. Eleanor, however, was a learned and an accomplished lady; not the heiress of lands and power only, but the heiress of much of the wisdom and culture of her time.

The Bastard of Champagne was at her wedding with Louis, and so too, according to tradition, was her younger sister Petronilla, and Raoul, count of Vermandois. Now how Petronilla, a girl of fourteen, should have seduced the princely Raoul and forced him to divorce his wife, and why the count of Champagne, who was brother-in-law to the divorced wife, should have made the pope annul the divorce, or why Petronilla, the sweet young thing, should have thought that this annulment increased her dishonor and should have caused Eleanor to become the enemy of Thibaut of Blois, I cannot say. Things like this had happened before, and I suppose they may have happened since. Eleanor's enmity was effective, and she persuaded her husband to engage in a new war. Therefore, several years later, he and his army were storming Vitry. Thirteen hundred old men, women, and children had taken refuge in the cathedral. Louis's army set fire to the town. The cathedral burned, and in it most of the thirteen hundred. Alas for Eleanor, now twenty-one years old and the mother of several daughters; alas for Louis! The burning of the

[26]

innocents at Vitry was a great scandal. Louis was repentant and made a hasty peace. Eleanor was scornful of her husband's weakness. She needed a man for a husband, not a priest. If God permitted a wooden church to burn, that was God's business. "By God's eyebrows," she cried, using a sweet maidenly oath in a voice which I fear was neither soft nor well modulated, "I'm a better king than you are." Perhaps she was right. Dear Eleanor!

Suger, Louis's counselor and friend, had at the beginning of the campaign withdrawn from the court. It was evident that Louis the king could not control Eleanor, and Suger the priest thought that it was equally evident that he, the representative of God, could not control her. She was a hard passionate woman, this girl of twenty-one, and in God's hands. Suger set to building St.-Denis in Paris. Perhaps later God would find a way. Then came the burning of the thirteen hundred innocents at Vitry. Bernard the saint was in Paris. He expostulated with Suger, and Suger took a hand. He played upon the sensibilities of Louis the pious. He pictured to him the torments of hell. Thirteen hundred Christians were not to be burned alive incontinently at a woman's whim. Louis was repentant. He gave over the war, shaved off his beard, and cut his hair. He became more priestly in his habits and more ascetic in his manner, and Eleanor wanted men around her, males who could fight and kill and sing songs and pay compliments, men who were living in this world, eager, strong, modern. Then St. Bernard preached the second crusade under the groined vault of the church at Vézelay.

3

St. Bernard was a man, a great strong man with a square chin, a ruler of men and a man of his time. "He was hot in burning love, humble in conversation, a well in flowing doctrine, a pit in deepness of science and well smelling in sweetness of fame." When his mother "bare the third son which was Bernard in her belly, she saw in her sleep a dream. . . . Her seemed she had in her belly a whelp, all white and red upon the back, barking in her belly. And a . . . holy man . . . prophesying: Thou art mother of a right noble whelp, which shall be a warden of the house of God, and shall give great barking against the enemies." Bernard was hot in love, but not in the love of women. One time "when he had holden his eyes and fixed them upon a woman, he had anon shame in himself and was a cruel venger of himself. For he leapt anon into a pond full of water and frozen, and was therein so long that almost he was frozen. And by the grace of God he was cooled from his carnal concupiscence."

He was a worker. He lost no time except when he slept. When he had eaten he would consider whether he had eaten more than was his custom or more than he needed to carry on God's work. When he had done this, if he found that he had overstepped the limits he had set, he would punish his mouth so that it lost the power of tasting and became a great black hole in his face. He would drink oil and think it was water. He preferred plain clothes to fine clothes and filth to cleanliness. His sister "was married into the world, and went into the monastery for to visit her brethren in a proud estate and great apparel. And he dreaded her as she had been the devil or his net for to take souls, nor would not go out for to see her. . . . One of her brethren said that she was a foul ordure, stinking, wrapped in gay array."

St. Bernard was a ruler. His rule over men was strong, his rule over himself was stronger, but strongest of all was his rule over devils. Never a devil in the world got the better of St. Bernard. He knew their ways and their tricks. When he could not drive them out by the words of the gospel or by holy relics, he got himself into a divine rage; and with his face all red with anger and his black brows close together in his fury, he drove them out with a thunderous excommunication from his black lips. There was a woman of Guienne, a countrywoman of Eleanor's, who was troubled by a devil of the kind that still seems to give the women of that land much concern. She told St. Bernard of her devil, weeping bitterly. "He said: Take this staff which is mine, and lay it in thy bed, and if he may do anything let him do it. . . . And he came anon but durst not go to his lecherous work accustomed but threatened her right eagerly." This threat she told to the saint, who "assembled the people that each man should hold a candle burning in his hand and went from one to the other and came at last to this devil and cursed him and excommunicated him and defended that never after he should so do to her ne to none other."

Call it hypnotism, if you wish, or divine force, or power of personality or what you will. Certain it is that people once believed in God and the devil with as much reason

[29]

as they now believe in germs and internal glandular secretions and "counter-indications" and the scientific method. And through this welter of belief forty-five-year-old men like Bernard and twenty-one-year-old girls like Eleanor saw their vision of the good life gleaming. Bernard fought his way to a place in the pantheon of the saints and Eleanor to a grave in the abbey at Fontevrault.

The first time Bernard preached the crusade to Louis it was in the church at Vézelay; the second time it was in the great hall of the fortress. Here it was that Louis took the cross from the hands of the saint; but the crowd was so great that the multitude was unable to see the king. A tower was built in the fields outside the fortress. Louis showed himself on it with the cross on his breast. The multitude took up the cry, "Praise to God," and all demanded crosses. The number that took the cross that day was so great that Bernard had to tear the clothes from his back to make crosses for them all; holy crosses they were, made of the vestments of the saint who preferred filth to cleanliness and who wore a hair shirt next to his skin.

4

What of Eleanor on that day, twenty-four years old, who for nine years had been queen of France, ruling her husband and his sycophants, his priests and enemies, like the eternal woman that she was? Hardly had the holy man left when she appeared with a band of her girl friends, armed head to foot, riding like warriors astride great chargers. They performed Amazonian exercises and follies in public and sent their distaffs, now useless, home to those knights and nobles they chose to consider as slackers. Entire villages were deserted by male inhabitants, and the land was left to be tilled by women and children.

Eleanor with her band of Amazons and Louis with his lords temporal and spiritual set out on foot and on horseback to save the sacred city and to bring back as much of the wealth of the Orient as they could steal from the good heathen who erroneously, no doubt, thought that having worked for it, they deserved to keep it. They went overland, young, debonair, gay; some of them saintly and some of them wicked; an average crowd surrounding a few personalities which were in their own way either great or amusing. They arrived, much harassed by the cavalry of the Arabs, the baggage of the ladies, and the whims of the queen, at Laodicea. The queen and her ladies were sent on ahead to occupy a barren hill. At their feet a romantic valley with lush grasses, flowing streams, and shady trees invited them. They camped in the valley. The Arabs camped on the hill and shut the king up in a narrow pass. Seven thousand knights perished in the affray, and the king was able to save himself only by climbing a tree. The baggage was lost and the army in confusion.

They turned into Antioch, now ruled by Eleanor's uncle, Raymond of Poitou, the handsomest man of his time, big, broad, and black, and expert in his manipulation of ladies for the purposes of war and politics. Even the confused army of Louis might be useful in extending the dominions of Raymond of Poitou. There was intrigue and counter-intrigue. Raymond plotted with Eleanor and Louis, and with Eleanor against Louis. Eleanor plotted with Raymond and the Saracens; Louis read his breviary, became pale at the elevation of the host, and meditated. One chronicler says that Eleanor fell in love with a handsome Saracen prince, and there has been much controversy as to the identity of his person. Another chronicler reports that she forgot herself *jusqu'à la foi due au lit conjugal*. A lady of the last century who wrote for the late Queen Victoria of the lives of that exemplary lady's predecessors seems to believe these scandals, and implies that Eleanor, in disgust after seeing her shaven husband up a tree hiding from his enemies, turned for consolation to her handsome and dashing uncle. What need had Eleanor of her uncle of Antioch or of handsome Saracen princes? There were men enough in her entourage. Finally, Louis stole her away one night, a protesting and crying female, and was commended later by Suger for his moderation. Evidently somebody believed the slander. Somebody always does.

Eleanor was brought back to Paris again with truck-loads of silks and jewels. She was kept in Paris; she was not permitted to visit her own country or the courts of love at Poitiers. She amused herself as best she could at the court at Paris, now entirely dominated by the clerics. . . . But there were compensations of a kind. An occasional saint or two would come storming into her apartments, his black brows working, his face pale with the whiteness of asceticism, to expostulate with her for her evil worldly ways or, maybe, to exorcise the devil who was supposed to be her familiar spirit. "From the Devil," said the English, "she came and to the Devil she will return." There is a *tenson* sometimes attributed to her, a gay, scurrilous, light-hearted, bitter little thing which begins:

> If I should marry a cleric,
> God forbid . . .

and continues in a way which unfortunately cannot be translated acceptably for the twentieth century.

5

But why did Eleanor travel in the year 1152 from Paris to Orléans and from Orléans to Beaugency, thence, even as you and I, down the Loire to Blois, to Tours, and further still to the noble city of Poitiers, where strange things have happened and strange things happen still? That too is scandal.

No capital of France could in the Middle Ages fall entirely under the control of saints and priests. There must always be politics, there must always be embassies and lords who pay scant attention to the mass, excommunicate, maybe, for having seized the lands of a rich abbey, or for having refused to admit the lords of Rome who came collecting taxes, or for putting off their old wives and putting on their new. One such embassy which made its entry ten years later has been described in some detail. It was the embassy of that young Thomas, later to win sainthood at Canterbury, but then the young man about town, worldly, shrewd, and the boon companion of Henry in his vices and escapades. When the embassy of Thomas entered Paris, the cortège was opened by two hundred and fifty young people singing national airs and clad in brocade. They were followed by his dogs, tied together in pairs, and by eight chariots, each drawn by five horses and driven by coachmen in black uniforms. Each chariot was covered with costly furs and protected by two guards and a huge dog, sometimes chained and sometimes at liberty. Two of the chariots bore casks of ale to be distributed among the populace; another carried everything necessary for the chapel of the young chancellor; a fourth, the furniture of his bedroom; a fifth, the necessaries of his kitchen; a sixth, his gold and silver plate and his wardrobe; and the last two carried the luggage of his followers and his companions. Behind these came twelve sumpter-horses. On the back of each was a monkey and a kneeling groom. Squires carrying the shields and leading the battle-horses of their knights followed; then more squires; then the children of gentlemen whose education was being completed in the household of the great man; then the falconers; then the officers of the household; then the knights and ecclesiastics, mounted and riding two by two; and finally, at the very end, came the chancellor himself, carrying on a gay conversation with several friends and apparently oblivious of the great impression he was creating.

For these crowds of gentlemen, there must be dinners in the great halls. There must be exchange of compliments and inquiries after "the health of our sister Petronilla" and "What of that Bastard of Champagne?" and gossip about the young exquisite who tried to maintain in open debate with the churchmen that a good God could not have created hell, and about that other who said that God was a poet who dreamed the universe or that one who maintained that the universe had dreamed God. . . . At these dinners Peire Vidal's latest escapade was, no doubt, discussed and a musician called to sing Peire's latest song, and, perhaps, to sing that naughty one by Eleanor's grandfather, now dead these many years in a hermit's cave in Compostella; and perhaps Eleanor herself, if the company were small enough, would entertain with one of her own songs. Eleanor probably had a gay enough life, even in Paris.

One day Geoffrey of Anjou, clad in light armor, rode through the gate of Paris. Behind him, with many knights, rode his son Henry, a lad of seventeen. They came to do homage for the county of Anjou and to see whether some plot might be arranged against his cousin by marriage, King Stephen of England. These Angevins were likely men, as the Angevins still are; not tall, but ruddy, worldly and active. Geoffrey was a great scholar; he came from Eleanor's part of the country; he brought news of friends, and the movements of her friends the poets; and his musicians could produce the latest song. They no doubt argued points of philosophy and esthetics, and to what extent was a man in love responsible for his actions, and whether women prefer clerics or soldiers as lovers, and why, and whether poetry should be written in a language so clear that a child could understand it or so intricate that only experts could unravel its complications; for in the same way that psychoanalysis and evolution and fundamentalism have swept the intellectual sea of our time, so similar fashions swept the intellectual seas of those, furnishing topics of

[35]

conversation for the afternoons in the great halls when the sun came through the traceries of the Gothic windows which then were a new fashion of architecture and very smart indeed.

There was gossip about Eleanor and "old" Geoffrey—he was about thirty-eight years old at this time, an old man and past his prime but still hearty—and some say that she forgot herself again. But that is mere gossip and based upon no evidence whatever. Eleanor was not the kind of a woman who forgets herself. What she did, she did with a clear consciousness, and, for all I know, with an equally clear conscience. Two years later Geoffrey of Anjou died and his son Henry came to Paris to do homage a second time for his inheritance, but this time it was his cortège and not his father's that accompanied him.

That Eleanor was sick of Paris there can be no doubt. "My husband," she said, "is more of a monk than a man." And here was a man at hand, an active man, heir to Anjou, claimant of Normandy, and pretender to the throne of England. He was a man who could hold her as no other man could hold her, who could reform her life for her, could make her a chaste and virtuous woman, and transform her passion and gaiety into an implacable hatred. She was a woman who wanted a ruler; a just providence brought her, in this stocky red-headed youth, a man who *could* rule her. And none could resist this wealthy woman of Aquitaine, this clever poet, this superb female, familiar with the devils of her own country and the devils of the Holy Land, and with saints and warriors and poets and priests besides. She is said to have placed her ships and treasures at his command. "When we are married," she said to him, "you will see what lovely things I brought from the Holy Land. I know the seven arts, and the methods of love in the East." Nor was Henry a man afraid of difficulties. He could take a castle in a night; he could hold together his rebellious barons and churchmen and ride three horses to death in a day. He could hold this woman, and perhaps the very difficulty which she presented attracted him the more. He was a courageous man, was Henry, unafraid of saints, devils, and Eleanor of Aquitaine.

When Henry of Anjou left Paris, Eleanor proceeded to divorce her husband, King Louis. The court, consisting of trains of mules and cart-loads of baggage and King Louis and his relatives and friends and her relatives and friends and prelates and knights and hangers-on, proceeded by slow journey from Paris to Orléans and from Orléans to Beaugency, where the king's marriage was dissolved on March 18, 1152.

6

To-day when you go from England or America to Tours and the country of the châteaux, you go from some place on the coast of Normandy or Flanders eastward to Paris, and from Paris you return westward to Tours. If you take the express at seven o'clock in the morning, you reach Orléans at nine, and by a quarter of ten you are in Beaugency. If you wish you can be in Tours for lunch and have a late tea at Poitiers. If you are one of those cynical souls who go in conducted parties, a large-mouthed guide will explain to you in demotic English the wonders of the French

Renaissance. Indeed, the entire country has been covered by the French Renaissance, which, I suppose, is beautiful in its way and testifies to the love which the kings of France and England and their favorites long after the death of Eleanor and her poets felt for the cooking of Touraine and the *vin rosé* of Anjou. But if you will look with attentive eye beneath the flowers of the Renaissance you will find the bare branches of another age, an age before towers were thought to be a pretty decoration on a façade and when walls had to be built strong and thick if they were to afford protection against the men-at-arms of a neighbor who cast envious eyes on one's wife or ox or ass or rich vineyards. You will, if you are light-hearted, leave Paris in the morning and get yourself as quickly as you may to Orléans and the Loire. There you will desert the railway and the broad highroad in boat or barge or raft to float down the Loire past La Chapelle, St.-Ay, and Château Meung-sur-Loire to Beaugency.

When Eleanor and her scandalized friends and family hurried from Orléans to Beaugency they probably followed the trail which wound beside the river and sent their luggage down by barge. The trail was very narrow and worn deeply into the earth. On rainy days it was a small river of mud, and even on pleasant days it presented difficulties. The company straggled out for many miles through the green fields, and there were gossip and jest and high words. Following behind, perhaps a day's journey, came Louis with horns well sprouted preparing for his halo, good pious Louis whose wife was too much for him, surrounded by his priests, whose shaven heads reflected the weak sunshine of

the early spring, sitting ungainly astride their horses, bob-
bing and nodding among themselves and offering the king
good, wise, and pious counsels, doing observance at the way-
side shrines and performing perhaps a miracle or two for
the glory of God.

Little time was wasted on the divorce at Beaugency.
The ground given was consanguinity. Eleanor and Louis
had lived together half a lifetime as lives were counted then,
and after fifteen years of tumultuous marriage Louis suddenly discovered that his wife was his fourth—some say
his seventh—cousin and demanded a divorce. For shame!
The queen would have no delay. Her first and eldest son
was to be born in August. She had to dispose of her husband and provide a father for the heir of Aquitaine. The
decree was pronounced with all the solemnity of a church
council: the clerk handed it to the bishop, and the bishop in
his fine robes, standing out from the altar in the shadow of
one of the pillars, made the decree permanent.

Eleanor left at once and in the early evening rode into
the white city of Blois, clean and bright on the river-bank,
but dingy and brown in the city, and straggly and Renaissance and nineteenth-century in the narrow streets that run
up to the château. There seem always to have been Counts
Thibaut at Blois, and they have been traditionally hospitable. The one who accompanied Eleanor from the church at
Beaugency, sending messengers ahead to prepare the rooms,
and ordering great entertainment for the illustrious grass-
widow, was perhaps not the first to make his hospitality
insistent.

Imagine Eleanor and her company riding down from

Beaugency. Imagine Thibaut riding at her horse's head, making ribald jokes at the expense of Louis, whispering to her of the declining popularity of his cousin, King Stephen of England, and reminiscing about Henry of Anjou.

These people had a great deal of talk in them. Being denied the doubtful benefits of universal education, few of them could read or write, and even if they could, books were very scarce and very expensive. As each book had to be copied carefully on vellum by the hand of monk or clerk, this was the age of limited editions, each edition being limited to one copy. Thus the people who took the pains to write took further pains that the thing written should be worth reading. There were no head-lines to announce that somebody's wife had run away with somebody's chauffeur. That the people in the Middle Ages were interested in these runnings-away is certain, but their information was confined to gossip in the window-niche. Under these conditions the stories could be elaborated as such stories should be elaborated, and, since there were no laws of libel, the story became a tradition, the tradition a saga, and the saga finally was worked into that curious kind of light literature which scholars unacquainted with the popular and no doubt equally bad novels of their own age refer to by the pompous and misleading title of medieval epic. Since most of the people of the twelfth century were unable to read, and even if they could, since books were very expensive, the chief amusement left to them after a strenuous day on the battle-field was talking. But again, do not be misled. Their conversations would make a Mississippi boatman blush with chagrin. It was of a crudeness, of a frankness, of a vivacity! The coarsest language of to-day is euphemism mere and pale.

Thus I would not tell you if I could what Thibaut said to Eleanor or she to him as they rode together from Beaugency to Blois on a road which, nearer the river than the present main road, runs directly through Tavers, Lestiou, Avarai, to Suèvres, where it joins the main road for a moment until it reaches the village of Cour-sur-Loire, where it joins it again. They left the road a little west of Blois to ride up the winding path to the old strong castle, a building which, too stolid for the splendors of the French Renaissance, was torn down many years ago. It made way for that other castle which, now the wonder of all comers, was inhabited by that other saintly Louis, the twelfth of the name. It is where Henri II superintended the butchering of the duc de Guise, remarking as he pushed the head away with his foot, "I had not thought he was so long." As they approached, the herald rode ahead with his banner and sounded the call. There was a scurrying within, and the officers of the castle strode out to welcome their master and his guests. Eleanor was shown to her room overlooking a garden of roses transplanted from Jericho, and, wearied by her day in the divorce court, was provided with a hot bath and a massage. Thibaut was the brave son of a brave father and was hospitable to excess. He did the best a gentleman of those days could do to a wealthy heiress traveling alone: he asked her to marry him. She refused. She may have said she would be his sister, and she certainly intended to become his cousin as soon as she could persuade Henry of Anjou to leave off burning cities and making widows and orphans long enough to come down and marry her. But Thibaut was insistent and persuaded Eleanor to spend several days with him at Blois. And who can blame her? "He who has not known lilac-time at Blois has not yet experienced the sweetness of living," says an old French proverb; and perhaps Eleanor found the gay little city which reflects its bright clear face in the Loire and the early spring days and the sound of her own language in her ears refreshing after the gloom of the capital. Oh, there were parties, I have no doubt; and debates, and serenades in the morning, clear-voiced musicians singing to the accompaniment of the guitar some new *aubade* to the rising sun and the singing of birds.

Then once more came the question, and once more the refusal. Perhaps Eleanor noted now that she was no longer permitted to be alone as much as before. Perhaps she heard orders given; or perhaps she was told simply, for this reason or that, that it would be wise not to leave her chambers. At any rate Eleanor disguised herself in the jerkin of a serving-man and escaped by minutes a plot to put her into seclusion, there to be kept until she could be persuaded by courteous or discourteous means to marry the count of Blois.

7

She left Blois by night and foiled her pursuers by slipping down the river in a boat. One should drift down the Loire on a soft spring night before the summer droughts have made the stream shallow and unpleasant. It is not only the sweet odor of flowers that makes it sweet, or the odor of the stream and the dankness of the air, but hanging over all this is the eternal odor of France, a composite of stale wine, sweaty boatmen, and, in these days, French national tobacco, than which there is none worse.

When she arrived at Tours, Eleanor said a prayer at the tomb of St. Martin; for with all her sins, or perhaps because of them, she believed in the saints. This Martin was a great good man, and he fought devils until the end of his life. When he was dying—this happened unfortunately in Poitiers and gave rise to a great struggle, and the Tourainians once again disgraced themselves—St. Martin was, for his holiness, lying on dust and ashes. He asked that his brethren would remove a little his body that he "might behold more of the heaven than the earth. Saying this he saw the devil that was there, and St. Martin said to him: 'Wherefore standest thou here, thou cruel beast? Thou shalt find in me nothing sinful ne mortal.'" After he died there arose a great altercation between the people of Poitiers and the people of Tours as to which might have the body. While the people of Poitiers slept, the Tourainians hurried the body out of a window and down the steep hill into a boat and took it down the stream to Tours.

St. Martin was a good man. "He was clad with sharp clothing, blue, and a great coarse mantle hanging here and there upon him"; and he always got what he wanted. Once there was a duke who, for his sins, refused to see the saint. Martin made himself lean with fasting, wrapped a haircloth about him, and threw ashes over his head and sat outside the palace gate. And simply by making himself as obnoxious as he could he forced the duke to receive him.

[43]

Even though he had power over beasts—he could make the dogs stop barking, the hares stop running, and the snakes stop doing whatever snakes do—he had his difficulties with the Tourainians, which, since the saint was a very abstemious man and the Tourainians wonderfully fond of their good cooking and their beautiful churches, can hardly be wondered at.

When Eleanor had said her prayer and rearranged her toilet and demanded safe-conduct from Henry of Anjou's younger brother Geoffrey, she seems to have thought herself safe and proceeded on her way. This part of her trip was by land. She made a straight line south to Montbazon, where a huge donjon-keep of the eleventh century rises above the village, and where, for what reason I know not, on the topmost rock sings a very small brave bird.

Her path continued south to Port des Piles and the river again, this time a small rippling stream that might have sung to Eleanor of safety, but her good angel, according to her earliest historian, warned her to beware. Henry's brother Geoffrey was waiting for her, and with Geoffrey was an armed band of knights-errant out, not indeed to save the hesitating maiden from the unwelcome attentions of a cruel enchanter, but to capture the fleeing maiden, lock her up in the donjon-keep of Montbazon, there to starve her into submission. This would have served her right, for according to the code of that day it was not proper for women to travel alone, unescorted by some member of their family. The chroniclers seem to know no more than I how Eleanor evaded Geoffrey and his good intentions, for they credit her with having turned south down an even smaller stream toward her own dominions. Since she was already going south and there was no small stream for her to take, this may have been somewhat difficult. She must have had a small company of men-at-arms in her train, and the warning of this good but anonymous angel may have given them opportunity to screw on their helmets, don a comfortable shirt of mail or two, and thus defend their mistress from the threatened attack. Or perhaps the threat of Geoffrey was mere gossip, and he did no more than plan the attack. (Poor Geoffrey! He was always planning attacks and never succeeding in getting very far with them. His cousin Stephen was too quick and his brother Henry was too shrewd; although he did succeed now and then in doing them dirt, which is not to be wondered at, since they succeeded in doing him much more dirt than he, with the best of intentions, was ever able to repay.) Eleanor seems to have escaped Geoffrey, and she must, in due time—for journeys were very slow in those days—have reached Châtellerault, which is a very nineteenth-century city, and later the proud city of Tours in her own country.

Here she was joined by Bernard de Ventadour, a young poet who had got into difficulties by his passionate and not too discreet love for Agnes de Montluçon, and later by Henry and Geoffrey, all smiles now and politic words; and in the high hall of the château at Poitiers she arranged for her second wedding at Bordeaux, many miles away. Her fine garments which she had stolen from the infidels in the Holy Land she sent north to Caen, where she was to hold her first court while she was waiting for her second husband to steal England from his cousin, Stephen the king.

Then she went southward in the spring, as all poets of this time seem to have gone, to a land where gray towers of an evening rise to a dark-blue sky: and because the sky is very blue and the towers are very gray and both are very old, they seem at times to merge and flow into each other. While one wonders about this, and why it should be just as it is, and how it is possible, and whether one should walk to the next town or take the train, the frogs set up— in the grassy moat—the same song that they sang underneath Eleanor's window, a song as much more permanent than the towers as her passionate life was more permanent than the body which led her astray and is now buried in the abbey at Fontevrault. One will walk after all.

Chapter III

The Trail of a Troubadour Errant

VENTADOUR TO POITIERS

CAEN TO LONDON

Castle of Falaise where William the Conqueror was born

Chapter III

1

BIOGRAPHERS who have treated the rather fluid and peripatetic life of Bernard de Ventadour have tried to infuse it with the wine of romance. The romance they choose is of the wrong vintage. It is the kind the late Lord Tennyson brewed to beguile the long evenings of a widowed queen. It is a syrupy draft. Men and women a thousand years ago are supposed to be something less, or, if you prefer, more, than men and women to-day. Bernard and his fellow-wanderers under the blue sky are supposed to have been high-souled English gentlemen whose arms were strengthened by the purity of their hearts. By committing wholesale murder, they extricated medieval flappers from situations in which these flappers should never have become involved. After having perpetrated this rather brutal heroic, these gentry, we are told, wandered in virginal and unchaperoned innocence through the forest, pausing on occasion to inquire from simple-minded peasants whether there were, in the neighborhood, knights who required murdering, while the pure maidens they collected jogged along behind on demure white asses.

That a certain amount of this kind of romance is extracted from the popular novels of the twelfth century written by Bernard's friends and contemporaries does not make it of value as data for the reconstruction of the social and moral history of the time. For popular novels of the twelfth century, like popular novels of the twentieth, pictured a world as we would like to have it rather than a world as it actually was, is, or will be. Galahad, Lancelot, and Tristan were literary myths created for the entertainment of the medieval flapper. Arthur was a stupid and complaisant husband, and Guinevere a thoroughly immoral woman. This immorality and this complaisancy were justified by various literary devices, some of them credible and some of them incredible; and out of the hard facts of life was woven a soft tissue. The authors of these novels presented certain universal problems and by their skill seemed to justify certain actions which then as now were recognized as wrong. Thus the reader was permitted to sin vicariously, and art, holding the mirror up to nature, shows nature inverted. Though good little girls may dream about being bad and bad little girls dream about being good, it is the dream which is preserved in the novels. The girls themselves are, unfortunately, dead. It is because scholars are pleased to ignore this truism that, looking at life as it boils about them, they insist that knee-length skirts cover less than waist-line morals and that the prevalence of divorce proves the substitution of individual passion for domestic patience. As they contemplate the aspirations toward a better life incorporated in the popular novels of the Middle Ages, they insist that since the Middle Ages were romantic, they must also have been pure.

[50]

As a matter of fact, the real men and women were much the same as we are: they knew what they would have liked to do if conditions had been different than they must have been and had they as individuals been different than they were. But this knowledge did not prevent them from carrying on the necessary and more or less unpleasant business of life; therefore Eleanor, the eternal and protean female, offered a poisoned bowl to one Rosamond Clifford whose youthful intimacy with King Henry II of England, Eleanor's husband, was apt to prove annoying; and Bernard the poet seduced the wife of his patron, Ebles II of Ventadour.

2

There was scandal in the Château de Ventadour, but had not one of the participants been destined to write the best poetry Europe had heard in a thousand years, scandal in Ventadour—where there was always more or less scandal— would have been quite unimportant. Ventadour is a small heap of stones on a small hill some three miles from Egletons, a village of less than two thousand souls, which itself is from two to four hours distant from Brive if you travel by what is euphemistically called a train and somewhat nearer if you walk. But when one has reached Brive, one is still several hours from Périgueux, which most tourists consider a bit of virginal and untouched France. Thus in order to reach Ventadour, where there was a nasty scandal in 1152, the tourist must go beyond the farthest known, there to find a small heap of stones not nearly so picturesque as the ruins left by the lesser men of a lesser age.

But the stones remember. Ventadour was at one time an important château. It witnessed siege; it housed passion; it was taken once by treachery and twice by assault; it was, in 1145, the home of Agnes de Montluçon, the very young bride of Ebles II of Ventadour. When she came to be mistress of the château she may have been thirteen or fourteen years old and an accomplished woman. Her husband Ebles, somewhat older, and in some respects the mirror of fashion, was one of those fine fighting barons of the Middle Ages who would knock you down in a tournament in the morning and take away your horse and armor, write a delicate and sophisticated love poem to your wife in the afternoon, lay siege to a castle at night, and, if the castle were weak enough to yield, slaughter the defenders, but return home in time to sing an *aubade* to your wife or the wife of somebody else before sunrise and early mass. He was a fine cultured gentleman, was Ebles II, but somewhat too old for Agnes. He seems to have permitted her to play about with his gifted friend, a lad called Bernard, the son of a smith, one of the lowest servants in the château.

The processes whereby an obscure youth came to be one of the members of the household of a great lord may be conjectured. The château of those days was a comparatively small place, surrounded by a wall and occupied by the lord, his lady, and the members of their household. Most of the things that one ate or wore or used were produced on the grounds. Although the population of the château may not have been larger than two or three hundred, these two or three hundred people lived together with a certain intimacy. There must have been a considerable amount of fraternizing between the lord and his servants; and although the lord probably insisted on absolute obedience—his was the power of life and death—he must from sheer boredom have permitted liberties and friendships. In the main street of the château and the village which grew up around it, tongues must have clacked and gossip spread. One could be dignified and distant with one's servants in the city, where one's servants had proper distraction; to be dignified or distant in the small world of the château, where the increasing size of one's belt was an event known not only to the tailor and his wife but to all his acquaintances, and where a smile at a peasant's daughter was magnified to a grin, to a leer, to a kiss, to—what you will, must have been difficult.

Nor is there any evidence that the country gentry insisted particularly upon the forms of subserviency; the substance was enough. The lord ruled by right of ability rather than by right of inheritance, and if he were too weak to hold both the land and the respect of his followers, an upstart, a stronger man would take them away. For these great lords were realists; they took what they could lay hands on to build up a duchy, a family, or a kingdom. Justification could come later; justification was the business of the scribes, the poets, the monks. But since a failure could not afford to pay the scribes, the great thing was to be successful; and to be successful, one needed shrewdness, ruthlessness, and an ability to discount the manner for the man.

In some way the ability to write poetry possessed by this youngster Bernard was brought to the attention of Ebles II of Ventadour, who, being a man of fashion and aware of the value of a poet, may have thought that since his estate could produce good wine and a fair number of fighting-men, it might also produce a poet or two. The boy must have been clever and is said to have been handsome. How close this friendship was, or when it began, I do not know. Bernard seems to have been made a member of the family, and he may have traveled with his master to Poitiers and Toulouse and Bordeaux. He may even have known William IX of Aquitaine, the earliest of the troubadours, and have learned from him much about the art and business of poetry. Although Ebles engaged in an occasional war to keep his weapons bright and clean, there were no great maneuvers to engage his attention at that time. Life was gay, frank, and sophisticated; and this gaiety, frankness, and sophistication are shown in Bernard's philosophy, which he stated in a single sentence: "That man is dead who does not feel in his heart the sweet savor of love; and he who lives without love is merely an irritation to his friend." The society that produced not one but several men of this creed is not the "society of barbarians who posed as civilized people," in the unhappy phrase which Mr. Van Loon uses to characterize the people of this time. It may have been a decadent, a cruel, an immoral society; but it was not a barbarous society; for a barbarous people do not devote their lives consciously to the pleasures of love or produce a subtle and philosophical lyric poetry. If a man's civilization be determined by what he understands rather than by what he wears, the civilization was in many respects in advance of the civilization of the nineteenth.

Bernard represents the first phase of troubadourism, the

phase in which the poets and their subjects regarded love realistically. The time was to come when men writing about love would be thinking of something else entirely. The concept of love in the next century was to become pale and philosophical and the technique of love "scientific." In the thirteenth century love was theoretically vicarious. The lover was to obtain complete emotional satisfaction in looking at his lady. The scandals of that century demonstrate, nevertheless, that the machinery of love was not entirely worn out. For Bernard, love was an intense physical passion with certain delicious emotional and psychical concomitants. It transformed the landscape and gave purpose and direction to life. Life without love was as unnatural and unhealthy as life without war or wine or those other amenities that civilization has made necessary to us.

Bernard's philosophy of love may at times threaten the sanctity of the home and hearth, and some may hold that Ebles was ill advised to permit his young wife to play about with a gifted poet. The inevitable occurred; although Ebles, the heavy husband, occupied with his own and more important matters, may not have observed its precise development. Bernard's early poems to Agnes were the conventional compliments of the time. The compliments became less conventional, the avowals less discreet, and when the humility of the suppliant gave way before the arrogance and exultation of the victor, tongues clacked and there was scandal in Ventadour. If you repeat often enough, and with enough variation, the phrase, "I love you," to a girl who is cultivated and charming and perhaps beautiful, you

[55]

may find in the end that sentence has become a sentiment and the sentiment a passion. And if the girl had been married to a man old enough to be her father at a time when girls of the twentieth century are still playing with dolls, the girl might believe that you actually did love her and might actually love you. These were the sinister chances that poets had to take.

Ebles seems to have been irritated, but his irritation was directed against his wife rather than against her lover. He would have been in his rights as they were defined at that barbarous time, and, I am told, they are still defined in this civilized twentieth century, had he killed Bernard. Instead of doing this he spanked his wife and sent her to bed without supper. Nor was the spanking theoretical; it was an actual spanking of his wife, the vicomtesse de Ventadour, who had so far forgotten herself as to grant favors to a poet. The spanking of the vicomtesse requires explanation. Ebles knew and Agnes should have known that the job of the poet was to make love and make it exquisitely. If he were exquisite enough, the lady, her husband, and the poet would all profit. The lady would become famous throughout the land and be boosted into the position of social leader. In an age when there were no social columns in the newspapers, no descriptions of entertainments or illustrated supplements, ladies expected poets to act as publicity agents. As songs about them spread throughout the land and their fame increased, important gentlemen would be attracted to their courts. They and their husbands and the poets would increase in power and wealth. This was an accepted and recognized fact. It was further admitted that since a poet needed a certain amount of fuel to keep his ardor at white heat, a certain amount was granted. It is, however, a law of all societies, written in red letters in all books of etiquette of all time, that a vicomtesse, if she be not respectable, must, at least, be discreet; or if she be indiscreet, that she choose as her companion a prince sufficiently powerful to protect her against the not unnatural chagrin of her husband. There were cases, as we shall see later, where this law was observed with a minute scrupulosity. When the poet says, "I have loved you since the day we first played together as children, and each day of the year my love for you has redoubled"— which Bernard actually did say to Agnes—the lady has no business believing him, even though she may feel a reciprocal passion. Bernard was in the right, as Ebles and all the world knew. He was doing his job, and Agnes was in the wrong. It was a hard world and a real world, and a man took what he could get.

Thus was the vicomtesse de Ventadour, the beautiful but indiscreet inspiration of a rising poet, spanked and locked up in her room. In parting, Bernard said: "Lady, when my eyes behold you no longer, remember that my heart is always near you. When your husband beats your body, do not let him beat your heart. If he humiliates you, take care that you humiliate him too. See that you do not return him good for evil. . . ."

3

Thus Bernard de Ventadour bade farewell to the first mistress of his heart, the one who according to some biographers retained the first place in his affections throughout his long career. For be it known that Bernard is supposed to have been absolutely faithful to at least three women at the same time. Biographers seem to argue that since he said he was faithful and is too nice a boy to tell a lie, therefore he must be faithful, which is as pleasant a way of looking at life as any I can imagine. When he set out to seek his fortune in the early spring of 1152, he turned north toward Poitiers and that other subject of much gossip who, too, was faithful in her fashion, Eleanor of Aquitaine, recently queen of France and now about to become queen of England. He traveled via Limoges, Bellac, and Chauvigny. A broad highway to-day follows the approximate course that he must have taken, although his actual trail diverges from it in some places, and to find it one needs a stout pair of boots and a stout heart.

His first stop was probably Egletons, a village owned by the counts of Ventadour. In the twelfth century the citizens of this village built themselves walls strong enough to stand for several thousands of years; and although the fashion has somewhat changed in walled cities, one can still climb the grassy steps on the portion which girds the western side of the town and look out over the barren country toward the Monts de Monédières.

From here Bernard went northwest through a stony and hilly country to St.-Yrieix-le-Déjalât, an old monastic village which has forgotten its past and is hopeless of its future, a village which was begun by a cluster of houses around the old abbey of St. Yrieix—as the people of that country mispronounce the good name of Aredius the saint

—and which never grew up. Then he crossed the mountains to reach the Vézère River, and on the river, with wall and gates and ruined castle and old houses, the village of Treignac. And as he crossed the low hills which are called mountains, he cursed and detested them.

One must distinguish in the works of these poets between a true and sincere love of spring in particular and a rather cold indifference toward nature in general. If one lived all winter in a castle, which is to say a stone house built on a hill open to the fiercest blasts and the most penetrating cold winds and heated by a large though inadequate fire built in one end of a very large and high room, one would have reason to rejoice at the return of the flowers in the spring. And if one traveled afoot or a-horseback three or four times across the continent of Europe, one could have reason to curse the mountains. The love of external nature, the love of the wild and desert places, is a bad habit like industrialism and democracy bequeathed to us by the sentimental nineteenth century. Even our recent ancestors of the eighteenth century had great difficulty in explaining why God let mountains grow over an otherwise pleasant landscape. For these, as for the people of the Middle Ages, the proper interest of mankind was man; and it was considered a proof of great holiness when a religiously minded person went out from the cities and the fraternity of his fellows there to live by meditation. For the common man, the house was merely a place to sleep, and the streets and the market-places, peopled by other interesting and gossipy common men, the places to live. The gentry of this period spent most of their time in the great hall of the castle, surrounded by a mob of undisciplined friends, dogs, servants, hangers-on, clerics, and men-at-arms. There was no privacy in the Middle Ages, nor did most people desire privacy. They enjoyed having people around them and hated loneliness. They hated the mountains and the deserts which were tiresome and difficult to cross, and they loved cities where one might gossip and play politics. Their admiration for the hermits who renounced the world and the fellowship of men was in part an admiration for people who demonstrated by their renunciation that they were possessed of a stronger will than the Middle Ages or the modern ages in general can boast of. The twelfth century loved men and was indifferent to mankind.

Beyond Treignac there is a small wood which is called a forest, and beyond that Mont Gargan Barnagaud and St.-Germain-les-Belles, and St.-Bonnet-la-Rix and Château-neuf and Limoges, which Bernard's successor, the powerful Bertrand de Born, was to visit some thirty years later on business connected with this same Eleanor whom Bernard de Ventadour was setting out hopefully to serve.

I do not know what road Bernard followed from Limoges to Bellac, for the old itineraries are silent, and there are no streams to give the clue. I suspect that it was the long road west of the present highway that slips through Nieu and Blond and châteaux of doubtful interest. I do know that on the spring evening when I followed this trail the sky suddenly became verdigris and a cold wind blew down in my face from the northwest and the rain was spray and the trees beat the air and the cattle in the fields went galloping with a strange excitement toward home. It was one of those magic storms in which, as described by medieval novelists, the knight strays into a forest for shelter and, following some strange decoy, is led into the presence of that curious lady who can make a hundred years seem as one short night. Scientists, acquainted only with her unlovely sister who can make one short evening seem like a hundred years, regard her as a superstition. It transformed the rather pretty landscape into a thing of beauty and reconstructed for me the city of Bellac, which, on a hill dominating the Vincou and surrounded by an amphitheater of hills, once stood a long siege. First there was a Roman fort. The fort was transformed into a château, and around the château, seeking protection and profit, there grew a large village, then a small city.

The château where Bernard stayed has been torn down, but it was a very old building when he arrived. It had been built originally by Boson le Vieux three hundred years earlier, when Boson, by his craft, gained for himself the kingdom of the Provence. But Boson had enemies, and one of these was his sometime friend, the king of France, who set out to break him. Boson retired with Ermengarde, his wife, to the château, and the armies of France gave it siege. The siege lasted for several years. That means, of course, that for several years the hostile army was more or less in evidence about the place. The inmates of the castle seem to have been able to go and come much as they pleased, but they were never able to go far away or take a large number of men or leave the place entirely undefended. Boson grew weary of the siege, and so did the king of France. They both set out for other worlds to conquer. The king left Boson's brother in charge of the siege, and Boson left his wife in charge of the castle. She held out for two years against her importunate brother-in-law and then surrendered to him. Boson paid her ransom and freed her from imprisonment when he remembered it. We in the twentieth century have become legally minded and talk a great deal of nonsense about women's rights and fail to distinguish between the rights of women and the right women; for the right women of all ages and in all societies seem to have been able to exercise their precious personalities in any way they pleased.

From Bellac the old trail follows the highroad to Poitiers as far as the Pont St.-Martin across the Gartempe, where it branches. If either of the branches were in the Middle Ages the more important, it was probably the one leading through Theix, which contains, for those who are interested, the ruins of four châteaux. Beyond Theix the trail loses itself again, but the road of the Middle Ages was probably one of those that followed the Gartempe northward to Montmorillon, whose château and fortifications were destroyed shortly after Bernard's visit and rebuilt to be destroyed a second time. There still remain some old churches and a curious twelfth-century tower which was, perhaps, once used as a kitchen. Here again is a main modern road which leads directly to Poitiers, but the Middle Ages, being more accustomed to travel than we, probably followed its course only as far as Lussac-les-Châteaux, where it meets another river, this time the Vienne.

At Vienne, Bernard probably turned north to Chauvigny, which huddles about a ruined donjon-keep and a church on the cliffs. At Chauvigny, if you are of a trusting spirit, you may find the ruins of five châteaux. If you are cynical, however, you may conclude that the small heap of stones about the donjon is not a château but what the masons forgot to pick up when they did their last job in that part of the town several centúries ago. But whether there were four or five châteaux at Chauvigny was of little concern to Bernard, for there was only one château in the town when he reached it, if indeed he ever did. There were many lords and ladies along the way in those days who would welcome a clever poet, and he may have turned off at a dozen points and taken a dozen short cuts.

Bernard probably never traveled more than a day at a time, and if the master or the mistress of the castle were pleasant, he probably spent several days or a week or two with them. If there were neither castle nor monastery near where he could spend the night, he took his chances at an inn; and if the innkeeper were fairly honest, Bernard, like the rest of us, might count himself fortunate. For the innkeepers of those days have bequeathed some of their intention though little of their skill to their descendants and practised methods of robbery which were less subtle but more efficient than those practised to-day.

There were two main rooms in these inns: one room was for eating, and here everybody ate from a large table; and the other was for sleeping, and here everybody slept, men and women together. In the winter when it was cold, the windows were kept tightly closed, and people slept without undressing; in the summer when it was hot, the windows were kept closed just the same, but everybody slept in the nude. A hundred years later a particularly modest lady was commended for waiting until the light was put out before she undressed; such modesty was remarkable. These people thought that love was one thing and nakedness was another. When you entered the castle as a visitor, your host showed you to your room and ordered a bath for you. The tubs and water would be brought in, and a maid-servant would stand near to help you off with your clothes and to rub your back. Sir Percival, one of the Arthurian knights, protested against this and was laughed at for his crudeness. The twelfth century thought that we were all God's creatures together and there was nothing more immoral about a naked body than about a naked face. Bernard and his colleagues the troubadours were the first who, for purely practical reasons, introduced the distinction between love and lust, a distinction which remained largely theoretical until some time later, when nature, striving always to model itself upon art, made it a reality.

At Chauvigny Bernard probably turned west to Poitiers, unless he followed the Vienne northwest to Châtellerault where it meets the Clain and then returned southwest along this river to Poitiers. This, however, is improbable.

That Bernard, having fallen into disfavor with the lord of Ventadour, should have turned at once to the court of the most powerful princess in western Europe is significant and, when properly understood, may explain a great many things about Bernard, about the poets, and about the Middle Ages. To-day, should a rising young poet suddenly attach himself to the household of one of the powerful industrial princesses, his action would be regarded by an amazed society as somewhat presumptuous; for this amazed and highly civilized society believes that people of wealth have no responsibility toward people of talent, and since people of wealth have little interest in the arts, their responsibility toward artists, one must admit, should be somewhat limited.

In the Middle Ages, however, no one would have thought it presumptuous for Bernard to attach himself to Eleanor, and that for two reasons. The great ones of those days were really interested in poetry. Strange as it may seem, these people actually enjoyed hearing a good poem produced with skill, finesse, and subtlety as much as we enjoy a game of bridge or of golf. In those barbarous days, a poet was something more than a sportsman and something less than a god. He occupied the position in middle air which at present is held by that strange creature called the super-journalist who can ruin a reputation by a misplaced comma and whose power over his audience and function in society are similar to the power and function of the medieval poet. There is, however, this difference, that the art of the journalist is exercised on less personal material. When the journalists of the twentieth century have all been forgotten —even the greatest, and some of them are very great indeed —Bernard de Ventadour's cry in a morning song to Agnes, "O God, that dawn should come so soon," will still have the power to thrill the pure and virtuous. This universal interest in poetry may have assured Bernard that he would be given a hearing, and, if his poetry pleased, that he might find employment either in the household of Eleanor herself

[65]

or in the household of one of the great lords who congregated about her.

Moreover Bernard may have known Eleanor. His master, Ebles of Ventadour, was a friend of her father, William X, and a protégé of her grandfather, the earliest troubadour. During Ebles's, Bernard's, and Eleanor's peregrinations through southern France, they may have met on this or that occasion and exchanged compliments. Further, though Bernard was a plebeian by birth, he was a poet by profession and a gentleman by training. The poems he had already written, which had been picked up and sung by more than one wandering minstrel, had already served to make him and Agnes de Montluçon known, though perhaps not famous, as social figures. Eleanor and her courtiers certainly knew Ebles, and if they did not know Agnes, they certainly knew her family. Since Bernard was certainly not in disgrace—what gentleman either medieval or modern could refuse to kiss the vicomtesse de Ventadour if she requested it, she being very young and very charming?—there could be no reason why both her friends and Ebles's friends should refuse to welcome a poet of known ability whose broken heart was waiting to be mended should it find a patron both charming and generous.

This patron it found in Eleanor, whose heart was made of unbreakable material, and whose generosity to the poets her colleagues—she herself was a poet of no mean achievements—was proverbial. She had recently undergone a rather trying experience. Her last husband, King Louis of France, was making difficulties over her proposed marriage to young Henry, duke of Anjou; and Henry, who was willing enough to marry her, was busy making war in the north. A few weeks after Bernard's arrival in Poitiers she succeeded in marrying young Henry in Bordeaux—from Poitiers to Bordeaux and back was a good two weeks' journey in those days—and during the next year and a half, Henry having already taken for himself the duchy of Normandy and formulated serious expectations toward the scepter of England by means of a strong army provided by Eleanor and liberal bribes also provided by her, she was to await the fruition of her husband's plans at Caen, which is the first important stop between Cherbourg and Paris and across the bay from the modern city of Le Havre.

4

When Eleanor held her Norman court in the great château at Caen, on the high hill above the old church of St.-Pierre, now replaced by a structure of the thirteenth century, it was in all probability the gayest court in western Europe. Students of that fashionable young exquisite, Abelard, were down from Paris. They practically denied the existence of sin and tried to prove that the world we live in and the God that made it were good, gay, and happy. And Eleanor thought that although she did not know a great deal about God, the world was a pretty fair world and she would be glad enough to see somebody abolish sin. She knew that she seemed to get into trouble as the sparks fly upward, and yet she did not think she had ever done anything which anybody could say was really wrong.

The château had been built by Eleanor's great-grandfather-in-law, William the Bastard, called by an English text-book that "great good man, William the Conqueror," who, with an army led by a poet, put the English to flight at Hastings. He and his wife Matilda built the other two most interesting buildings at Caen, the Abbaye-aux-Hommes and the Abbaye-aux-Dames, and, desiring to keep the good monks and nuns out of temptation, built the two abbeys at opposite ends of the town. These buildings had been erected as expiations for sin. William and Matilda were cousins and had married without the sanction of the church. The churchmen and perhaps God were somewhat appeased by the dedication to them—and Him—of these two pretentious foundations. They had also been erected as thank-offerings for sinners. William had been successful, beyond the wildest dreams of the most fortunate brigand, in his project of stealing England, and, by creating a comparatively stable government which the English did not desire, in assisting the progress of civilization.

William was buried with some difficulty in the Abbaye-aux-Hommes. He died in Rouen, the traditional capital of Normandy. As soon as he was dead, his court with the cry, "Long live the king," set out to intrigue for favor with one or more of the princes who hoped to succeed to the throne. The residence was deserted except for the servants, who, following the custom of the time, set out to plunder it of jewels, plate, and furniture. When this was accomplished, they took from the dead king the clothes he was wearing and left him naked on the floor. Later his son Henry found him, and he was transported to Caen for burial. The royal cortège had just reached the church, however, when news arrived that fire had broken out in that quarter of the town and threatened the abbey. The monks, ecclesiastics, and nobles, more concerned with the preservation of the abbey than with the routine of burial, left the dead king in the middle of the road until the fire had been extinguished, when the business of interment was resumed. The body was taken to the altar of the church, and the priests began to read the service. Then there was another uproar. This time it was caused by Anselm Fitzarthur, who forbade the interment. "This spot," he said, "was the site of my father's house, which this dead duke took violently from him, and here, upon part of my inheritance, founded this church. This ground I therefore challenge; and I charge ye all, as ye shall answer for it at the great and dreadful day of judgment, that ye lay not the bones of the despoiler on the hearth of my fathers." William's sons, who were probably less concerned with the justice of the claim than with pacifying the Normans whom they hoped to make their subjects, bargained with Fitzarthur, while the priests waited with the service, and finally agreed to pay him a hundred pounds, which, in those days, was a fabulous sum of money for a piece of land. In the meantime the workmen removed boards which had been placed over the grave, and the funeral party was assailed with such a stench that the service was mumbled over and hurried through in any way so that the king could be rolled in his grave and covered up as soon as possible.

That had happened in 1090. Since then Caen had been increasing in power and in wealth and in importance. By 1154 these events had been forgotten, and Eleanor was having a gay time in the château, and well she deserved it.

It was to be the last of those gay times which made her famous as the queen of the troubadours. The next years were to bring a change. The fogs were to subdue her; the coldness of the English atmosphere was to restrain her impulses. She was to learn how difficult it is to dissipate in England with a running nose and to be gay in a strange language. Many children were to appear and at brief intervals. Henry's dominant will was to put hers into hibernation, a hibernation that would last for twenty years, from which it was to emerge strangely different from what it had been but still formidable.

At Eleanor's court in Caen one might have met the youth and beauty of the world. Everybody of importance was there except the young king, now arrived at the mature age of twenty-one, busy in the northwest with a small revolution. Students from the north, poets from the south, lords and squires, ladies and knights and statesmen speaking a strange medley of Romance languages and dialects, all were gathered of an afternoon in the great hall at the château on the hill with the city clustering around its feet and the cathedral spire half-way between it and the earth beneath. There must have been intrigue, bold words, hilarious voices, and above it all, a musician singing the latest song of Bernard de Ventadour, a song which sounded over the multitude, a song which said only half of what it meant, which struggled with the accompaniment, too loud by far, and which quarreled with the din of the room, a clear-voiced song with the refrain:

> She in this world whom I love most . . .
> With all my heart and in good faith . . .

May she hear and grant my prayers,
May she receive and remember my words;
If one can die of too much love
      I shall die . . .
For in my heart I bear for her
A love so true, such perfect love,
That other love compared to it
      Is false and base. . . .

This song or one like it was certainly sung at that court, and Bernard, standing perhaps a little away from the crowd where he might catch the queen's eye, may have made clear to her that this was his homage, and the queen, flattered, may have said, "You will sing that for us again in England"; to which Bernard, since the southern Frenchman of those days regarded England as a wild country inhabited only by barbarians and not fit for civilized people, may have muttered, "God save my soul."

All the world that counted knew in the early fall of 1154 that one of two important events was about to happen in the history of England: either King Stephen would be deposed, or he would die. As death was the less humiliating, he died; and young Henry, who in two years had risen from the inconspicuous duchy of Anjou to become the ruler of the largest territory held by a single man in western Europe, made great preparations to take his queen, her infant son, courtiers and poets, and who knows how many scullions, ladies, servants, dogs, lords, and what not to England for the coronation.

Channel crossings in those days were much as they are now, only somewhat worse. The short crossings between

Calais and Dover were not feasible. To reach Calais a long and tedious overland journey through hostile or doubtful territory would have been necessary. The favorite crossing was either from Honfleur at the mouth of the Seine or from Barfleur near Cherbourg. One went in a Norman ship, that is to say, in a boat about twice as large as a Newfoundland dory, but, even so, small and very much at the mercy of the wind. A lucky crossing would require no more than fourteen hours, but if the crossing were unlucky, one might be tossed about for a day or two.

At one end of the boat was a cabin, richly wainscoted for the royal party. The masts and the sails were bravely decorated with pennants and medallions. "When the horses were in the ship," says a chronicler, speaking of another embarkation, "our master mariner called to his seamen who stood in the prow and said, 'Are you ready?' and they answered 'Aye, sir—let the clerks and priests come forward!' As soon as these had come forward he called to them, 'Sing for God's sake!' and they all with one voice chanted. . . .

"Then he called to his seamen, 'Unfurl the sails for God's sake!' and they did so.

"In a short space the wind had filled our sails and borne us out of sight of land, so that we saw naught save sky and water, and every hour the wind carried us farther from the land where we were born. And these things I tell you that you may understand how foolhardy is that man who dares, having other's chattels in his possession, or being in mortal sin, to place himself in such peril, seeing that, when you lie down to sleep at night on shipboard, you lie down not knowing whether, in the morning, you may find yourself at the bottom of the sea. . . ."

They had to wait an entire month before they dared even to embark, for, as all the world knows, October and November are the worst of all the bad months of the year to cross to England. And when they finally did venture forth, the wind so separated the fleet of thirty-six ships that when they arrived at the English coast, the party had to wait several days until everybody could be collected again.

There were, of course, the usual deck sports: flirting, drinking, gaming, and intriguing. Many years before, the famous White Ship containing Henry of Anjou's uncle had sailed from Barfleur at night, and all the passengers and crew were so hilariously intoxicated that the ship was sunk and all were lost. There were investigations, and had there been a "Times" there would have been letters in it, and new regulations were passed; but human nature being what it is, people persisted in distracting themselves as best they might on the long crossing. In Eleanor's party, too, there must have been gaiety—or as much gaiety as the rough weather permitted. The only lines in Bernard's writing which seem to refer to the crossing relate that this poem "has been written far beyond the lands of Normandy on the deep and wild ocean. Although I am far distant from my lady, she draws me to her as a lover draws his mistress . . . May God protect her!"

Henry and Eleanor received at Winchester the homage of the southern lords of England and then proceeded to Westminster, where "they were blessed to king." It was a gorgeous coronation. Eleanor, fresh from Paris and beyond, displayed to the natives the latest fashions in silks, brocades, and underwear. She had relieved the Saracens and Constantinopolitans of a great portion of their silks and had had these made up in novel styles. In the Middle Ages it was customary for a lady to have in a lifetime no more than two or three dresses, and these were passed on as heirlooms from mother to daughter. The amount of linen a lady had was directly proportionate to her lineage. As the line grew longer and the blood grew thinner, the wardrobes grew fatter. The following incident, which occurred some fifty years later, is illustrative. Joinville, the friend of St. Louis of France, is speaking:

The king came down after dinner [he says] into the court below the chapel, and was talking at the entrance of the door to the Count of Brittany, the father of the Count that now is—whom may God preserve!—when Master Robert of Sorbonne came to fetch me thither, and took me by the skirt of my mantle and led me to the king; and all the other knights came after us. Then I said to Master Robert, "Master Robert, what do you want with me?" He said, "I wish to ask you whether, if the king were seated in this court, and you were to seat yourself on his bench, and at a higher place than he, ought you to be greatly blamed?" And I said, "Yes." And he said, "Then are you to be blamed when you go more nobly appareled than the king, for you dress yourself in fur and green cloth and the king does not do so." And I replied, "Master Robert, saving your grace, I do nothing blameworthy when I clothe myself in green cloth and fur, for this cloth was left to me by my father and mother. But you are to blame, for you are the son of a common man and a common woman, and you have abandoned the vesture worn by your father and mother, and wear richer woolen cloth than the king himself." Then I took the skirt of his surcoat and the surcoat of the king and said, "See if I am not speaking sooth."

The wealth of the Orient which flowed into Europe as a result of the Crusades—an interesting commercial enterprise wherein men's original love of God was modified somewhat by a greed for wealth—was bringing about a great sartorial as well as a tonsorial change. Eleanor and Henry were among the early fruits of this change. At her coronation, Eleanor wore a wimple or close veil running over her head and fastening beneath her chin. Around this was a circlet of gems. Her dress was a kirtle or close gown gathered at the throat. Over this was a pelisson or loose outer robe of brocaded silk lined with ermine; Westminster, where the coronation was solemnized, was an unheated building. The brocaded sleeves of this pelisson were very large and showed the beautiful lawn of the tight sleeves underneath. Her husband wore mustaches but no beard and an Angevin doublet or short coat which the English, in those days somewhat provincial, thought ridiculous. His dalmatic or outer robe was of rich brocade covered with gold embroidery. The ecclesiastics, too, wore robes of cloth of gold, silk, and brocade.

Thus here in the old Westminster was crowned this boy of twenty-one, who knew not a word of English but by bribes, theft, threat, and promise had made himself the legal master of a territory stretching from Scotland to Spain. Beside him was the queen he had stolen—a poet, we are told, though not an authentic work of hers exists—and in her train was at least one and perhaps many another poet from southern France.

Bernard de Ventadour stayed with Eleanor for four years, and for two of these, he says, he wrote not a single poem.

Chapter IV

The Trail of a Hopeful Poet

LONDON TO ALENÇON

Chapter IV

1

THERE is the best evidence in the world for concluding that in the fall of 1158 Bernard de Ventadour, the troubadour, decided that he would not under any circumstances consent to spend another winter in England. Northern winters, he may have argued, are bad enough; but another winter in England in the service of a queen who has already seen her best days (in the twelfth century a woman of thirty-six was an old woman), and is now devoting her time and energy to the breeding of a group of young princes who are destined to be the death of their father, is an intolerable prospect. Since all Englishmen who can afford it go to the south of France as early in the fall as they can afford to and stay as long as they can, and since English gentlemen prove their love for England by spending most of their time elsewhere, Bernard, who was an adaptable creature, decided to follow their example.

England in those days was a wealthy and barbaric kingdom. It was an outpost of civilization, still only partly civilized. In those days poets were not made welcome in

England except at the court—England has now corrected that condition—and here, where there were not enough ladies to go around, poets were likely to be pushed aside by eager and warlike noblemen. Most of the natives were unable to understand French, and when they did understand it—the kind of delicate, complimentary, flattering French Bernard used—they were likely to misunderstand it. The knights thought a compliment was an indecent advance, and the ladies expected inhuman prowess of a troubadour in the service of the queen. It is in the English character to believe that women are pure and in the French temperament to hope that they will be discreet.

The knights spent their time quarreling and grumbling. If they were not quarreling with the king or setting up a new king in the hope that the old one would be killed, they were quarreling with the church. When they could find no pretext for a quarrel with the church, the king, or their wives, they would, out of sheer good nature, set to quarreling with each other. Instead of helping a king who, in his own right and his wife's, controlled the largest empire in the world—all of England and western France from Scotland to Spain—instead of realizing that England was a little piece of nothing at all tucked away in a corner, good enough to provide revenue but barbaric and uncivilized, they earnestly tried to make all the trouble they could for the foreigners, and their earnestness was not without its reward.

Centuries before, England had had a civilization. In the time of Alfred poets and scholars and statesmen had flocked to the court at Winchester, had transcribed laws and written histories, and in the green fields had wondered whether life was worth living and why, and engaged in those exercises which make man nobler, more civilized, and less happy than his brethren in the fields, the ox and the ass. But a decadence had set in, or rather, the English had fallen behind the French. They were unaware of the perfection to which the fine art of living had been brought by the southern Gauls. A hot bath to them was a silly luxury. Private lavatories and individual bedrooms were vanities. Pleasant conversation, delicate compliment and intrigue, were effeminate, which is to say immoral. Theirs was a manly race, but crude; they were good fighters, but lacking in finesse and polish, in civilization.

The English did not take kindly to civilization. Their consciousness of the superior physical comfort of life among the Gauls was dimmed by the realization that English money paid for foreign comforts, that these comforts were not necessary to keep an honest Englishman alive, and that if the Gauls thought France was better than England they could go back to where they came from. But most important of all, and the fact that irritated them most, was that the foreigners were collecting and spending the graft that free-born Englishmen might justly claim by the right of precedence. England was not the place that an Aquitanian poet would visit unless he had business there, and to Bernard's credit let it be said that I have no evidence to prove that he ever wanted to go to England, or ever would have gone had not circumstances and Queen Eleanor, who was a circumstance of another order and used to having her own way, forced him to.

[81]

2

Despite the eternal discomforts of life in England under an English climate, life with Queen Eleanor in her palace at Bermondsey, which was a country village on the south bank of the Thames, may have been pleasant enough. The palace, originally built in the Saxon style, had probably been rearranged for the Aquitanian princess. Across the river, on rising ground, encircled by a wall over which peered the spires of some hundred churches, was the city of London. On the east was the Tower, newly built; on the west was the spire of the old St. Paul's and the center of the life of the city. Beyond that was the old Temple, the pleasant country road of the Strand, the villas of the wealthy merchants and gentry, and further still, even as now, the village of Westminster. As the streets were narrow and crowded, and the pleasant country road was not particularly well built, the best way to get from Westminster or Bermondsey or from any part of the city to any other part was by boat; and to conduct almost any business in London one had to pass by or through old St. Paul's, which was almost crushed by the press of houses, shops, and booths that were huddled about it. London was famous for its "crowds of pimps and bands of gamesters. Its bullies are more numerous than those of France, and it is full of actors, buffoons, eunuchs, flatterers, pages, effeminates, dancing girls, favorites, apothecaries, witches, vultures, owls, magicians, mimes and mendicants." Evidently England was on the highroad to civilization, although this account, written by a man not friendly to the French, who seems to have had a slight attack of dyspeptic misanthropy, may be somewhat exaggerated. With the accession of Eleanor, brisk trade was made possible with Bordeaux, and claret dropped to the comfortable price of fourpence a gallon.

Here for a few months Eleanor seems to have been comparatively tranquil. While her husband was rushing from London to Normandy, to Wales, to Beaucaire, to Poitiers; besieging castles, negotiating treaties, chopping off the heads of those who betrayed him and buying the friendship of those who were to betray others; conferring with Eleanor's mother-in-law, the formidable Matilda, sometime empress of Germany; arguing with bishops and clerks, dictating constitutions, setting precedents, building castles, keeping a wary eye out for federal interference, which in those days meant interference from Rome, holding his large possessions together as best he might, reducing his expenses when he could, increasing his revenues when chance offered, busy as any president of the United States and much more active, Eleanor, his wife, spent her time during these years in London, Westminster, Oxford, Winchester, and Normandy, raising the children who were to be the death of their father, who were to avenge her for having married at her own choice the only man in Europe strong enough to break her, and entertaining herself with Bernard de Ventadour, Bernard the Handsome, Bernard the Hopeful, the son of the lowest servant in an obscure château and one of the best poets in Europe. She was cultivating the arts and the artists, and for the first time in her life was keeping herself free from scandal. Henry, Rosámond Clifford, young

Thomas Becket who was to die a saint, and others were providing that; and she seems to have felt that so long as one member of the family was scandalous, she might devote her energies to the production of proud, noisy, meddlesome children.

However well London agreed with Eleanor, Bernard de Ventadour seems to have found it difficult. About 1158 he admitted that for two years he had made no new songs, and this admission is significant, for Bernard was the kind of person who wrote poetry on any provocation. He says in one song: "When the blossoms appear beneath the green leaf, when the air is clear and the sky serene; when the sweet birds sing in the woods in their fashion, I too can sing; I have more joy in my heart than they: all of my days are joy and song, I think of no other thing."

Many explanations have been advanced to account for Bernard's silence. The school of literary critics called meteorological, because they are not meteoric but believe that the level of art rises and falls with the barometer, gloat over Bernard's admission that he needed serene skies and clear air for the production of poetry. (Last year summer in England was on a Monday morning and the year before that on a Wednesday afternoon.) Critics point out that although there may be occasional perfect days in England —these usually occur when one is safe in the sunshine of southern France and thus dares to long "to be in England now that April's there"— the enthusiasm with which poets describe these days proves both their rarity and the need of recording them for the information of posterity. A boastful contemporary of Bernard's uses the generous phrase "on pleasant days" and says that these were sometimes the occasions of celebrations. Then "the streets are cleaned and decorated by hangings and garlands; they are thronged by rich burgesses in holiday attire and there are entertainments of gleemen and jugglers." Another group of literary "scientists," the gastronomes, who say, "Show me what you write and I will tell you what you eat"— a bit of information which would seem to be somewhat supererogatory— insist that English cooking is and always was ruinous to the digestion and point out that there are only three kinds of vegetables in England and that two of these are cabbage. This, they say, accounts for the traditionally phlegmatic temperament of the Englishman and for the silence of Bernard.

In the winter of 1158 Bernard begins to hint that he is unhappy. Some critics suggest that he was recalled by Agnes de Montluçon, vicomtesse de Ventadour and his first love. They do not think it improbable, and perhaps they are right, that he was faithful in his fashion to both the vicomtesse and the queen and that he loved them both faithfully and both at the same time. I do not suggest that the queen granted him the liberties that Agnes seems to have granted. In one place he mentions the "evil speakers," but whether these people spoke evil about him and the queen or about him and somebody else is not clear. Critics believe that the following lines were addressed to the queen:

My heart is so full of joy that everything seems to have changed its nature. It seems to me that the cold winter is full of flowers: white, vermilion, and yellow. My happiness grows with the bitter wind and the cold rain. I raise my voice. I build my song. My prowess increases. I bear in my heart so much of joy and of sweetness that the winter seems to be filled with flowers and the snow is a green tapestry.

I could go unclothed into the coldness for my perfect love would protect me against the bitter winds. . . .

But alas! I have placed my hope on her who succors me so little that I am lifted and dropped like a boat on the waves. . . .

I do not know whither to flee to evade the evils which crush me. Love has brought me more sorrow than it brought the lover Tristan in his love for Isolt the blond. . . .

Eleanor spent Christmas day with her husband and family and full court at Cherbourg, and here, it may be, Bernard had his minstrels sing to her his farewell song. As it was as disastrous in the twelfth century as it is now for an ambitious young man to spend four years away from his friends in a barbarous country, and as Bernard may have feared that his acquaintances in the south may have forgotten him entirely, he introduced in this song a peculiar request, a request for a letter of recommendation from the queen. He said:

I am awakened by the sweet song which the nightingale makes at night whilst I am slumbering. I am lost in joy; my soul is filled with amorous dreams; for I have dedicated my life to the love of joy, and joyously my song begin.

If people knew the joy which is mine and if I could make them understand, all other joy in the world would be small in comparison with it. Some vaunt their joy and think they are rich and superior in perfect love. Their love is equal to only half of mine. . . .

Frequently I contemplate in thought the gracious and well made body of my lady. She is distinguished by her courtesy. She knows well the art of gentle speech. It would require an entire year for me to tell you all the good qualities of my lady. She has so much courtesy and distinction!

Lady, I am your knight, and I shall be your knight forever, always ready for your service. You are my first love, and you will be my last . . . as long as life endures.

Those who think I will be separated from her do not know how easily souls can find each other however distant the bodies may be.

Know, ye speakers of evil, that the best messenger to her that I have is a thought which reminds me of her beauty.

I leave you and I am melancholy. I do not know when I shall see you again. It is for you that I have left the king. Grant me this grace: let me not suffer because of our separation, when I present myself at a strange court, courteously among knights and ladies. . . .

One may explain in many ways the departure from the court of Eleanor of Aquitaine of Bernard the troubadour poet of Ventadour. Perhaps he was driven away by evil speakers. Perhaps he had begun to bore her, or perhaps he had found her tiresome. Perhaps he had found the young princes a nuisance, or perhaps the climate of England was too much for him; or perhaps, as his more sentimental biographers suggest, he actually had received a message from Agnes de Montluçon, his first passion, and he had set out for the south, in that naïve hopefulness which is the privilege of poets, to find her again or to recreate her image out of those imperfect details which our senses bring to us and from which we build the personality of the ideal. For Bernard de Ventadour loved many women in his time. One he had loved—and he had loved her well and calamitously—before he met the English queen at whose court he remained songless for two years. Others he was to love, great

[87]

ladies and experienced in the arts of *courtoisie* and *belle parler;* but who can say that each was not in some way a reflection of that image to which he was eternally as faithful as it is fitting that any man should be whose flesh hungers and thirsts for nourishment and whose spirit hungers and thirsts for beauty?

3

There is a quality of prettiness, a sensuous richness as of butter and eggs, a fecundity, fertility, and smugness in the undulations of the wooded plain which Normandy throws out, wave upon wave, toward the British Channel and the south coast of England. The old Normandy casts an oblique eye upon her ungrateful daughter England, whose white chalk cliffs flash back in a triumphant smile. A tall, brown-haired, blue-eyed Norman peasant said to me as he drew a glass of sparkling cider one summer day: *"Eh bien!* The English! We're the same blood as they and the same race." And a teacher in one of the schools at Argenton asked: "And your English architecture, whence does it come? Isn't it after all merely an exaggeration of the Norman style? Was there an architecture before the Normans came to England? Was there even an English nation?"

Many of the towns and most of the country of northern Normandy through which Bernard passed are English towns and English country; the people are, in many respects, English people. The Normans gave to the mild Anglo-Saxons, from whom they stole England, a shrewdness, an intellectual agility, and the gift for playing a game which at its best is called diplomacy and at its worst trickery. English vices and English virtues are also Norman vices and Norman virtues. In Normandy one finds the same boisterous satire of human vices and human follies which is to be found in much of the most characteristic English literature; in the first Butler, Fielding, and Chaucer. In the churches of Normandy in the spring were once celebrated curious pagan festivals. In the festival of the drunken deacons, the deacons elected a "bishop of fools"; they burned before him incense of smoldering leather; they chanted obscene songs and ate on the altar. At Evreux the first of May was the festival of St. Vital and the festival of cuckolds. The priests wore their surplices inside out and threw starch into each other's eyes. At Beauvais a girl and a child rode an ass into the church, and the choir chanted as refrain the edifying word "Heehaw." The people of this country and time were a vital race, whose passions, long suppressed, demanded violent and boisterous expression.

If Bernard de Ventadour went by land rather than by sea, his first stop must have been Valognes, whose beauty dates from the seventeenth rather than the twelfth century. But even in towns like Valognes one may see here and there, if one wanders through the small streets or studies the town plan with an attentive eye, a pile of stones or a bit of wall or—as at Montebourg some eight miles further—an old abbey founded and built by the Norman or Angevin kings, Bernard's patrons. Beyond this the country flattens out and becomes a country of lowing cattle, butter and eggs, and very placid streams over which gnarled trees lean like

[89]

women brushing their bosoms in the water. And all of these towns through which Bernard must have passed, either on this trip or on those other trips when he rode with Eleanor or Henry on their royal business, are towns over which the great ones of those days growled and fought and killed each other. Before them many an honest man-at-arms lost his life; and in the sacking of them, many a thrifty burgess lost his wife and wealth and daughters in order that the prestige of the English kings might be raised and the wealth of the English coffers might increase. Carentan, the next town on the great main road toward the south, was taken by Geoffrey Plantagenet after a siege and was sacked; here he built the château in which he never lived; and beyond Carentan, on a rock hill rising from the right bank of the river Vire, is St.-Lô, which suffered a disastrous siege in 1142. Beyond that is Tessy, and still further, embraced on three sides by the meandering river, is the ancient city of Vire. On a hill is the donjon built by the first Henry, the grandfather of Eleanor's husband, that it might dominate the four valleys of which this is the center. The donjon and the fortified gates still stand, and the citizens of Vire are busy in the manufacture of fresh white sheets.

To the southwest of Vire is the city of Tinchebrai, where there was once a famous battle of which you will hear more in a moment; and directly to the south a city which in the twelfth century was much more important, the city of Mortain, held, when Bernard passed through, by William III, the last descendant of the malodorous Stephen from whom Henry II had taken the crown of England. From the earliest times, the county of Mortain was one of the most important in this part of Normandy. It was always assigned to one of the brothers of the Norman duke, much as Wales to-day is assigned to the English crown prince. When William the Conqueror took England, he granted the earldom of Cornwall to Robert, count of Mortain. Later this same Robert rebelled against William's successor, William Rufus; and Robert's son, William of Mortain, led the rebellion of the barons against his cousin, Henry I, Eleanor of Aquitaine's grandfather-in-law.

The politicians of that age had not yet formulated the comfortable policy of majority rule, and the minority had not yet learned to chew the cud of its discomforts placidly until somebody died. If a minority of those days wanted a thing badly enough, it would fight for it and die for it if need be, and sometimes, because the majority of these majorities is usually made up of people who want to be on the winning side, it would get what it wanted. In this famous rebellion the barons lost, not, however, because their arms were weaker, but because their purpose was less obdurate.

The first two Henries, kings of England, were shrewd men. They were the first to discover the advantages of diplomacy over war and the first to make the king of England something more than the first baron of the land. Before their time the barons had lived together in a more or less argumentative complacence. They held what they could hold and stole what they could get. The king was no more than the chief baron among them, and his actions were rigidly limited by the good nature of the lords who were willing, from a desire for gain or from vanity, to put themselves out to help him or to hurt him. Henry I and Henry II were shrewder than their followers, and before they died they had succeeded by bribery and murder, which are dignified in history texts by the emasculate words "persuasion" and "punishment," in giving the king of England a position which approximated that of a ruler. The barons were not particularly happy.

In the beginning of the twelfth century Henry I was waving a precarious scepter over England, and his brother Robert, ostensibly independent of Henry's sovereignty, was duke of Normandy. In Robert's castles and the castles of his friends were a host of malcontents who were progressives and firm believers in the doctrine of change. Chief among these were Robert himself and William, count of Mortain, Henry's cousin. Normandy was a sore whose suppurations infected the happiness of England, but most particularly of England's king. It wanted cleaning. The adventures of the campaign were many, but the dramatic moment came before Tinchebrai, one of the castles held by Mortain. Henry took it from its small band of defenders and left in it his own garrison. Mortain returned, recaptured the castle, and locked the garrison up. Then Henry reappeared and laid siege. Mortain called all his friends, and when the two armies were assembled, the leaders, the duke of Normandy and the king of England, began to discuss terms. As they could not agree on terms, they decided that the quickest way of settling their differences was to fight them out. Their armies fought for an hour. During the battle the count of Bellême, evidently persuaded by one of Henry's agents, fled. The army of Mortain and Normandy surrendered. Henry captured four hundred knights and ten thousand burgesses, and "no man concerned himself to count the number of their fellows who fell in the fight." Henry lost few men of rank and virtually no knights, and Normandy lost not more than a score of knights in the battle. The count of Mortain was sentenced to life imprisonment and had both of his eyes put out. Mortain now is a city of two thousand, and on the left bank of the river are the vestiges of the old château.

Although the progressive and energetic spirit of the Normans has somewhat obscured the work of the twelfth century—the Normans frequently prefer, and that not without reason, the comforts of a modern house to the discomforts of a medieval castle—the town of Domfront, a few hours beyond Mortain and in Bernard's time the second or third most important city of that district, still presents to the universe a face which is vaguely medieval. It is on a hill some two hundred feet above the valley; it has a wall and vine-clad towers, and a ruined château. Because it is in the border-land between Anjou and Normandy, it has witnessed many sieges and many battles. When William Rufus, king of England, was having trouble with this same Robert of Normandy, young Henry, who later became Henry I, promised Rufus to attack the city of Eu some miles beyond Dieppe. He left Domfront, where he had taken refuge to repair his fortunes, and rode out gaily to the city of Avranches, where he took ship. Instead of attacking Eu, however, he appeared suddenly in England, and here, professing friendship to Rufus, he succeeded in squeezing from that unhappy monarch supplies of men and money sufficient to launch his own blow at the English throne. Matilda, Henry II's mother, also seems to have thought Domfront a good place in which to be ambitious, for she and her husband Geoffrey arrived here after Henry I, her father, died; but Stephen was too quick or Geoffrey was too slow, and his army from Anjou began quarreling with the Normans and after a great fight in the streets east of Domfront was driven out, and with it its ambitious masters.

The Domfrontains are very friendly and very cordial. They make you feel that you are doing them a favor by being there and that you must always be their friend. They persuaded Henry I and Henry II and several other Englishmen by adoption always to be their friends and never to desert them and always to protect them against their wicked enemies. And the English kings seem to have remembered their promises to the Domfrontains. They deserted Domfront when they found it profitable, and protected Domfront when they felt like it, and treated the town after the manner of the aristocracy, which is with negligence.

Half of the twenty-four towers that once studded the city wall silhouette themselves nightly against the western sky and defy the insidious attack of the small roots which slip in between the stones, and the cold frost of winter, and the heat of summer, as they once defied hostile armies or welcomed ambitious princes. One night as I watched the sun set there, a stone broke loose and thundered down into the valley. The stones that were left settled themselves comfortably murmuring to await their turn. When they are all gone and the ugly new church whose yellow skeleton screams against the eastern sky has become old—for God, whose wisdom passes the comprehension of men, is as tolerant of ugliness as of beauty—the Domfrontains will still gossip in the Place de la Mairie. They will tell you that the new church has already cost them more than a million and a half francs, which were raised by the sale of butter and eggs. The hostess of the tavern thinks that a million and a half francs is a great deal of money and that the old church did very well. And so do I.

Bernard then proceeded southeast, through rolling fields and over gentle streams to Domfront's sister city, Alençon. When Domfront had a new château, Alençon had a new château. When Domfront fell before an army, Alençon also fell. Here William of Normandy, while he was still William the Bastard and before he had attained to the eminence of the Conqueror, once avenged bitterly a bitter insult. William's father was Robert the Devil, and his mother was pretty Arlette, the daughter of a furrier, who bore to Robert and others many a count who succeeded in disturbing the serenity of the Norman landscape. William was besieging Alencon. When the defenders realized that they could hold out no longer they collected on the walls and shouted, *"A la pel! A la pel!"* intending to humiliate him by reference to his grandfather's occupation. About fifty years ago before Bernard reached Alencon, Henry I built the donjon which still stands. Later he gave the city to the father of the same Thibaut of Blois who entertained Eleanor on her flight from Paris to

[95]

Poitiers. Once Alençon was held by one William Talvas. Robert the Devil, who was duke of Normandy at that time, took it away from him for some offense. William Talvas, in order to regain it, had to approach Robert the Devil on his knees and barefooted. He was clad only in a chemise, and he bore a saddle on his back. This kind of humiliating punishment was not so childish in the Middle Ages as it is now. In those days, a man's power depended largely on his ability to hold the respect of his followers; that is, on what passed in the Middle Ages for personal dignity. You could not have a great deal of respect for a man whom you had seen groveling on the ground. Later, William Talvas had his revenge; but that is another story.

Some hundred years after Bernard visited it, Alençon was the setting for one of those domestic triangles which created a certain amount of gossip and finally terminated in the polite sport of the time, the wager of battle. Attached to the household of the earl of Alençon were a knight called John of Carougne and a squire called Jaques de Grys. Sir John went oversea for the advancement of his honor, and left his lady in the castle. On his return she told him that shortly after his departure his friend Jaques de Grys paid a visit to her, made excuses to be alone with her, and then, by force, dishonored her. The knight called his and her friends together and asked their counsel as to what he should do. He took his complaint to the earl of Alençon. The squire proved that on four o'clock of the morning on which the offense was supposed to have been committed he was at his lord's the earl's house, and the earl stated that at the same morning he was present at the levee. The alibi seemed perfect.

Whereupon the Earl said that she did but dream it, wherefore he would maintain his squire and commanded the lady to speak no more of the matter. But the knight, who was of great courage and well trusted and believed his wife, would not agree to that opinion, but he went to Paris and showed the matter there to the parliament.

The contest continued for more than a year and a half. Finally

the parliament determined that there should be a battle at utterance between them. . . .

Then the lists were made at a place called St. Katherine behind the Temple. There was so much people that it was a marvel to behold; and on the one side of the lists there was made great scaffolds, that the lords might the better see the battle of the two champions; so they both came to the field, armed in all places, and there each of them was set in their chair.

The Earl of St. Paul governed John of Carougne and the Earl of Alençon's company was with Jaques de Grys. And when the knight entered the field he came first to his wife who was sitting in a chair covered in black, and he said to her thus:—Dame, by your information and your quarrel do I put my life in adventure as to fight with Jaques de Grys; ye know if the cause be just and true. Sir, said the lady, it is as I have said; wherefore ye may fight surely, the cause is good and true. With those words the knight kissed the lady and then took her by the hand and blessed her, and so entered into the field. The lady sat still in the black chair in her prayers to God and the Virgin Mary, humbly praying them, by their special grace, to send her husband the victory according

[97]

to the right he was in. The lady was in great heaviness for she was not sure of her life; for if her husband should have been discomfited she was judged without remedy to be brent and her husband hanged. I cannot say whether she repented or not, yet the matter was so forward that both she and her husband were in great peril; howbeit finally she must as then abide the adventure. And so these two champions were set one against the other, and so mounted on their horses and behaved them nobly, for they knew what pertained to deeds of arms. There were many knights and lords of France that were come thither to see that battle: the two champions parted at their first meeting but neither of them did hurt other; and upon the jousts they alighted on foot to perform the battle, and so fought valiantly; and first John of Carougne was hurt in the thigh wherebye all his friends were in great fear; but after that he fought so valiantly he beat down his adversary to the earth, and thrust his sword in his body and so slew him on the field, and then he demanded if he had done his devoir or not; and they answered that he had valiantly achieved his battle. Then Jaques de Grys was delivered to the hangman of Paris, and he drew him to the gibbet of Montfaucon and there hanged him up. Then John of Carougne came before the king and kneeled down and the king made him to stand up before him and the same day the king caused to be delivered to him a thousand francs, and retained him to be one of his chamber with a pension of two hundred pounds by the year, during the term of his life; then he thanked the king and the lords and went to his wife and kissed her and then they went together to the church of Our Lady of Paris, and made their offering and then returned to their lodgings.

When John of Carougne plunged his sword into the body of Jaques de Grys he was defending his property and not propriety, which is a much later conception; he was thinking of a real thing, to save his life and kill his enemy, and not of an abstract thing, such as saving his own face

[98]

and ruining his enemy's reputation. The Middle Ages knew that there were some women who seduced men because they were made that way, and since John of Carougne would make no compromise, the parliament let him fight it out as best he might. Nor was John of Carougne needlessly cruel or bloodthirsty. It is much less cruel, in a way, to kill a man under the blue sky and in public than it is to shut him up in a room with poisonous gases or torture him in the electric chair.

From Alençon Bernard went south to Le Mans over the last trail that his young master Henry II ever followed, and thence onward over the trail of Henry's greedy and poetic son Richard, via Saumur and Poitiers and thence further and further into the south and into the spring over trails worn deep by the feet of many poets, until one morning he found himself on a naked white road. Above him was a sky of cobalt blue. At his left was a yellow cottage; and before him, rising tier upon tier above the city walls, were the spires of Toulouse. Of the friends he met there and the things they did, you shall hear later if you care to read.

Chapter V

The Trail of a Petulant Prince

LE MANS TO POITIERS

Chapter V

1

THE king fought with his sons. The whelps ate their sire. There were gatherings of the barons and knights, of the kings and bishops; there were leagues against the kings; the bishops fought each other; and the barons swayed from side to side as the gold jingled. Over the fair face of France was danced a saraband; the dancers slipped across the English Channel; they danced through the lush green fields of Normandy; they rushed through Touraine, Limousine, and Aquitaine. They combined with each other; they broke; they shouted. The age of chivalry was in its flower. It was a "great sight to see the moats filled with the bodies of the dead, to see a great charger limping through the forest with a lance hanging in his side." There were blood and blows, curses and obscenity. And during the dance the continental empire of England weakened and crashed.

There were five principals in this dance, of which the mazes are so intricate that only the professional historian can disentangle them or the professional psychologist make clear the obscure motives which were, no doubt, as little understood in those days as they are now. Around Poitiers,

Tours, Le Mans, Périgueux, over as much space as the flat thumb of a man will cover on a small map in France, the figures were thickest and the dancing was most intense. Rushing through this country, with occasional vivid dashes to Normandy or London on the north, to Paris in the west, or to Toulouse in the south were four young men, all sons of King Henry II of England and his wife, Eleanor of Aquitaine. Richard of the Lion Heart was stupid in politics but shrewd, cruel, and indomitable in warfare. He was a maker of poems and was called, by courtesy, a troubadour. Henry, the young king, had been crowned while his father was still alive to insure succession and to keep the scepter from the hands of his mother's darling, Richard. The third of these charming gentlemen was John Lackland, still a shadowy figure. He pirouetted, frequently alone, in the marches of Brittany and stepped furtively through the massed warriors to the court at Paris. The fourth of these was Count Geoffrey, who supported during these years the maneuvers of young King Henry. The princes and their followers formed, in the central part of France, one figure in the dance. "It is the custom in my family," said Richard cynically, "for the sons to make war on their father." Geoffrey announced, "We hate our father only slightly more than we hate each other."

The next dancer is the fat king himself, Henry II of England. He has become so fat that he is grotesque; yet despite this obesity he is never quiet, he never sits down, he is always a-horse. "Where will we find a bed large enough for this creature?" cried the French when he visited Paris. He is a Falstaffian king, a very mountain of flesh. But underneath this is a shrewd hard mind, the mind of the Middle Ages, eclipsed now by the more modern intelligence of Philip of France. His secretary said that he was more violent than a lion; when he became angry his blue eyes filled with blood, his face became purple, and his voice trembled with emotion. In an access of fury he bit one of his pages in the shoulder. Humet, his favorite, once contradicted him. The king rushed at the courtier, who fled down the stairs. The king tore up a plank from the floor and threw it after the knight. "Never," said a cardinal after a long conversation with the king, "have I seen a man lie so hardily." Grotesque Henry II, whose wife and sons were in league against him and against each other, rushed through Normandy and Aquitaine, followed by a rout of histriones and parasites, pimps and prostitutes, men-at-arms, churchmen, and the bully boys of the world. He was trying to hold his vast kingdoms together against the attacks of his sons, of his wife, of Philip of France, of the barons of England and elsewhere, and of the church at Rome and Avignon, all of whom wanted it for themselves. He had held it together for twenty years, but now the whelps were gouging at his entrails and the king of France was beating him at every move.

The third, dancing solo, between Le Mans, Saumur, Chinon, and Poitiers, is a *danseuse*, a bitter old hag of a woman, Eleanor, by the grace of God, queen of England. She is listed among the troubadours; she was granddaughter of one of the earliest and mother of one of the worst. She made a cuckold of her first husband, the king of France; then she cast him aside as too weak and chose as her master the strongest man she could find, Henry, the young duke of Anjou. She brought wealth and power, men, ships, and lands, for his shrewd intelligence to use; but even when supported by all these, he could not break her. All he could do was to hold her in leash as he had held his turbulent barons in leash for a span of years. For this she never forgave him, and her hatred followed him to his grave. She was too weak herself to master her lord, so she bred him a race of sons and taught them the custom of their family. She is now sixty years old and a very old woman indeed. Eleanor the hag danced, and ever as she danced she whetted the appetite of her darling son Richard for the blood of his father. It was grotesque.

The king and his wife and their sons were moderns, people of their own age. The fourth dancer was "advanced." He was Philip the crafty, Philip Augustus of France, the son of Eleanor's first husband. He was a quiet man but shrewd. He preferred directing battles to fighting them. When he was a boy on a hunting party he was separated one day from his companions. He wandered alone in the forest for many hours and was found overcome by terror. His life was despaired of. Louis VII, his father and Eleanor's first husband, made a personal pilgrimage to Canterbury to pray for him. St. Thomas à Becket, the patron of Canterbury, had once led a splendid embassy to Paris to treat with King Louis; the king now paid his respects to the dead saint. King Henry II rode all night from London to meet Louis at Dover and later entertained him at London and Winchester, where Eleanor was kept safely locked in her tower. As part of the celebration, bushels of silver pieces were heaped on the floor, and the knights were told to take as many as they pleased. Philip recovered. He played the princes against the king, the church against them all. He organized a pop·· ular secret society. The members had to vow to protect the country against foreigners and to preserve the peace. The costume was a linen hood. In 1183 the organization con- tained seven thousand tramps and cutthroats and fifteen hundred prostitutes. "They burned monasteries and churches and drove along before them the priests and the nuns. . . ." Their concubines, according to another chron- icle, made chemises of altar-cloths. They wanted to pro- tect France against foreigners; they wanted to preserve the peace, and they were 100 per cent pure. Mass was chanted for Philip at all hours of the day and night. Whoever was the enemy of Henry of England was the friend of Philip of France.

Finally, Bertrand de Born, the last of the principals in this dance, is a slighter figure and less important. If you will go to hell with Dante you will see him carrying his head in his arms suffering eternal punishment for having stirred up strife between Henry and his sons, as though any- body could stir up strife between those elemental forces created to make war on each other. Sitting sideways on his horse, with a cynical smile on his face, he has gone to the Christmas court at Le Mans where the dancers are massed for a moment before entering in solemn procession the great cathedral on the hill where they will celebrate God's birthday. There is a spark and a flame. Richard spurts south to Saumur and on to Poitiers, where he prepares for a siege. Bertrand de Born pauses to sing a song to the Princess Matilda. There is another flash. Bertrand spurs his horse to the southwest, to his great castle at Haute-fort near Périgueux. As he goes he sings war-songs and inflames the hatred of the barons against Richard. From Hautefort he makes the grand circle and sings at every castle, Ventadour, Cambron, Ségur, Turenne, Montfort, Gordon, Puyguilhem, Clarensac, Astier, Angoulême, Ber-nay, Givaudon, Armagnac, Tartas, and hundreds of others in the rough triangle Périgueux, Bordeaux, Toulouse.

The Christmas court began only one of the many move-ments of the maze and that one not the most important. You will see the young king die a traitor, and the old king, broken at last by his wife and her sons, turn his face to the wall with the words, "He too has deserted me? Let me die."

2

The king is holding court at Le Mans. The birthday of God is being made the occasion of subtle maneuvering for position. He who can dance longest and quickest will secure for his pains the sovereignty of western Europe. There was solemn music in the cathedral which is now all that remains of the feudal pride of Le Mans. On the summit of an eminence it looks down on the one side over the Sarthe and the green valleys and the peasant women washing their clothes in the river; and on the other side over the modern city that has grown up at its feet. Opposite the cathedral was once the château where Henry II was born, and down the street was a house which tradition assigns to Queen

[108]

Berengaria, the wife of Henry's rebellious son, Richard the Lion-Heart. But to reconstruct these things one must cut away ruthlessly the pleasant eighteenth-century houses that cluster around the cathedral and with them the seventeenth, sixteenth, fifteenth, fourteenth, and thirteenth century foundations upon which the modern houses were built. One must cut away the transept of the church, which is thirteenth-century, and leave only the Romanesque nave, which is a great church in itself but was in Henry's time already old-fashioned, out-dated, and in need of renovation. The old nave was left standing but was called the transept. The new Gothic nave was built on to it at right angles. The old nave, now the transept, is good enough for God, who is very old himself; the new nave is for the world.

Into the church streamed a motley company of dancers. The old king waddled on legs bowed with too much riding; the young king, Henry, the flower of chivalry, walked proudly close to his father. There followed Richard, suspicious of this new amiability of his father's, fearing and expecting some move to be made against his lordship over Aquitaine, acquired from his mother, the old queen. Perhaps Berengaria was there, a saintly maiden and a figure peculiarly improper in this gallery of rogues. There too was Bertrand de Born, the troubadour, the journalist, the trouble-maker. He was a shrewd observer of affairs and was amusing himself this season with the Princess Matilda, sister to these violent brethren, who was completing her education at the court of her father.

Following these come others: nobles, barons, clerks,

poets; the rout of prostitutes that always darted like flies about the courts of Henry and his sons, now crowding into the church to atone by a moment of prayer for a year of sin. The church is too small. They need a larger church, a modern church. The crowd is thick on the steps; it spreads out into the square. An old woman faints; a cavalier slips up behind a young wife and whispers in her ear. She pretends not to hear him. Her lips move in prayer or in assignation. The sanctus bell rings and announces to the mob that can neither hear nor see the service that the host is being elevated. Two monks look slyly at the choir-boy. There is an angry shout when several knights who have stepped on each other's toes swear by God's bonnet that the insult shall be wiped out in blood. Pushing and worming through the crowd are begging friars, imploring alms for the love of God, and loosening, when they can, jeweled bits from the brocaded dresses of the knights and ladies. Henry is restless. The stench of humanity, unbathed for generations, mingles with incense and floats out of the door of the cathedral. There is solemn chanting. Emasculate clerks with the torsos of full-grown men and the voices of women sing the soprano. Henry is restless. There are councils to be arranged, barons to be persuaded, work to be done. . . .The priest chants Nunc Dimittis— "Now let thy servant depart in peace." Then the benediction . . . "In the Name of the Father, the Son . . ." Henry and his party leave, cross the square to the hall of the château.

In order to understand the kind of square they crossed, it is necessary to reconstruct to a certain extent the attitude of the Middle Ages toward streets and roads. We of the present time like to look back on the medieval city as a small, clean, compact place. Then there were no elevated trains to violate the afternoon; nor did soot from factories cover your face with a veil when you left the house. One thinks of neat, clean little Rothenburg, built in the sixteenth century, and of the polished cobblestones of Monaco on the rock opposite Monte Carlo, and one thinks wrong. For Rothenburg and Monaco are medieval only in architecture and not very medieval even in that. The life of these cities is dominated and directed by the heresies of the twentieth century, that "cleanliness is next to godliness," and the germ theory. To see the medieval street in its glory, one should walk fifty miles into the hills behind Monaco, or into some of the villages near Würzburg, Germany, or into the walled cities of China. Here the Middle Ages still live, worldly, pious, and unashamed. The streets, like the square which the royal party crossed to return to the château, bear upon their bosoms the filth of the ages. If one could have dug down deeply enough through the mud and slime, one would have found cobblestones scattered here and there, the refuse from the large blocks that went into building the houses. The square was simply the place where nothing had been built. It was every man's club. It was the place where the common people lived. The house was the place where they slept. The square which the royal party crossed was not a bright clean little square between a picture château and a picture cathedral. It was a medieval square, which is to say, a dirty square.

In the hall of the château, a large oblong room, raftered, with a balcony at one end and windows cut in the thick walls forming large alcoves, dinner was served; but since meats of many kinds were the only dishes, Bernard and his friends called it more properly sitting at meat. Long heavy tables had been pushed into the center of the room, which was now filled to overflowing with all manner and ranks of hungry creatures, flea-bitten dogs, flea-bitten nobles snarling for charters and grants, unwashed servants, hangers-on, suitors, effeminate young men who hoped to become favorites of the king and his sons, and other effeminate young men who were favorites of the king and his sons; people from all conceivable ranks of society, sitting at meat with the fat king of the ingrowing toe-nail. The atmosphere was uproarious. Everybody was shouting and wrangling in a dozen different dialects, in all the dialects of western Europe except English, the language of a conquered race which none of its kings of that century could speak. Ragout was served in large bowls which were placed at intervals along the table. Everybody dipped in with his ladle. Everybody spilled it over everybody's clothes, over the clothes of everybody's neighbor, and spat upon the floor for the hungry dogs pieces of bone and gristle. The dish was highly spiced. Meat, in the days before the arts of refrigeration had been developed to their present subtlety, wanted spices to make it palatable. The Crusades which were then in progress had brought into France in a single year more spices than France had imported during the five hundred years preceding. Although the king of England, fabulously wealthy, could no doubt have squandered his wealth in spices when an ounce cost a duke's ransom, now that spices were cheap, his cooks spiced it with spendthrift hands. The roast meats, smoky and burned, were served on the spit. The knights whipped out their knives and began carving. They tore the meat off with their fingers and stuffed it into their faces.

At the upper end of the room on a slight dais was the king's table. He stood—Henry seldom sat, even at meat— surrounded by his counselors and body-guard. One carved for him, another tasted for him, and then he ate. While he ate, he argued fundamentalism with one of his nobles, a disciple of Abelard's. The fire of fundamentalism, fanned by the blood and fat of an occasional eager revolutionary who overstepped the limits of propriety, was burning more brightly in those days than it is now. In the beginning of the century, Abelard, a young exquisite of good family, attempted to rationalize religion. He spoke of the mysteries of God in terms that the lords and ladies could understand. He pointed out that a sin committed in ignorance is not a sin, that the soldiers who, ignorant of Christ's nature, nailed him to the cross were not sinning. As modern liberalists, working with a cruder logic, attempted to abolish hell, so Abelard, gallant, sophisticated, and worldly, attempted to abolish sin. Christ's act of redemption was an act of pure love. Thus God is a kindly gentleman, a fastidious judge, and his passion is love. Henry, with his fat belly, his ingrowing toe-nail, and his gross manners, liked to argue these subtleties with his courtiers and his clerks. He and his friends built up the civilization, debated the doctrines, and evolved the principles which envelop us in the twentieth century. The difference is not a difference of fundamental vision; it is a difference of technique.

After meat the tables were cleared and the hall was transformed into a council-room. The king and his bodyguard, still watchful for attempts at murder, stood on the dais and argued. Young Henry, about to receive the homage of his barons, stood a little at one side talking to the ambassador of his good friend the king of France. On the other side was Richard, cordially hating the world. Beside him was Matilda, his mother's representative, Bertrand de Born, and Marcabrun the troubadour making epigrams. "I have never loved," said Marcabrun, "and I never shall." "Love is a worse curse than war, epidemic, or famine." "He who makes a bargain with love," he continued, "makes a bargain with the devil." "Love stings no more than a mosquito, but the cure is much more difficult." Other things he said too, things not to be translated, for the mind of the Middle Ages was of a certain frankness which has been lost to the mind of the twentieth century.

A herald announced that young King Henry would receive the oath of fealty from his barons. The first to be called was his brother Richard, lord of Aquitaine. There was a moment of suspense. The break that was coming had been anticipated by all the world. Some hoped that young Henry would show a politic disposition and not demand the oath from his brother. Others like Bertrand de Born who were made for trouble smiled as Richard clapped Marcabrun on the back and whispered in his ear.

The herald called again, and still Richard paid no attention. Henry II, a man of scant ceremony even in those times, called to him that young Henry was ready to accept the oath of allegiance. What Richard replied is not known. His argument, however, was that he held Aquitaine by direct gift from his mother. It had come to her from William IX of Aquitaine with the stipulation that it was to remain always in her gift. Henry II had served there merely as regent. Richard was now an independent duke, and by God's body he would swear allegiance for it to no b— English king. Bertrand de Born was bored by the crudities of this court. The Princess Matilda was solicitous. "There is neither true laughter nor gaiety at this court," said Bertrand, "and a court without these is merely a park for barons. Boredom and stupidity would have murdered me without doubt," he continued, "had not the sweet compassion, the complaisance, and the conversation of your Highness saved my life."

Richard left the hall and went to the cathedral, there for a moment he was safe from the attacks of his brother's friends and refused to see anybody. Several clerics tried to pacify him, and others tried to pacify young Henry. "Forgive him his oath," they urged the young king; "today his allegiance is merely a form. He might have taken the oath with the intention of breaking it. Overlook the fault."

Young Henry, however, said: "If I forgive him the oath now, I leave him free to offer it to Philip of France. Philip, to be sure, is at present my good friend; but he is equally eager to be the good friend of Richard. Nothing

[115]

would delight France more than to get control of Aquitaine. Moreover, if I forgive him now, the shrewd fox my father will make up to him. I will remain forever a king without land." Henry ordered the cathedral surrounded and commanded his men to arrest Richard when he tried to leave.

To Richard the peacemakers said: "What after all is it that the young king demands? It is merely an oath of fealty. The young king is powerless and holds his title in name only. The lord of Aquitaine is rich in money and men; he is still free to do as he pleases." Richard finally consented and sent word that he would take the oath his father and brother saw fit to force upon him. Henry refused to accept an oath under these conditions, and Richard stormed out of the vestiary, broke through the circle of men-at-arms set to guard him, leaped on his horse, and, breathing threats and contumely on his brother and father, fled southward to Saumur.

3

If you wish to follow his route to-day, you must leave Le Mans by the road that runs along the railroad-track toward Parigné. Where the road turns toward the left, you continue straight ahead until the place where the road branches in three directions. The road at the left is the short cut to La Flèche, and the road at the right is a more or less direct road to Tours. The dim bicycle-path between them, however, which leads through the forests of Les Mortes Œuvres and Les Guégilets to reach ultimately the Château l'Hermitage and the main road, is the one followed by Richard the Lion-Heart when he fled from the court of his father and brother that Christmas day. At the Château l'Hermitage he crossed the main road and passed the modern village of Requeil, where, if you can find the hostess of the tavern, she may give you a bottle of her own special *vin rouge* to drink with your bread and cheese, a *vin rouge* which will put wings beneath your feet as you proceed south by west through green prairies and forests to La Flèche and an afternoon's walk further to Baugé.

Now there are two Baugés, and let you not be mistaken by them. One is the modern city, a kind of Manchester, bustling and busy, gossipy and well fed. The other is Le Viel Baugé. It too is on the Loire, hardly a village and hardly worth the attention of the modern tourist except for its creeping streets and its general air of somnolence. A few kilometers further is the Château de Bois Bure. There is a sleepiness about these cities, disturbed sometimes when a wealthy American buys them up and renovates the castle or when a party of tourists, on excursion from Tours, comes clacking up the quiet hills. Then for a moment there is tumult in the hills again and the clicking of cameras. But for the most part, as my hostess said, *"On dort bien ici!"* And indeed, if one is trying to follow the turbulent dance danced by those lords a thousand years ago, one needs to sleep well. . . .

From Le Viel Baugé Richard the Lion-Heart passed southward another eight leagues to Saumur through the country of smiles and laziness. Countless favorites of countless French kings took this country as theirs by right of nature and covered it thick with châteaux of a comparatively modern period. In the middle of August here the fields are as lush and green as in the beginning of May, a fact which makes the country pleasant to look at; but if one is fleeing for one's life through the by-paths of the lowlands, the country is heartbreaking.

The château of Saumur, built by Henry II to be a stronghold for his barons, rises from the plain a stark monument. When Richard reached there, it was still comparatively new and the latest thing in military architecture. Although it has been restored in recent years, its plan remains much as it was when Richard drove his horse up the high hill to the great south entrance now closed. Some fifty years after the conclusion of the saraband in which Richard participated, there was a dinner in Saumur which bears description.

It was the year 1242 when Louis of France held

a full court there, and I was there and can testify that it was the best ordered court that ever I saw. For, at the king's table, ate after him, the Count of Poitiers, whom he had newly made knight at the Feast of St. John; and after the Count of Poitiers ate the Count of Dreux . . . and before the king's table, opposite the Count of Dreux, ate my lord the king of Navarre, in tunic and mantle of samite, well bedight with a belt and clasp, and a cap of gold; and I carved before him.

Before the king, the Count of Artois, his brother, served the meat, and before the king the good Count John of Soissons carved with the knife. In order to guard the king's table, there were my lord Imbert of Beaujeu . . . and my lord Enguerra of Coucy, and my lord Archambaud of Bourbon. Behind these barons stood some thirty of their knights, in tunics of silken cloth to keep guard over them; and behind these knights there was a great quantity of sergeants bearing on their clothing the arms of the Count of Poitiers

[118]

embroidered in taffeta. The king was clothed in a tunic of blue satin, and surcoat and mantle of vermeil samite lined with ermine, and he had a cotton cap on his head which suited him very badly, because he was at that time a young man.

The king held his banquets in the great halls of Saumur which had been built, so it was said, by the great king Henry of England in order that he might hold his great banquets therein; and this hall is built after the fashion of the cloisters of the white monks of the Cistercian order. But I think there is none other hall so large and by a great deal. And I will tell you why I think so— it is because by the wall of the cloister where the king ate, surrounded by his knights and sergeants who occupied a great space, there was also room for a great table where ate twenty bishops and archbishops. The Queen Blanche, the king's mother, ate near their table at the head of the cloister at the other side from the king.

And to serve the queen there was the Count of Bologne who afterwards became the king of Portugal, and the good Count Hugh of St. Paul, and a German the age of eighteen years, who was said to be the son of St. Elizabeth of Thuringia, for which cause it is told that the Queen Blanche kissed him on the forehead, as an act of devotion because she thought that his mother must ofttimes have kissed him there. . . .

At the end of the cloister on the other side, were the kitchens and cellars, the pantries and the butteries; from this end were served to the king and to the queen meats and wine and bread. And in the wings and in the central court ate the knights in such numbers that I knew not how to count them. And many said they had never at any feast seen together so many surcoats and other garments, of cloth of gold and of silk; and it was said also that no less than three thousand knights were there present.

When Richard the Lion-Heart reached Saumur he found it held by a garrison of barons which his father had left there in readiness for activities against his restless subjects.

Richard prepared the castle for siege, and sent out embassies to the comparatively small number of lords in that part of the country on whose loyalty he could count. During his lifetime Richard had comparatively few friends. His popularity is largely posthumous. Although the Aquitanian lords feared Henry II, they both hated and feared Henry's son Richard. Henry was stern but just and had the gift of winning confidence. Richard was stern, suspicious, and arrogant. Although his virtues show with comparative brilliance against the vices of his brother John, his vices are black against the brilliance of his father's genius.

There are two roads which Richard may have followed on his angry ride from Saumur to Poitiers. One is now merely a little country road, well made as all French roads are, but obscure and unimportant. That it was once a thoroughfare is indicated by two facts. It runs through a country dotted by old castles, broken-down monasteries now used as farm-houses and barns, and churches which were built in another era. It follows a streamlet called La Dive out of Saumur, twists from one side to the other, gets lost in marshland, turns its back on the river, then, suddenly changing its mind, runs suddenly into it again near Moncontour, which contains an old donjon and keep. Since medieval roads cost nothing at all to build, and the trail which was used least was frequently less worn than the highroads, the traveler may have turned off, if he followed this trail, at a dozen or so châteaux to sow discontent against his father, to urge the barons to remain loyal to him, and to build fences.

If Richard went directly southwest on this trail or as

directly as the trail would permit, he passed within a league or two of Thouars, which has preserved its walls and a gate or two. The viscount of Thouars was just then rising to political power. A few years later he was to play an important though not a particularly savory part in the fall of the English continental power. Despite this viscount Thouars remained English for another two hundred years. When all of Aquitaine, Poitiers the proud, Angoumois and Saintonge, had driven out the English and had capitulated on terms which were very satisfactory to the lords of these cities, all the loyal English nobles left in the country gathered at Thouars, where they stood a bitter siege. Du Guesclin, the French general, agreed to an armistice. "If help does not reach us before November," said the English, "we will capitulate." The old king Edward III and the Black Prince set out from Southampton in the teeth of the autumn gales. For weeks they struggled against the wind, and finally, on November 1, the day of capitulation, realizing that the English power in France had finally been broken, they put back to England.

4

Beyond Moncontour the trail has been made into a highroad and joins at Mirebeau the national route which is the other trail Richard may have followed between Saumur and Poitiers. This national route runs east from Saumur, up the Loire, under the hills dotted with caves where the good red wine of the district is being ripened to a luscious sweetness and smoothness. At Montsorbeau the road turns south to the famous abbey of Fontevrault.

[121]

The curious dichotomy in the religious thought of all times shown by the existence of a religious consciousness which expresses itself both by elaborate ritual, magnificent pomp, and display, and also by an insistence on a complete annihilation of physical demonstration and a denial of ritual and pomp, seems to have been more marked in the twelfth century than it is to-day only because the twelfth century failed to reach perfection and balance eight hundred years earlier than we. These eight hundred years are an imperfect glass through which we see only the extremes of the Middle Ages. We miss the infinitely small variations and gradations of thought. God is, after all, both body and spirit, and both those who exalt God's body and those who praise his soul may find justification. Thus, in the century of the troubadours, bishops attired in cloth of gold studded with precious jewels carved their meat on silver platters and listened to and loved monks whose bodies were emaciated by fasting and religious passion. And the monks loved and listened to the bishops and the popes.

Robert d'Arbrissel, a Breton, was one of these fanatics. He understood the soul of God, and he pitied the bodies of men and women. After mastering the art of debate, he spent his youth exercising his talents against the lechery and simony of the prelates his masters. Failing to find martyrdom in this, he retired from the world. He went into the forest, built himself a hut of leaves, and, trusting to the antiseptic love of God, went unbathed for two years. In a land of superb wines he drank only water, and when his clothes wore out he covered his nakedness and what was left of his emaciated body with a sack. The keenness of his intellect, his remarkable gift of words, his acts of faith, as well as the undoubted mercy of God in protecting and preserving him in his asceticism, attracted to his retreat a crowd of followers and the notice of Pope Urban II, who commanded him to evangelize the surrounding country.

Imagine him then, Robert the Breton, with matted beard and sunken eyes, with skinny arms protruding from a coat of sacking, paddling on bare feet and bare legs through the mud and slime of the medieval villages of the district, preaching hell-fire and damnation on the church steps, exhorting sinners to repentance and performing miracles. His labors were rewarded. He was followed by a mob of old and young, of men and women. Married women left their homes and good husbands to follow him; prostitutes deserted their ancient profession; mothers left their children. Rich and poor, saints and sinners, left their accustomed tasks to hang on his words and join in the halleluiah chorus. But there were, as usual, gossips. Husbands raised some protests when their young wives left comfortable homes to follow this wild man through the fields of Aquitaine. Husbands in those days knew what they knew about wives, and when the young gallants of the city whom husbands had no reason to trust were also fired by this religious zeal and joined the mad rout, the husbands of an age where public morals were controlled neither by police-court regulations nor societies for the improvement of public manners knew what they thought and said what they knew.

[123]

Robert himself was sensitive on the subject of their complaints. He therefore chose a "wild and barbarous desert inhabited only by wild beasts and robbers," half-way between the important castles of Saumur and Chinon, and there at Fontevrault established his order. In one place he built huts of leaves for the women, and some distance away—not more than a four or five minute journey —he built other huts of leaves for the men. The men were set to work in the fields to support the women, who spent their time keeping house and singing hymns. Even this arrangement had its drawbacks, and, as the settlement increased, Robert found himself forced to build a stone abbey for the women and another for the men and to separate these abbeys by a thick high wall. But another difficulty arose. For some reason reformed prostitutes began joining the order in large numbers. The "respectable women of the order" protested, and Robert had to build still another abbey not far away where the magdalens found asylum. The popularity of this abbey increased mightily during the eleventh century. The Angevin dukes and the Angevin kings treated it with particular charity, and when Richard passed it on his trip southward it was an institution of great fame. Later he was to return to it, and fat old Henry was to be carried in feet foremost; and bitter old Eleanor—but that is another story.

5

There is a short cut between Fontevrault and Chinon and a good old road from Chinon to Tours, but Richard probably pressed southward to the city of Mirebeau where, twenty years later, his mother and his friends were to enact one episode in a great drama. In that strange family, where all well bred sons spent the greater part of their lives striking at their parents, it happened that Eleanor, whose bitter spirit would not face death, found herself one fine day at Mirebeau besieged by her grandson, the young Prince Arthur of Brittany, a stripling of sixteen, whose ambition to be sole lord of western France was supported by King Philip and opposed by the old queen and her son, the reigning King John. Young Arthur's army, which contained a goodly number of rebel knights, had already penetrated the outer walls of the city when her messengers reached John at Le Mans. John, by forced marches (he traveled via Saumur and Fontevrault), covered the forty leagues between Le Mans and Mirebeau in three days, and succeeded not only in saving his city and his mother, but also in capturing many knights and the young Prince Arthur himself. Those knights who could pay ransom and take the oath of fealty, which to be sure was little more than a form, were released. Others were released after having their arms and legs chopped off; others were killed outright; and still others—a comparatively small number— were sent to England.

John had promised to save Arthur's life, and what actually did happen to that impudent young prince is still a matter for conjecture. Scholars are agreed on only one point: he never got out of John's hands. Some say that his eyes were put out and that he finally lost his life in trying to escape. Others pretend that John murdered him with his own hands and threw the body into the Seine.

[125]

It is rather difficult to be fair both to Prince Arthur and to King John with the words of Shakspere and the pathetic and unhistorical figure of the young boy before us. Yet when one has admitted that John was no more cruel than his predecessors and contemporaries, one does not by that declare that John could have learned from them to look on death with the repugnance of a well bred English vicar or that his or their manners were those of the English gentleman of good family. Arthur was a trouble-maker and must be put out of the way. The fact that he was only sixteen years old does not count in his favor. Lads of sixteen in those days were accounted men and were thought to be responsible for their acts. The Aquitanian revolt was broken, and the great outcry that was raised by the beaten barons has been the cause for the shedding of many tears over the fate of the unfortunate Arthur. Although to this day nobody knows exactly what happened to the young prince, John is supposed to have perpetrated terrible atrocities. The putting out of eyes and the cutting off of legs and arms were among the amenities of chivalrous warfare. The Norman barons, John's supporters, were disappointed that their king should by this stroke of luck have acquired sudden power. With Arthur out of the way, the king's power was no longer dependent on the affability of his barons. Finally, political murder was not a new device then, nor is it entirely unknown to-day. During the last decade in France two important parties have carried out successful assassinations, and though both assassins were tried before legal courts, neither was convicted.

It must have been a great sight to see John's men come riding down from Le Mans to Mirebeau, forty leagues in three days. There must have been a pretty scrap when Arthur's men found themselves hemmed in between the outer and the inner walls of the city, caught like rats and cut down like wheat. There must have been screams and curses and brave words. Many a young boy there fought his first battle, and many an old warrior his last. Eleanor from her tower, part of which is still standing, grinned down on the battle, bitter old Eleanor, doddering now through the last steps of her long and tiresome dance. She had known many a young man in her time; she had seen many a young man killed. In her girlhood she had been called queen of the troubadours; in her womanhood she was queen of France; and now, in her haghood, she signed herself, Eleanor, by the grace of God, queen of England. Poor Eleanor.

All of these things were to happen in twenty years after Richard the Lion-Heart clattered into Mirebeau vowing, like a good son, curses and damnation on his father and worse than that on his brother Henry who was trying to do him out of a duchy. From Mirebeau it is but a step to the south to Poitiers the proud, famous for its vipers and devils, its beautiful women, its good church or two, and its hospitality to saints and troubadours.

Chapter VI

The Trail of a Furious Viscount—I

POITIERS TO PÉRIGUEUX

Périgueux

Chapter VI

1

WHEN the afternoon sun strikes the west façade of the cathedral at Le Mans, it sends through the window a brilliant ray which collects like liquid light directly in front of the altar. The dust-motes rise in it and flow upward and outward through the window. A minor and very senile cleric loiters about the tomb of St. Julian; an old woman reminds you that life is bitter; she hints that the chastely erotic aspirations of her youth were illusory and urges you to buy a candle in honor of the patron saint both of Le Mans and her humble self—St. Julian, particularly beloved by Henry II of England. Unfortunately I cannot assure you that the ray of light fell in exactly the same way on that Christmas afternoon when Henry and his whelps quarreled after parading in pomp through the crowded church; nor can I assure you that an old woman bedeviled some casual Anglo-Saxon visitor who fled from the turmoil of the great hall for a moment of peace. These things are dark, and no man may say for certain whether they did or did not happen. Whatever the facts may be—because the sun strikes the church to-day in much the same way it struck it in 1183, and because old women are pure because

[131]

life is hard, I believe the facts are much as I have suggested—this is certain, that when Richard the Lion-Heart,
hating his father and brother, broke through a circle of
men-at-arms and fled from this same church southward to
Poitiers as you have heard, he left in the great hall three
and perhaps four of the dancers who participated in the
tumultuous and in many respects tragic political saraband
of the twelfth century. He left his fat father, King Henry
II of England, the man who had never been defeated, fretting and fuming at the impudence of the young pup. He
left his brother, handsome young Henry, who recently and
arrogantly had been crowned king of England in order
that Richard by treason and trickery might not get possession of the crown—as by treason and trickery he ultimately did get it; he left, finally, cynical Bertrand, viscount de Born, master of the castle of Hautefort, a young
man well brought up who was at the same time aristocrat
and journalist, patriot and traitor, sycophant and trouble-
maker, man of affairs and time-server.

These three may have taken counsel in one of the re-
cesses of the hall, that is to say in one of the embrasures
formed by cutting the windows in the walls of the building. These walls were so thick that when a window was
cut it was necessary to make a small alcove in the room, an
alcove large enough to be made into a retiring-room which
could be shut off from the rest of the hall. These windows, the larger ones of the room, always faced the court
of the château and looked out upon the manifold activities
of the community, the loitering servants idling about their
work, a groom exercising a horse or a page polishing the

armor or sharpening the sword of his master, an infinite number of dogs fighting and snarling over bits of refuse or snapping at the meat being carried from storehouse to kitchen. Through the windows and into the room came the noise of activity and the hum of talk, the indescribable sound of the busy business of keeping one's self human and amused, the sound of that curious activity characteristic of all times and places, the activity of being modern and up-to-date.

Each of these three, the old king, the young king, and the Viscount Bertrand, were moderns. The old king was a modern, and for those who care more for events than for character, he may have been the most modern of the three. One may say what one likes about the theory of sexual morality which led or rather followed this man into various temptations to each of which he seems to have succumbed—not in turn, but simultaneously, he is said to have violated several of his daughters-in-law and to have planned to marry one of them himself—one may point out that his religious convictions were peculiar and that his conversation was not suitable to the modern drawing-room either in tone or intention; and yet the fact remains that this mountain of flesh and iniquity did understand the theory of the modern state better than any of his contemporaries, and that out of the anarchy which was England when he landed there emerged the English nation. Philip the comely of France beat old Henry in the end, and beat him by carrying old Henry's methods a step further; but Philip, the son of Henry's old rival in love and war, represented the new generation that had learned a thing or two from the old. The old king refused to take sides in this quarrel with his sons. Young Henry, his favorite, had given him trouble enough; let the youngster see what he could do. If the young man were chastened in the struggle which was to ensue, it would be a valuable lesson to him; and if Richard were overcome, so much the worse for Richard. After all, the quarrel was within the family. The old king jigged northward through Domfront and Caen to London, there to watch the progress of events.

Young Henry too was a modern; but he represented the social aspect of the modernity of the time. Young Henry was the fine blossom of chivalry, the hero of the tournament, the last word in social elegance. To-day institutions have changed; the tournament has been supplanted by the more refined sports of polo and golf, and chivalry has no more to do with the horse which gave the rank its original dignity than the rough horse-play which concludes a bootleg party. The human spirit seeking its own comfort and aggrandizement has forgotten those things about the age of chivalry which might be unpleasant and has remembered only those other things which envelop it with the oil of unction. The medieval tournaments of which young Henry was the hero were of a brutality as much worse than the brutality of a Spanish bull-fight as the lives of two men are more significant than the life of a bull. Although it was no doubt pleasant to sit of a spring day on the bleachers and watch the royal pavilion thronged with lovely ladies and hear the sonorous herald and watch the knights ride down the field six abreast with lances poised, it may have been less pleasant to see a man run through the body by a spear, to see the spear—by a thrust which was, no doubt, strong and true—run through a man's throat and break off, and to know that the blare of the trumpets were to cover his choking cries as he writhed on the ground like a fantastic thing. Young Henry was the hero of tournaments. If you killed your man, you got his horse and armor, which were valuable. If you were killed you lost your horse and armor, for which in the nature of things you could have few regrets. Tournaments were good business.

Bertrand de Born allied himself with young Henry and took charge of the publicity of the war. He undertook to urge upon his friends the injustices which they had suffered under Richard, although all concerned knew that Richard's misrule had been no worse than Henry's would have been. He kept Henry's ardor at white heat by pointing out that although he was king in title he possessed no lands, castle, or revenue; whereas his brother, Richard, a mere duke, was in effect the king of a large territory. He persuaded the young king that all the Aquitanian barons would rise against Richard if Henry led them into battle. He himself, Bertrand de Born, the young head of an old and important family and a poet of some note, promised by his poetry to inflame the hatred which he said the Aquitanian barons felt for Richard. He placed himself and his service at Henry's command.

He affected great anger with Richard, whom he called a profligate, and with the old king, whom he called much worse. There is in his poetry some faint gleam of that passion which in more recent years has been called patriotism; but one must not be deceived. The more or less altruistic love of country which is one of the highest civic virtues to-day was unknown at a time when the conception of country had not yet been formed. One's country was one's own estate. The thousand or so castles and counties that constituted the duchy of Aquitaine were not united in any common interest except the interest that each felt in its own aggrandizement. They were no more than a thousand or so castles and counties that were forced by expediency to pay more or less unwilling homage to a central duke. The more frequently the person of the duke changed, the more frequently would the knights and chatelaines by the devious methods of back-stairs politics be able to enlarge their various rights and powers. "When the big ones fight," said Bertrand de Born, "the small ones grow rich."

Young Henry decided upon war; and Bertrand, pretending great fury against Richard and the old king, spent the next three months traveling, chanting his war-songs at every château, and inflaming the knights and chatelaines to revolt.

Although there is much doubt as to the exact trail that he followed, the evidence is clear that he stopped at Angoulême, Périgueux, his own castle of Hautefort, and then proceeded south via Rocamadour to Cahors and thence east to Toulouse. The trail from Hautefort to Toulouse formed one leg of the triangle. From Toulouse he turned westward to Bordeaux along the old Roman road. Thence he probably turned northeast again to Périgueux. The last leg of the triangle is so vague that I am inclined to think he sent out ambassadors and musicians to sing in his place and that he returned north by some shorter route. There is little doubt that Bertrand himself went as far as Toulouse between Christmas and the early spring, when the actual fighting began. If an ambassador was sent to Bordeaux, it may well have been Henry's brother Geoffrey, who at that time was in love with the poet Jaufre Rudel, whose own posthumous passion for an unseen mistress has stimulated the philosophic imaginations of Robert Browning, Rostand, and others. But of Jaufre Rudel there will be something to say later.

2

Shortly after Richard broke away from the crush of dancers gathered at the château of Le Mans to pirouette southward, the old king with his ingrowing toe-nails jigged off to England, and Bertrand de Born a day or two later set off on Richard's trail for the south. There is no reason why he should not have called on Richard at Poitiers; they had been friends from boyhood, and Bertrand had here an opportunity to harden Richard's heart against Henry and make certain that a war would be fought, an opportunity which a man like Bertrand delighted to make use of. At Poitiers too he would have the opportunity of paying his respects to the troubadours who thronged the court of Richard, and of spending, in order to cement their friendship, some of the money which Henry probably gave him. Two of these poets, Gaucelm Faidit and Folquet de Marseille, were certainly with Richard at this time. A third, Marcabrun, may have been a member of the party.

Gaucelm Faidit was a fashionable poet and profligate. His father was a bourgeois and was connected, during Gaucelm's boyhood, with the legation at Avignon, which during this century was the seat of the papacy. He sang, according to his biographer, "the best of any man in the world, he composed very well both the words and the music of the songs, and his contemporaries said that he could match good words with good sounds." Another biographer adds that Gaucelm was a "man of good cheer, living carelessly, for which reason he lost his entire fortune by playing at dice." He became a "comedian," which means, probably, an actor manager, and sold the tragedies and comedies which he made at two or three thousand pounds and sometimes at more, "according to their invention." He himself arranged the scene and composed both words and music. Thus he could take for himself the entire revenue. "He was so liberal, prodigious and gourmand in his eating and drinking that he spent all the profits of his poetry and became immeasurably fat." He married a lady called Guillhaumone de Soliers, whom by his sweet words he had seduced from a monastery at Aix en Provence. "For twenty years she followed him through the courts of the princes, and she was very beautiful, well trained in all the virtues, and sang very well all the songs which her Gaucelm made for her. . . . But because of the dissolute life they led together she became as fat as he and, surprised by a malady, she died."

[138]

Together they wandered over the narrow and friendly medieval trails, fat Gaucelm with his Gargantuan laughter and his weakness for the ivories, for pretty words, and for pretty Guillhaumone, who was connected perhaps intimately with the proud Soliers of the Château de Soliers in the south. On warm summer afternoons they would lie under the trees laughing in the sunshine. On cold or rainy days when Guillhaumone grew tired he would put his arm around her and help her over the muddy roads. When, in the days of their poverty, they came to a tavern, they would enter with a flourish: "I am Gaucelm Faidit the singer of songs, and this is Guillhaumone de Soliers who sings divinely." They would do their little act and hope for a bed and a meal. When Gaucelm lost his money his reputation as a poet decreased, and when Guillhaumone left the convent her friends snubbed her. "For a long time they were unfortunate and miserably poor, receiving no gifts or honours from any knight until"—after Guillhaumone's death—"Duke Richard with whom he lived until 1189 took pity on him."

Another biographer presents a slightly different account. Here Gaucelm is said to have been the son of a bourgeois in Uzerche in the bishopric of Limoges "who sang the worst of any man in the world." He is said to have received thirty, fifty, or sixty livres—sums more worthy of credence than the fortunes mentioned by the other writer—for his comedies and tragedies. Both agree that Gaucelm was immeasurably fat. The second biographer declares that Gaucelm married *une soldade*, a certain Guillaume d'Alest, whom he seduced from a monastery of nuns. After the death of Duke Richard, Gaucelm stayed with the marquis of Montferrat, who was so charmed by the comedy, "L'Heregia dals Preyres," that he gave Gaucelm "rich and precious gifts of clothing and of harness and put a good price on his inventions." The best though not the most characteristic of his poems that I have seen shows a regrettable cynicism. It begins:

> Many a man is much more generous
> In gifts of evil than gifts of good. . . .

If Gaucelm Faidit represented the Bohemianism of Richard's court, Folquet de Marseille, like Bertrand de Born, represented its eminent respectability. Folquet was the son of a very wealthy merchant of Marseilles. After his father's death he devoted his time and his fortune to the services of "valiant men and arrived with them to great honour." He was extremely wealthy and composed very well and sweetly in the Provençal tongue, although he is said to have sung better than he wrote. He was pleasant and liberal in his manner and beautiful in his person, which latter fact may account for his friendship with Richard, who shared his mother's passion for handsome young men. At one time he, like Peire Vidal, was enamoured of the fair Adalasia, the powerful countess of Les Baux. As she was blessed with an impenetrable chastity Folquet devoted his talents to the extirpation of heretics (he was the leader in the prosecution of a group of men who believed that man was not created in an instant in the Garden of Eden but was the result of a slower development) and died, if not in the order of sanctity, at least enveloped by the odor of respectability, an archbishop of Toulouse.

Poitiers is no longer the rendezvous for poets, either fat or respectable, but there must have been a great party there one spring when that exquisite and fashionable young gentleman, the viscount de Born, rode over the drawbridge and, with his secretary and singer, a beautiful lad from Périgueux whom he was training in the art of poetry, was shown into the high-raftered hall and welcomed by Duke Richard. Marcabrun the cynic was probably in the hall with the others, although whether he was on the side of Richard or of Bertrand is uncertain. This, however, is recorded, that when Richard, Bertrand, and Marcabrun met on this occasion or another, Richard swore by all the saints that Marcabrun was a better poet than Bertrand, and Bertrand swore that he was not. Richard had the two poets locked in their rooms and gave them forty-eight hours to show their art. At the critical moment, Bertrand's inspiration failed him. He spent two days playing chess with his singer and listening to his rival, in an adjoining room, committing his new poem to memory. Bertrand, too, learned the poem and, requesting that in the tournament of song he be permitted to sing first, anticipated his rival. Marcabrun was furious until Bertrand pacified him by the explanation that in his zeal to please Richard he had become so dissatisfied with everything he had done that he had decided to join his friend Marcabrun, whom he admitted to be his master in the art of poetry in doing homage to the puissant duke.

3

From Poitiers Bertrand de Born proceeded southward toward Angoulême and the country of the honest Angoumois. The trail he probably followed is now covered by a secondary road, and accompanied—now on one side and now on the other—by the railway which leaves it at St.-Maurice-la-Clouère on the north side of a river and Gençay on the south. St.-Maurice was the sometime home of a formidable saint, now all but forgotten, and Gençay was the seat of a powerful castle now in ruins. "Maurice," says the Golden Legend, "is of amarus, that is bitter, and cis, that is to say vomiting odour, or hard, or of us, that is to say counsellor or hasty. He had bitterness for his evil idolatry and dilation of his country; he was vomiting by covetise of things superfluous; hard and firm to suffer torments; counsellor by the admonishment of his knights and fellows; hasty by ardour and multiplying of good works; black by despising himself." He was one of the 6666 knights who were slain defending Christianity against Maximian; and the remains of these saints, like those of the thousand virgins of Cologne, were scattered all over western Europe and did great miracles. If placed on the sea during a storm, they will still the waves; they can revive the dead. The relics of Maurice demand a proper observation of the Sabbath. Once when a "paynim workman" insisted on repairing the church where part of Maurice was buried and insisted on doing this on Sunday, the only day of the week when he would do any work at all, and worked during the hour while mass was being celebrated, the saints appeared to him all shining in light and beat him and admonished him so that thereafter he gave up his evil practices and did not work even on Sundays and was christened and became a good Christian.

At Gençay the road branches and runs southwest through Civray and Ruffec, the native home of the mystic *truffe* to St.-Amand-de-Boixe, where, five hundred years earlier, Theodobert, the son of Chilperic, perished, and on to Angoulême on the hill.

Angoulême was the home of Gerard, the bishop, who became involved in a quarrel with William of Aquitaine and the papal authorities and was chastened in a remarkable manner by St. Bernard. The château of Angoulême, except a tower and a stairway, has been destroyed to make room for a modern court-house; and the cathedral, although it still retains much of the grandeur of the Romanesque style, has been rebuilt at least twice. However, when Bertrand de Born, coming in on the road from Ruffec, climbed the hill to enter the city by the northern gate and by what is now the Rue de Paris just above the grotto in the cliffs, where the holy St. Cyprian is said to have achieved holiness, when he had paid his respects first to the chatelaine and then to God as was the custom in those days, he must have felt, if he felt about those things at all, that the cathedral which was in his time relatively new and the château which was old and formidable were both, in all respects, adequate.

As one proceeds south from Caen and the Abbaye-aux-Hommes, for example, to the Mediterranean, the architecture loses that nervous irritability of spirit which is

[143]

characteristic of much of the Gothic with its aspiration after things unknown and its suggestion of architectural catharsis, to assume broader, more placid, more realistic expressions. The old wooden church at Angoulême, built on the site of an older pagan temple, had been destroyed in the early part of the century; the new stone structure had been completed only a few years before Bertrand's arrival. Here as elsewhere there was a sense of newness about the world: a new poetry was being made; new philosophies were being preached; new churches were being built in new ways; and every day or two there were new political bosses. This sense of change which in our own epoch we dignify by the name of progress, this newness and freshness that clothed the body of the earth and the thoughts of men, has led sentimental historians to believe that the people of the twelfth century were naïve and simple. As a matter of fact, they were simply, even as you and I, modern and up-to-date.

Although Bertrand evidently persuaded the lords of Angoulême[1] to participate in the struggle against Richard, their participation was not whole-hearted. To their defection—and Bertrand gives a long list of traitors—is attributed the failure of the campaign.

When Bertrand left Angoulême, he traveled east by

[1] Angoulême is not the capital of Anjou, as is reported by Henry James in his "A Little Tour in France," p. 124, but is the capital of the ancient duchy of Angoumois. The political geography of France in the twelfth century in broad outline was as follows: proceeding from north to south, the duchies were Normandy; Maine (chief city, Le Mans); Anjou (chief city, Angers); Poitou, which takes us as close to Mr. Cabell's Poictesme as any human foot may come (chief city, Poitiers); Périgord (chief city, Périgueux).

north toward Limoges via a short cut which took him past the Château de Rochefoucauld, where he enlisted the co-operation in the plot of an early ancestor of the moralist Rochefoucauld. The warrior lord has been forgotten, although the château which he built and the descendant whom he begot are still ours. He may have been a distant relative of Bertrand's. From Rouchefoucauld, Bertrand proceeded to Rochechouart and thence northeast to St.-Junien, where there are churches and a bridge of the twelfth century and paper-mills and glove-factories of the twentieth.

4

Bertrand's next stop, and it was relatively long, was Limoges. For an entire day, from St.-Junien, he had been traversing broad and rich forests and green fields in the rain which raineth every day, the eternal rain of the Limousin. Here and there rising abruptly from the flat plains are rounded granite hills with, maybe, a church on top or a small village with the walls of another civilization still intact, and at times the fields give way to the purple of the heather. The north, the center, and the south of France are each distinguished by a particular landscape and a particular historic rhythm. In the north one is active and practical. One builds protections against the winter cold, one creates, one plays complicated games for the sheer fun of being alive and alert. The landscape in the summer is rich and green. In the south one is indolent. One realizes that nothing, after all, is worth doing; that it is well to sit in a café and sip syrups and to read the "Action Française" and to grow fat and slightly blasphemous in a world which,

[145]

if not the best possible world, it is, at any rate, tolerable, if one takes it as it comes, good and bad together. Limoges is neither of the north nor of the south but of both. The inhabitants are, in their way, as decent as most, but they are not quite certain whether it is worth while being decent. They would like to get out and hustle and do things; but after they have made a fair start, it occurs to them that nothing after all is quite worth while doing, or one group decides that it wants to do one thing and another that it wants to do another thing. Then there are great arguments and a broken head or two, and both sides remain just where they were or go to the tavern to repair their heads and differences.

When Bertrand came to Limoges there were two towns. One of them was "the city"; it was fully fortified, closely and compactly walled, and had been built many hundreds of years earlier around the church, now the cathedral of St.-Etienne. The other was "the town." It had grown up out of the agglomeration of houses, monasteries, and chapels which collected about the tomb of that vital saint called Martin who spent his life in restoring people who should have remained dead and in carrying on edifying if somewhat platitudinous conversations with the devils who caused the ladies of his town much concern.

The tradition of St. Martin is as confused as the other traditions that cluster about Limoges. The saint is said to have been one of the crowd that heard Christ preach. He was a friend of St. Peter and was sent to Limoges to Christianize the heathen. The governor of Limoges was a cousin of that Nero whose fondness for feminine finery and

[146]

violin playing has become proverbial. He is credited with having burned more martyrs, that is to say with having made more saints, that is to say with having, by his influence, converted more pagans, than any other man in history. He has doubtless been given some suitable reward in heaven, although I am told that Nero actually burned fewer Christians than he is credited with and that the claims of his enthusiastic biographers are somewhat exaggerated.

On his way from Rome to Limoges, St. Martin stopped at Tulle, where he learned that the lord's daughter was being persecuted by "an ugly heathen devil." The devil on seeing the saint approach knew that his time was up and begged humbly and politely not to be sent to the "ugly abysm of hell"; and the saint, being at heart a kindly though a just man, sent him to a "place desert where bird, ne fowl, ne person dwelleth." He uttered this command in so terrible a voice that the maiden was literally scared to death. She fell over lifeless. Death, however, was nothing to this saint. He took the maiden by the hand and in a kindly voice told her to arise. She arose and was converted and became a good Christian.

When he arrived at Limoges, where he found many devils to exorcise, he was taken up by one Susanna, and he healed one that "was frenetic." He went to the temple, probably the temple of Jupiter which stood on the site of the present cathedral, and, like a good Christian and member of a superior civilization, began breaking the idols of ivory and marble and gold and silver. The priests seem to have been somewhat irritated by this summary method of procedure. They set upon St. Martin one and all and bound him and put him into prison. But the saint was potent. With the help of God he killed many of the heathen and frightened the others so badly that they came to him in his cell and began to bargain with him for his freedom. They said, "If you bring back our friends to life, we will set you free and permit you to baptize us." St. Martin agreed and in one day baptized twelve thousand creatures, men and women together.

At her death, Susanna commended to the saint's care her daughter Valérienne, who learned in some mysterious way that a man called Stephen was coming to Limoges. Now whether she knew that men called Stephen were dangerous or whether she had heard that this particular Stephen had designs upon her is not clear; but as soon as she heard of his coming, she took protective measures. They were useless. As soon as Stephen saw her he wanted her. She explained that she was busy doing other things, but in vain. Stephen gave orders, and all things stopped together. His squire, who cut off Valérienne's head, heard angels singing as her virginal soul was borne into heaven; he came back to his master and told about it and fell down dead. Stephen was so frightened by these events that he clad himself in hair garments and begged the saint to restore the squire to life, and the saint did, and Stephen and all his followers were baptized. Valérienne, the pure maiden, was permitted to remain dead. The wicked squire was restored to life.

Even the devils played fair with this saint. Once he was dedicating a church in Limoges, perhaps the church now called St.-Michel-des-Lions, and had commanded all the people there assembled to be in a state of perfect chasity. A knight and a lady evidently possessed of devils were brought before him. St. Martin said to the devils, "Why did you take possession of these people?" The devils answered, "You commanded that all your congregation should be in perfect chastity; but these have been doing evil things, and we thought that since they had not obeyed you, we might do as we pleased." Then St. Martin, seeing that they were civil devils, asked the lord of the country what should be done. The lord said that the devils should be driven out, and that the knight and lady had had a good lesson and would obey the saint next time. The saint drove the devils to a desert place, where, no doubt, they still remain, gibbering through the moor, unhappy, desolate. He was a potent, pleasant, kindly man, was St. Martin, and is said to have been the child on whose head Christ laid His hand when He said, "Except ye be converted and become as little children, ye shall not enter into the kingdom of heaven."

Limoges and the surrounding country of Limousin are the place where many poets have chosen to be born. Bernard de Rascas, a "sedate and well poised" poet, won great fame at Avignon after giving himself to the writing of poetry during his youth. "He despised the state of marriage, and all the great and learned men who visited Avignon to see the splendours of the papal court would call on Rascas to see him and hear him speak." Giraut de Bondelh was also of Limoges. "He was born of poor parents, was well behaved, had good sense and became the best poet in the Provençal tongue. He was called the master of the troubadours and was well liked by all valiant men and wise, and by the lovely and learned ladies who knew how to enjoy and make poems in the Provençal tongue. All winter he spent studying poetry and literature, and in the spring he took with him two excellent musicians and made the tour of the courts. He always refused to put himself in the service of the rich princes, but they offered him much money and gave him rich presents. He said that he disdained both the loves of the most beautiful ladies of his time and the yoke of matrimony. He was most sober in words and continent in person, surmounting in these virtues all the poets who have lived before or since. . . ."

At Limoges Bertrand de Born was in his own country and speaking his own dialect. Here he became more than the ambassador he had pretended to be while surrounded by men who might be friendly to Richard. Here he knew his people, and here he began the series of war-songs, the exhortations, and the arguments that kept the great ones in the saddle, fighting each other, in some cases, to the death. The appeal made by the advertising man of the twelfth century is strikingly similar to the appeal of his modern descendants. He regretted the brutality of war but insisted on its necessity. He appealed to self-interest. He called upon his countrymen to right their own wrongs and to rescue from misery the unfortunate Eleanor. Self-interest, vanity, and sentiment were aroused for the cause of Henry. "Do not believe," he cried in one of his poems, "that my humor is bellicose merely because I like to see the great ones charge each other lance in hand. It is only when the great ones fight that the lords and vassals"—and perhaps too the poet ambassadors—"are prosperous, for I swear to you that the great ones are larger of heart, more generous of hand and more complacent in words when they are at war than when they are at peace." "The danger is great," he said in another place, "but the profit is greater."

He sang a song for Eleanor, a song which is the more irritating because it adds little to our knowledge of Eleanor's position. All that is known of Eleanor at this period is that the old king had put her away somewhere for safe-keeping but that he had been unable to keep her quite safe enough to prevent her from intriguing with her sons and supporters. Yet if her sons had wished to see her free they might easily have done so; but Henry was not his mother's favorite and had little to hope for from her, and Richard may have been busy with other things, or, more probably, had a fairly clear conception of the extent of his mother's power and was glad enough to keep her out of his way.

Bertrand's musicians sang:

Rejoice, thou land of Aquitania. Rejoice, ye Poitevin barons. The scepter of the eagle king [Henry] will be removed. Maledictions and curses upon him who has dared to raise his sword against his master the king of the south.

Tell me, double eagle [Eleanor], tell me where you were when the eaglets fluttering from the paternal nest dared to bury their beaks in the bosom of the eagle king. Why have you been raped from your country and borne away into a strange land? Songs have been changed to tears. The sound of the cithern has been replaced by the funeral chant. Nourished during your warm

youth in royal liberty, you sang with your companions or danced
to the sound of the soft guitar; but now you mourn, you weep, you
consume yourself with sorrow. Return if you can, return to your
cities, poor prisoner. . . .

From Limoges, Bertrand de Born went south to Périgueux. He left by the southwest gate along the road which
is now called Avenue Baudin and followed the Vienne River
westward for a league and a half, where he turned south
into Nexon through a gate which still looks much as it
must have looked when he saw it except that now it has
machicolations and when he entered it was simply a plain
gate in a plain wall. Here he turned west to Châlus, a
poor place, held a few years later by one Vidomar, a sturdy
man who knew well how to stand up for his rights. There
is still something sinister about Châlus. Two ruined keeps
dominate the village, and the village itself fawns about their
feet. When I walked into the tavern there a year ago—
thirty-five-odd kilometers is a longish walk on a warm
indolent spring afternoon—I heard the *garçon* cry: "Mon
Dieu! Un Anglais!" (One must not forget that tourists
who look English are, to these people, Englishmen. Philosophy and the arts died in this region a few years after
Columbus discovered America.) The *garçon* led me to a
bedroom with an odor. The odor was hearty and friendly.
It prognosticated hundreds of merry little bedfellows. I
declined with thanks and bought a bottle of wine, a slab
of cheese, and a yard or so of French bread. I washed my
face and hands in the little stream a few yards above
the municipal laundry, where a good wife on hands and

knees was transforming her husband's Sunday shirt—who knows how in the muddy water—to a pristine whiteness and proceeded up the hill to the keep. Here I carried on a one-sided conversation with the present lord of the castle, a sleepy lizard.

What hospitality Bertrand met in Châlus I do not know; but some thirty years later, after Bertrand's little dance had been danced and the young king and the old king were both dead, Richard the Lion-Heart came before Châlus, Richard the Lion-Heart and his faithful queen Berengaria, Berengaria of the yellow hair. It was the last trip they took together.

Richard must have been an amiable fellow. His poets, Gaucelm Faidit and Blondel, whom he paid well for their work, have said many pleasant things about him; and the poets who honored him with their friendship, Folquet and the exquisites who were setting the fashion in singing, fighting, and love-making, found him a good fellow and capable of anything. He had a witty tongue, and although he could fly into insane rages, he was willing to forgive any fault if it could be made the subject of an epigram. When, upon his return from the Crusades, he had driven the minions of his usurping brother John from the kingdom and John was brought to him for forgiveness, Richard said, "I forgive you, John, and I wish I could as easily forget your offense as you will forget my pardon." At another time a revivalist friar urged Richard to give in marriage his three evil daughters. "Thou liest," said Richard, "for I have no daughters." "In sooth," replied the preacher, "thou hast three evil daughters, Pride and Avarice and Luxury."

[153]

"Then," said Richard quickly, "I will give my pride to the Knights Templar, my service to the Cistercian monks, and my luxury to the bishops."

It was avarice that brought Richard to Châlus. Word had been sent to him in Poitiers that a peasant of the estate of Vidomar had, while plowing, discovered a Roman treasure hoard. Richard sent word demanding half the treasure, his due, as overlord of the country. Vidomar answered that the treasure was merely a handful of Roman coins, to which Richard was welcome. Richard, who in the nature of things could know nothing at all about it, insisted that the treasure consisted of golden statues of an emperor and his family seated at a golden table. Accompanied by his queen Berengaria and a small body of troops, Richard paid a visit to Châlus and, if he had been lucky, would have taken the castle in place of the treasure. While he was inspecting the fortifications one of Vidomar's men, whose name was Gourdon, let fly an arrow from the ramparts and was fortunate enough to pierce Richard's shoulder. A wound in the shoulder in those days was of no particular importance, and it was not until the castle had been taken that the awkwardness of Richard's doctors came to notice. The wound began to mortify. Berengaria of the yellow hair is said to have tried to suck the poison out with her lips; ladies in those days were capable of acts of devotion, and Berengaria's faithfulness was proverbial. Richard had deserted her once for the wild women of Poitiers, the gay companions of his youth, and after she forgave him, she took good care that he should never again be out of her sight.

[154]

The day the castle fell all the garrison except Gourdon, who had fired the fatal arrow, were hanged on the walls. When Gourdon was brought before Richard and questioned, he boasted of his deed. "It is thou," he said, "who didst slay my father and my brothers. Now slay me. I do not fear thy tortures." Richard forgave the man and gave him a sum of money, a chivalrous action which the sentimentalists remember. He sent him with a letter to his lovely sister, Joanna of Toulouse, whose charm and beauty have been sung by many a poet. She, with characteristic Angevin tact, had the skin neatly removed from his body by an art which is known as "flaying alive," from which operation Gourdon died. The operation must have required some skill and a steady hand. It could be performed in two ways. Sometimes the practitioner began at the shoulders. The skin was removed in inch strips to the waist. Then the prisoner was set free and lashed with whips. As he ran he would trip and fall on his own skin, which hung down and impeded his flight. Other practitioners began at the feet and the skin was left comparatively intact. When the victim became noisy, the apron of skin was thrown up over his head.

Let you not forget that this is the age of chivalry, the age when one was as courteous to one's enemies as to one's friends, when brave knights rescued trembling maidens, when irresponsible knights-errant wandered through the country fighting with anybody who showed resistance, and when steel clanged on steel in fair fight. The age of chivalry was an age when maidens changed hands with sometimes alarming frequency. When the knights fought, they won for their pains sometimes a castle or perhaps merely an armor or a horse, but the point is that when they won they won something more than the smile of their sovereign or their mistress. The smile of the sovereign was of little value unless the sovereign had something to give away. The age of chivalry, which was also the age of the troubadours, was a hard-bitten and realistic age, and the flower of chivalry was a blue flower dreamed about by a group of rather effeminate poets who sang for the amusement of young ladies who were resting from the more serious business of life.

There were no ghosts on that night when Bertrand de Born stayed at Châlus, but could this viscount who delighted in the misfortunes of his friends and enemies have foreseen the events which were to happen there later his spirit would have gloated.

From Châlus Bertrand went on southward through Thiviers and Savignac-les-Eglises, and what he said I do not know, and what he saw I have forgotten. Finally he reached Périgueux. He was ferried across the river Isle near the present Place de l'Abattoir and followed the street that now bears his name to the château, which had been begun two hundred years before he was born and was not completed until four hundred years after he was dead. The Perigordians are an obstinate race. When the Romans came to the place they built themselves walls and a villa. Later the Romans were driven out and the Gauls entered; and they built themselves a villa at exactly the same spot, and they said, like many a modern Perigordian, "If this place was good enough for the Romans it is good enough for us." But they could never make the place really suit them. They built and changed and modernized and brought up-to-date and remodeled and rebuilt until the Huguenots in fury—or despair—tore it down a couple of centuries ago—all except two towers.

At Périgueux, Bertrand was kept busy, for the Perigordians are slow to take hold of a new idea. He played upon their sympathies. "Daughter of Aquitania, raise thy voice like a trumpet that thy sons may hear it, for thy day is approaching and thy son shall deliver thee and thou shalt see again thy native land. Thy tears are thy bread both day and night. Where is thy royal court? Thy band of poets? Thy counselors of state? Many of them have been dragged to a foreign land, many have suffered ignominious death, others have been deprived of sight and wander alone in a strange land. . . ." Under the influence of Bertrand and his friends, Périgueux entered the war. When it learned that the forces of Richard were victorious, it withdrew, with characteristic caution, and thus saved itself the humiliation and expense of defeat. Brave Périgueux! It stood two sieges but never was taken.

To-day Périgueux has a dual personality. The old portion, the section of the château and St.-Etienne, is no longer the center of affairs that it must have been in the twelfth century. Then the town around the château was one city; and the town around the monastery, now the cathedral of St.-Front, which, by the way, is very like St. Mark's in Venice, was another. As the town grew, the old city was superseded by the monastic town. The busy Perigordians never tear down. There are the remains of Roman ramparts and a Roman arena and vestiges of the old wall. On one of the arches the moss has grown into a pillow, and one afternoon I shall return there and smoke a pipe or two between showers under a deep blue sky.

Chapter VII

The Trail of a Furious Viscount—II

PÉRIGUEUX TO TOULOUSE

Chapter VII

1

T<small>HE</small> twelfth century was interested in the salvation of both the flesh and the spirit; between the poles of this interest may be ranged all conceivable human activities. Later centuries, lacking that self-sufficiency and intellectual freedom which gave the men of the twelfth century their indiscriminate and almost universal curiosity, passion, and knowledge, became interested in one or more aspects of the flesh—the flesh carnal, for example, in the fourteenth century—or in one or more aspects of the spirit. We of the twentieth century, fascinated by our sudden ability to develop great physical power, have forgotten the meaning of the term "cultivation." Our interest in physical power has brought with it another interest, an interest in speed. We have tried to annihilate time in order to increase our control of space, and this attempt has involved our conception of the arts. Literature has been reduced to large-scale journalism, and a man's power is judged by the geographical distribution of his readers rather than by their historical distribution, by their distribution through space rather than their distribution through time. Since we are no longer interested in the spirit, we have discarded the spirit or explained it away. Religion and love have been reduced to the sexual impulse. We have been tamed to civilization, and our civilization has therefore become tame.

Because Bertrand de Born and his friends believed in the real existence of the flesh and the real existence of the spirit and were concerned with the simultaneous salvation of both—although they had great doubts as to the means whereby this salvation was to be effected—they found time, in a life which averaged about half the years our lives average, to achieve two or three times as much as we can achieve, and to achieve this despite physical conditions which would enervate the best athlete we can produce. Thus when I say that Bertrand de Born came from Le Mans to Périgueux as young King Henry's publicity agent, I find it impossible to present an adequate picture of the difficulty of the trip: the danger from bandits, for example, or knights-errant who would be happy to capture a wealthy young viscount and hold him for ransom; the precautions to be taken when passing through or near the territory of an ancient enemy; the politic allusions to his task which must be made when visiting a knight who could, out of friendship for Richard or political ambition, throw Bertrand into prison as a traitor to his overlord and hold him there long years without ransom. It is equally difficult to make clear to one's self or one's readers, both bred in a century immersed in the contemplation of its own body, the subtle intellectual sophistication of a time that could make of poetry an art so complicated and withal so precise that future ages have drawn from it their standards of conduct; of a time that could give to social procedure a finesse and a gloss that no other age has approached. I am forced to explain the interest of these people in the art of poetry by analogy to games and interests which the twentieth century can understand and to reduce the sophistication of the twelfth century to its origins, which makes it over-simple and somewhat vulgar.

2

When Bertrand de Born left Périgueux he went east to his own castle of Hautefort and then south, via Brive, Gourdon, Figeac, and Montauban, to Toulouse. If you wish to follow the trail he followed, you must be prepared for many a disappointment and many a surprise. On every hill you will see ruins of fifteenth-century châteaux. Most of these were built on the ruins of twelfth-century castles, which in turn were made from the débris of Saracen fortifications; these were little more than the transformations of Visigothic fortresses which were built on sites occupied by Roman soldiers. It is a warm, mountainous country. Frequently it is arid. It is somnolent. One never tears down. When one is forced by circumstances, one merely adds to the things one already possesses. In the rock caverns of this region you will see the remains of men who lived here during the glacial period. In the cafés, taking their pleasure of a summer evening, you will see the descendants of these same men. The old and the new understand each other. They are all men together. You will penetrate regions which few tourists have penetrated before. You will, no doubt, lose your way, for the castles Bertrand visited were frequently isolated, and in order to go from one to the other you will have to follow foot-paths. Bertrand de Born did not mind this, for in his day main traveled roads were frequently worn so deep by the traffic that a foot-path was preferable and offered quicker traveling.

Bertrand left Périgueux as he had entered it, via the Boulevard Bertrand de Born, crossed the river and took the road to Ribeyrol and Cubjac. This road follows a petulant streamlet, the Auvézère, which flows in all directions at once until one feels, when one sees it now on the right and now on the left, flowing first against one and then with one, reflecting indiscriminately the infinite placidity of the sky and the infinite placidity of a herd of cattle, that the Auvézère would be capable of anything. One is not surprised, therefore, to see half of it disappear at Cubjac to emerge four kilometers away and turn the wheels of a mill, which, fortunately for the mill owner, happens to be situated at that exact spot. Not far from Cubjac, Bertrand passed the ancient hamlets, Ste.-Eulalie-d'Ans and St.-Pantaly-d'Ans. Ste.-Eulalie is the larger; it has 698 souls, and St.-Pantaly has only 416, men and women together, which, since St. Pantaly is the patron saint of midwives and doctors, is hard to explain.

How St. Eulalia, who is the patroness of Madrid, crossed the Pyrenees and traveled the rocky roads to this village near Périgueux must be told in another place; but I have my doubts as to the character of St. Pantaly. The orthodox, attested, and accredited history of this redoubtable hero runs somewhat as follows. He is supposed to have lived in the third century and to have been offered the privilege of martyrdom, a great privilege surely, since for a few hours of suffering he might have achieved eternal bliss. But

St. Pantaly was a difficult and mercurial martyr. They
tried to feed him to the wild beasts on a Roman holiday,
but the beasts fawned upon him and demanded his blessing;
they tried to break him on the wheel, but the ropes miraculously fell off. They tied a huge stone to him and threw
him into the sea, but the stone floated and with it the
good saint. When they tried to burn him alive, the torches
refused to light; when they tried to chop off his head, the
sword broke; when they tried to throw him into a caldron
of burning lead, Christ miraculously appeared beside him
and the lead hardened. He refused to accept martyrdom
until he felt like it. He was particularly fond of the goats
and cattle, of new milk, of the fields and rocky places. In
a barren and untraveled country, about a hundred miles
north of Nice, not far from the Italian border, is celebrated
the festival of the Pipes of St. Pantaly; and in a deserted
shrine, a day's journey by foot from this village, is a curious figure with a wizened face and a horned head. St.
Pantaly may now be a good Christian, looking with offi-
cious eye at the work of midwives and the fertility of flocks;
but he was once a Roman god, looking through the rushes
and licking his lips with a little red tongue while the
maidens bathed in a shady pool.

The old trail follows the trail to Chambon, but the new
road cuts straight across one of its loops to Hautefort. There
may have been a short cut here in the twelfth century, but
the road which was most frequented must have passed Chambon, for this was the place where the archpriest Anzème
founded a priory. Anzème was a modern and was suspected
of having been a friend to that liberal, Abelard. The chances

are that Anzème would establish his priory not far from the main road which led directly between the castle of that sophisticated and gallant gentleman Bertrand de Born and the important city of Périgueux. When the elegant Perigordian poets called on Bertrand, and when Bertrand returned the call, they would stop at the priory for a friendly chat. Thus Anzème pursued a life of religious ease and scholarly meditation.

From Chambon, the two leagues to Hautefort can be covered in a long hour and a half, and Bertrand, on horse, probably covered them in much less. He passed Tourtoirac, which to-day is guarded by a fortified gate of the fourteenth century, as in Bertrand's time it was guarded by a gate of the tenth century or older. These problems are mysteries. The hills have forgotten the answers, and the people of Tourtoirac, interested in their search for truffles, are singularly uncommunicative.

3

He who looks at Hautefort for the civilization of the twelfth century will be disappointed. The Borns were an up-and-coming, a progressive, family. After Bertrand's death the château was rebuilt many times until some beribboned and beruffled gentleman of the seventeenth century decided that it would do as it was, that the court at Paris was more amusing than the court at Périgueux, and that the levee of the Roi Soleil at Versailles was more exciting than the rising of his humble servant, the sun, at Hautefort. Although the luster of the twelfth century has been obscured by the brilliance of the sixteenth at Hautefort, the

names and achievements of Bertrand's friends still shine un-
dimmed.

One of these friends was Arnaut de Mareuil. There are
three accounts of Arnaut's life, and none of them is particularly trustworthy. It seems that his father had a
château at Aix-en-Provence, not far from Marseilles, and
falling into poverty was constrained to sell it. Arnaut
was born at the Château de Mareuil not far from Périgueux
and was put into training for the church; but "finding that
he could neither earn his living nor keep himself in good
repair by his learning, he set out to travel through the
world." He frequented the company of poets and from
them learned how to make poems in the Provençal tongue.
The manuscript says that he was very "coming" (*advenant*)
in his manner, that he pleased everybody, and that he knew
how to read the romances very effectively. Peire Vidal, one
of the most meteoric of the troubadours, knew him well
when he was involved with the countess of Béziers and
Alfonso II of Aragon. This was at a later period.

Arnaut de Mareuil's conception of love was very similar
to the conception of Bernard de Ventadour, whose first mistress, Agnes de Montluçon, lived with her husband, Ebles
II, at Ventadour, not many miles away. For him, love was
the chief and only inspiration of poetry, and he carried the
art of love and the art of compliment to a high perfection.
All other troubadours, he said, insist that their ladies are
the most beautiful in the world. "I am well satisfied with
this, for thus my honest poems will pass unnoticed amidst
their idle boasts. I and love only have been true to our
oaths." If at any time he were tempted to forget his oath,

[167]

he was reminded of it by a faithful and discreet messenger, his heart, who, by poetic convention, is supposed to have remained behind with his lady when he was sent away.

I am afflicted, lady [he cried], when my eyes are unable to gaze upon your beauty; but my heart has remained with you since the day I first saw you, and it has never left your gracious presence. . . . Day and night it is near you, wherever you may be; day and night it pays court to you. . . . When I think of other things, there is sent to me a courteous message, sent by my heart who is your guest.

This messenger reminds him not only of the high moral virtues of his lady but also of her beauty, and this is the ideal of feminine beauty which was before the eyes of the twelfth century, an ideal not only recorded in poems but painted in hundreds of miniatures hidden in illuminated manuscripts of the time.

The gentle messenger who is my heart displays to me your gracious body, your glorious blond hair, and your forehead more white than a lily; it shows me your beautiful eyes, clear and smiling, your straight and well made nose, and the freshness of your face, which is both white and more ruddy than a rose.

Loves takes dominion over him. He is unable to speak. He closes his eyes, he sighs, and he lives half asleep in a starry dream.

All of this indicates that Arnaut de Mareuil assumed the attitude and expressed the sentiments which, as defined by such books as "The Art of Honest Loving" and "The Breviary of Love," written long after this time, when the

[168]

art was in danger of decay, were considered proper to the aristocratic young man who either from choice or economic necessity found it necessary to keep the restless virgins and the dissatisfied wives who lived in the innumerable castles in this part of the world amused while their husbands, in most cases lads only a few years older than they, were busy defending the sanctity of their own homes or violating the sanctity of others'. That Arnaut de Mareuil happened to be a poet, that he had an exquisite sense of words and a good ear for melody, is to our advantage chiefly because most of his contemporaries had neither sense nor ear.

In another poem this friend of Bertrand de Born presents a picture of the perfect gentleman and the perfect lady. Perfect gentlemen, he says, come from three classes of society: the class of the bourgeoisie, the clerics, or the nobility. The middle-class gentleman, or more properly the independent gentleman, may be brave, but bravery is not part of his profession. He must be courteous and amiable; he must know how to present himself at court; he must know the art of paying compliments to ladies, the art of dancing, and the art of saying agreeable things. If he is wealthy, he must be generous. Clerks, and by clerks Arnaut refers to members of the religious orders, are distinguished less by their religious sentiments than by their charming manners and their gift of speech. Although knights must be amiable, courteous, brave, and faithful in service to their sovereign, they are most distinguished by their generosity, their largess. It is this theory of largess which made medieval civilization possible. There were in those days no fixed system of coinage and no minimum wage laws. Everything was worth what you had to pay for it, in service, in gold, or in gifts. Nobody ever received a salary for anything, and although you might be put on a pension you were lucky if you could collect a tenth of it. The poet's job was to please his lord and lady. If he pleased them sufficiently, he would receive gifts of clothing, horses, armor, or golden chains. The chief characteristic of the perfect lady, according to this authority more important than virtue, beauty, agreeable conversation, charming manners, or wealth, was the virtue of knowledge and wisdom, particularly the virtue of discretion. The English, as we have said, have always hoped that their women would be virtuous; Arnaut, a good Frenchman, was content to hope that his mistresses might be discreet.

Although Bertrand de Born may or may not have met Arnaut de Mareuil on this trip, he certainly knew Arnaut, and Arnaut certainly visited Hautefort on at least one occasion. At Hautefort, Bertrand is supposed to have composed some additional songs for purposes of propaganda, but his stay must have been comparatively short, for he still had a long trip to take before returning to his young king in the north.

He went from Hautefort to Brive probably by the small road that follows the railroad-track rather vaguely as far as Terrasson and then follows the Corrèze River until in the twelfth century the church of St. Martin's of Brive and the château now destroyed and forgotten rose above the walls and the cluster of houses that clung to them. The walls have been transformed into elm-shaded boulevards, but the streets and many of the houses of Brive are still the same as they were in the twelfth century. Shortly after Bertrand's visit, the city was besieged by the viscount de Turenne, and for a hundred years Brive was the stake of a small war which the counts of Turenne waged intermittently with the counts of Malemort, the lords bishops of Limoges. The count of Turenne had been a good friend of Bertrand's, but he is listed among the traitors to the young king. It may be that Turenne decided to join the war against Richard but remembered in time Bertrand's own assurance that the small lords grow fat when the great ones fight and decided to make the best of his opportunity to assure himself of the sovereignty of a rich city.

A single very small road leads through a country that becomes more and more rocky and barren from Brive to Turenne, a city built around a scarped hill surmounted by the ruins of a château. For many years Turenne was able to retain the friendship of both England and France. The kings of both nations exempted it from taxation and the duty of furnishing men and arms, and both granted it the right to coin its own money and make its own laws. The lords of Turenne were shrewd and able, and, as is shown by the history of Brive, when they wanted a thing they went after it.

4

There is only one trail into Turenne and one trail out. The trail in comes from Brive, and the trail out follows the river and the railway to Carrenac, the sometime home of another traitor to young Henry. All that is left of the twelfth century in Carrenac is a few rocks on the hill where the château stood, and around the château streets which are very old and always dirty, and an old man—also dirty—who spoke no French that I could understand, but only the local patois which is also very old, much older than the French of your academicians and your smart Parisian clubs, a language which, when Bertrand and his friends used it, had the glamour of spring, the smartness of a new epigram, the richness of good wine. It was the language of kings. The kings of England knew no other, and although Richard's ancestor, William the Conqueror, tried to learn English he gave it up after a short time. Richard is said to have mastered in the forty-four years of his disgraceful life only one English sentence, and that was more of an exclamation than a sentence. The language of Carrenac has grown old with the town and like the town has changed and decayed. To-day it has the perfume of an old and almost forgotten souvenir, which, if you like to be reminded of past gaieties, is pleasant enough.

The old man with his old patois showed me, as he or his son or his grandson will show you, the great statue of Christ with its curious figures of symbolic beasts, carved by some forgotten mason who was not trying—as the sentimental historians affect to believe—to deny the lusts of the flesh, but rather was trying to bring them under the domination of those infinitely more terrible and ruthless lusts, the lusts of the spirit. By these lusts the men of the twelfth century sought to control the body, to make it the disciplined, obsequious, subservient thing it is now. By these they have learned how to substitute commands for deeds, symbols for actions, the imagined formula for the real form. And these men succeeded. When a wife of the twelfth century was annoying, her husband spanked her and sent her to bed without any supper; the modern gentleman talks her over with the judge and the reporters and gets a divorce. Once a real world of real passions and enthusiasms, crude and cruel but none the less vital and authentic, a world young in its passions but old in its knowledge of passion, was directed by young men. To-day the disciplined traffic of a puppet world is directed by a puppet policeman. The flesh and the spirit were at war, and this warfare is made manifest in the symbolic and tortured beasts about the Christ in the village of Carrenac, which perhaps no tourist will ever see again until the mistral has worn it away to a memory and a suggestion.

The old trail follows the river from Carrenac to the Grottes de Salpêtre and thence turns south to Gourdon. You may find it, if you are lucky. I failed in two attempts and had pleasant sunny days in the heather and discovered two ruined châteaux which I have not been able to identify. It may be, for this is a mysterious country and many a one before me has wandered in the land of faerie, that they were as unreal as the sky and the yellow stones. I do not know. Gourdon, on a hill overooking La Bleu River, is real enough. It has an Avenue Gambetta and, I suppose, though I have forgotten, a Place de la République and a very small boy intent on shying a stone at a very fat sparrow.

The present city of Gourdon is fifteenth-century, and the château where Bertrand de Born stopped to sing a song or two is in débris near the church of St.-Pierre, which was built largely from the stones of the château.

Between Gourdon and Figeac, the châteaux where Bertrand probably did not stop are more interesting than those where he did. One leaves Gourdon as one entered, by the road which passes Les Capucines and continues until one reaches Peyrebrune. Here one strikes into the mountains, or rather into the rocks which were once mountains but now have a tired and worn look about them, in an attempt to find Ginuillac, which, since it is a very small village and perhaps not worth the trouble of looking for, is very hard to find. There is only one road to the west out of Ginuillac, past the Cointe Château over the mountains to Le Carlucet Grange and down again to the main road and the village of Bastit. Thence there are two roads, a cycle-path and a donkey-path. The cycle-path to Reillhac must be the better, because I did not follow it; thence, if you are tired, it is only four miles to the railway, or, if you are not, eleven miles to Livernon and the Château d'Assier.

5

In the Château d'Assier, which did not become important in history until four hundred years later, one might always find in the twelfth century a poet or two, for the chatelain was a courteous and a liberal gentleman and the chatelaine was a charming lady. Arnaut de Mareuil had visited here, and also Giraut de Bornelh of Limoges, the man who disdained love and marriage. Giraut once made a poem on one of Arnaut's themes which is perhaps worth quoting despite the paleness which our stubborn English with its paucity of rimes and absence of inflections gives to the productions of a more gracious tongue:

When my eyes no longer may
Gaze upon your loveliness
I am saddened. Lady, pray
Send to me of your largess
Messages of kindliness.
Bid your guest, my heart, to stay
Still your guest that my distress
May be lightened night and day
By his unfailing courteousness.

He reminds me of the gay
Glamour of your happiness;
Of your smiling eyes;
The way your features show straightforwardness,
And the graceful lines your dress
Falls in when you kneel to pray;
And your pale cheek's ruddiness
When in tournament or fray
Your hero proves his courteousness.

This message will transform the day,
Make sunlight out of fogginess,
Change January into May,
Translate to sweet my bitterness.
I shall walk in forgetfulness
Of time and season, night and day.
Thinking of your sweet courteousness
I shall pass lords and ladies gay
In a starry dream of happiness.

[175]

Lady, in your kindness, pray,
In your radiant loveliness,
Smile on me this dreary day,
Make happy my unhappiness.

Giraut's contemporaries vied with each other in praising him; his excellence consisted in his virtuosity in treating difficult forms, a limpidity of language, and a suggestiveness of style, virtues which the translation does not even suggest. Dante, however, preferred the poetry of Arnaut Daniel; and when Dante expressed his opinion, a hundred and fifty years later, the tide turned and washed out almost all traces of Giraut's achievements. The following lines by Giraut are perhaps more characteristic than those quoted above; they may have been addressed to the chatelaine of Limoges, who was kind to Giraut until her husband in sudden fury burned Giraut's library containing all his manuscripts, or they may have been addressed to one other; it makes no great difference:

When I remember how love can keep
My passionate heart forever true,
I know I was a child, asleep
Before I met my love and you.
Once I dreamed, when the year was new,
Of armies of roses, a thousand deep,
And the fleur-de-lis whispered of you. . . .
    Then I awoke from my boyish sleep.

To her I sing, to her I weep,
I send my prayers to her and you

In Limousin where you two keep
Splendor and beauty and courtesy too.
Noblest of all great ladies are you,
High-born, well mannered, chaste and sweet,
Kindly and virtuous, learned and true. . . .
  Alas, that I woke from my boyish sleep!

Alas for me, I am forced to keep
My secret hid from the world and you.
Speakers of evil jealously peep
And deride a love that is pure and true.
If I honestly gave you your honest due
The slanderous world which makes love cheap
Would deride the passion I feel for you.
  Alas, that I woke from my childish sleep!

But when from the crush of the crowd I creep
Away to the window which looks toward you
I sing in my heart—and that song is true—
  Thank God that I woke from my childish sleep.

6

From Assier, whose old château fort has been transformed
into a sixteenth-century castle and historic monument, the
country road leads southwest of Cardaillac, where it meets
the main road, and later to Figeac, which dreams in an
amphitheater of wooded and vine-clad hills of a past which
was greater than its present. There are, as usual, two
cities in Figeac: the old city, on the left bank, clustered
around a hill which once bore a château; and the town, on
the right bank, which grew around the monastery and the
church of the potent St.-Sauveur. This monastery, which

originally belonged to the Benedictine order, became in the tenth century one of the important centers of Cluniac reform; and here, as elsewhere, under the influence of that peculiar spiritual renaissance, the arts and sciences flourished and the flesh and spirit dwelt together in the honor of God. The flesh and the spirit, however, were sometimes at war, for the monastics honored God in a way which the pious townspeople sometimes resented. Sometimes the townspeople felt themselves oppressed by the zeal of the clerics; and sometimes the clerics, relying on their right of trial in ecclesiastical courts, would take from the townspeople those pretty and amiable things which all men treasure and which none can deny make manifest to all the world the greatness and goodness of the Creator. About the time that Bertrand entered Figeac with the intention of persuading the knights of that district to supplant the men who held power with the men who would like to hold power, the people of the town and the people of the monastery agreed to compose their differences.

On the Rue Griffoul—unfortunately I do not know what it was called in Bertrand's day—are still several houses that were new when Bertrand came to town, and near St.-Sauveur is the bridge which he crossed when with his bodyguard, his secretary, and his sweet singers he clattered up the hill to the château. The streets are narrow and filled with the ordure of centuries; and one wonders, as one wades through them and escapes by a hair's breadth the emptying of a chamber-pot from an upstairs window, whether they could possibly have been dirtier a thousand years ago. Ah, well for Bertrand de Born and his friends that they never

[178]

heard of the germ theory, that cleanliness was not yet placed next to godliness, and that the entire world was more or less democratically dirty.

Three miles to the south is Capdenac, with a modern château but with old, old walls that crown a steep hill. The château is and probably always was at the north gate, which is guarded by two towers. From the top of these towers, a watchman can note the approach of any considerable body of knights, their bright armor heliographing news of their position; and the tourist with an hour or two to spare can look down over the valley of the Lot—on the quiet vineyards of the hills, the rich green of the valleys threaded by chalky white roads.

Somewhere in this sector Bertrand received word from Henry. Exactly how this announcement was made is unknown, but the purport was that Henry had withdrawn his demands upon Richard and with vacillating spirit— now engaged, probably, in some new venture—wished to withdraw from the war. Bertrand sent back a musician instead of a letter. He had coached the musician in a song and sent word that if Henry withdrew the musician would spread this song throughout the length and breadth of the country. The song contained among other things the following complimentary lines:

> I'll help the vassals understand
> That Henry the king is a king without land
> Because he's the king of cowards.
> I'll spread the fame throughout the land
> Of the doughty king of cowards.

When the musician returned, he brought word that Henry had declared the war on Richard again, and begged his friend to withdraw his insulting poem and substitute for it one more calculated to sooth his master's vanity. Bertrand sang:

With gaily colored helm and spear
And freshly polished shield
The knights ride in from far and near
And hold their ground,
    And scorn to yield;
       And the horses in thunder
           Drag fallen riders through the field.
The Aquitanian castles reel
With the battle's thunder.
 And all the vassals in the fray
 And all the true knights wonder
    How many heads they'll break this day.

I do not love my ease and meat,
A soft bed, and good food to eat
As well as when on chargers fleet
Armies intent on battle meet
    And riderless horses scream. . . .
Then shouts of hate and oaths resound,
Foemen's bodies carpet the ground,
And many a brave one goes to rest
With a long spear growing in his chest
    And riderless horses scream.

This is one of those gay, light-hearted relics of the twelfth century which should help us to understand that the age of chivalry was not an age where two gentlemen met on an open field, slapped each other's wrists, and then retired to a shady grove to drink a dish of tea in honor of their respective mistresses. The age of true chivalry, curiously enough, is always an age or two earlier than the age in which we live. Modern writers think that the age of chivalry is in the twelfth century. Writers of the twelfth century thought that the age of chivalry was the eighth or ninth century, and the gentlemen of those years thought, no doubt, that it was still earlier. The twelfth century cannot, however, free itself from responsibility. The men of the twelfth century were the first to record an ideal of chivalric conduct; and this ideal formulation, this dream, this series of euphemisms, prepared for the entertainment of high-born ladies and *jeunes filles bien élevées* and accepted by them as amusing articles and pleasant ways of saying unpleasant things, had to wait for the scientific nineteenth century to mistake euphemism for the fact, the dream for the reality. And now the ideal of conduct contained in the poems of the twelfth century—not those written by Bertrand de Born, who was a realist and something of a cynic, but by his friends and companions—has been accepted not only as a social code which directs the actions of all gentlemen—it had always been that—but as a fair picture of the life of the time.

7

The Middle Ages have almost entirely disappeared from Montauban. Hardly a stone is left of the city Bertrand de Born visited when Rixende de Montauban lived in the château which had been begun a hundred years earlier by the counts of Toulouse, which was to be continued by the Black Prince in the fourteenth century and completed by Bishop de Berthier in the seventeenth. Although there was probably a bridge over the Tarn when Bertrand rode out of the city toward Toulouse, the present bridge with seven Gothic arches, well fortified against the attacks of hostile armies from the north and west and warlike monks from the monastery across the river, was built twenty years after Bertrand left the city.

Before there had been a city of Montauban, there had been a town of Montauriol, which had been built sometime after 820 by the great good man St. Theodard; and before there had been a town of Montauriol, there had been, sometime about the year 200 or 300 the Roman camp of Mons Albanus. We must not forget that the four centuries between 820 and 1220 were as long to the people of the Middle Ages as the four centuries between 1520—when America had been discovered only thirty years—and 1920 are to us. There was trouble of a kind between the monks of the monastery and their vassals. The counts of Toulouse made capital of this quarrel, and realizing that the White Mountain would be an excellent site for a fortress, seized a large part of the monastic lands and founded a town across the river. They made propositions to the tenants of the monastic lands, offered them home-seekers' rates, freedom from taxation, power rights, and other modern advantages. Most of Montauriol moved to Montauban, and the monks were sorely tempted to use strong language.

When Bertrand was at Montauban, the chatelaine was perhaps the same Rixende or Richilde who a few years later inspired a sinister passion in the bosom of the poet Roolet de Gassin. Roolet's enemies said that he was a babbler, a charlatan, ugly, unpleasant, misanthropic, disagreeable, and afflicted by divers other infirmities. His friends said that he was a remarkable gentleman, handsome of feature, pleasant and gracious of manner, and a good poet in all languages. He was involved in the Albigensian heresy, an interesting form of ultra-fundamentalism. Roolet was "well liked by the ladies and princesses who understood the charms of poetry. They gave him rich gifts of horses, armor, clothing, and gold according to the custom of the time." At Montpellier, where he was attending a convention, he was "surprised by love of a gentle lady of the Provence called Rixende de Montauban." She, however, like a false deceiver, made fun of his dress and manners. She laughed at him in public and said unprintable things about him to her friends. Nevertheless, "she was lovely, wise, virtuous, and well learned in the arts of poetry." Roolet, who was "incredibly taken by his love for this lady, forgot all the art of compliment in which he had excelled and, filled with a poetic furor, made a song against this lady, a song of base ingratitude and deadly insult." The friends of this "false deceiver" were powerful, and Roolet was persuaded to leave Montpellier suddenly and at night. His future as a poet had been ruined by this hasty and discourteous action. He took refuge in the most austere monastery in the world. Austerity seems not to have agreed with him. At any rate, he left the monastic life a few years later, bought a pleasant château, married a virtuous wife, begot children, burned heretics, and prospered.

[183]

There is a story told to all French children of one Renaut de Montauban who had in his service a great magician and a magic horse that could fly through the air. He is said to have killed the son of Charlemagne with a chess-board, and he and his friends lived in outlawry for many years like Robin Hood, helping the poor and robbing the rich. By a lucky chance, they helped the king of Bordeaux against the Saracens, and Renaut married the king's sister and lived in the château of Montauban. M. Bédier, whose work on these problems none may question, thinks that the Montauban of this legend is not the one Bertrand de Born visited but another Montauban several hundred miles further west. M. Bédier thinks that the novel was written about the time Bertrand made his trip, and there can be no doubt that the customs and social situations in the novel were drawn from models furnished by the twelfth century.

From Montauban it is but a step to Toulouse, whence Bertrand turned west for the other two legs of his journey, if he did not return at once to his castle in Hautefort, there or further north to meet young Henry and engage with him in his last and most important war.

Chapter VIII

The Trail of a Broken King

LE MANS TO FONTEVRAULT

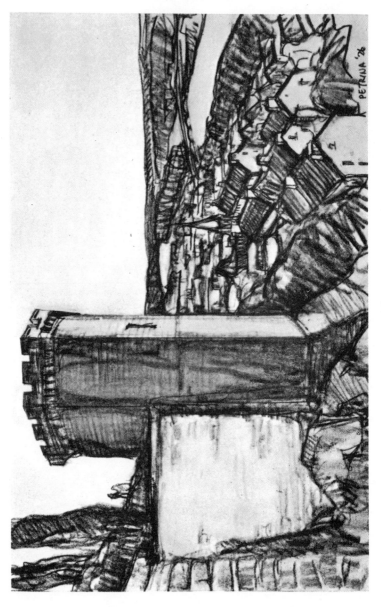

Chinon

Chapter VIII

1

K<small>ING</small> Henry II of England, like Humpty-Dumpty, to
whom he bore a striking resemblance—both were oval in
body, tending toward the round—had a great fall; and since
his and Humpty's falls were from the heights, none of his
horses and none of his men could ever put him together
again. When he fell he thought it was God taking ven-
geance on him for his various misdeeds and misdemeanors.
In this thought he failed to do justice to his demoniac wife,
Eleanor of Aquitaine, said to have been born of the devil,
sometime queen of the troubadours, the old woman of the
tower, who, too weak herself to wreak her spite on her husband, had borne from her body a pack of angry, proud,
noisy, suspicious, and quarrelsome sons, who, as Henry himself said, pecked at his heart like young eaglets at raw meat.
Finally the old heart broke, and Henry, breathing defiance
to the God of the Christians, turned his face to the wall.

Henry was the superman of the age of the troubadours,
and his successes were phenomenal and characteristic of
his time. While he was still a young man, he succeeded
where his father had failed in seducing Eleanor of Aquitaine, the wealthy wife of King Louis of France. She
threw her wealth in his lap, a toy for him to play with,
a stake for him to throw on the table in his big game which

finally brought him the crown of England. He was victorious in his struggles with his relatives, the barons of France, England, and Normandy; he was victorious in his struggles with those other barons who were not his relatives; he was successful in his struggles with two French kings, and with the church at Rome. Where other men would have lost a battle, he won it; where other men would have wasted weeks besieging a city, he took it in a single night; where other men would have been betrayed, he caught the traitor in the act. He launched defiance at the church and at God. The struggle was bitter, and for a time, when Thomas Becket was murdered, the world thought that Henry the superman was to be defeated; but from this too he drew new strength and lived to see the day when the great lords spiritual came begging at his door and he sent them about their business with a cynical oath. He was even successful in that more bitter struggle from which no man emerges unscathed, the struggle with his wife, the demoniac woman from Aquitaine, said to have been born of the devil but certainly the daughter of a nun raped from a convent. But this superman was superior to his fellows only in having more intensely than they the great human virtues and vices. He was shrewd enough to make strength out of his weaknesses. He was more concerned, said a contemporary, about a dead soldier than a living knight; and this, in a century of universal warfare and slaughter, was a great weakness. Partly because of his sympathy with his soldiers, and partly because, like Mr. Shaw, he was a good housekeeper and disliked to see things wasted, he avoided battle whenever he could make diplomacy or bribery do the work.

Both he and his grandfather, Henry I, realized very clearly that a bribed enemy is worth a thousand dead followers.

Henry II was the fool of nature. He began life as a man. At an age when our youths are being exposed to courses of lectures carefully arranged to "teach a moral lesson and at the same time maintain the student's interest," Henry had blossomed into the superman of Europe. It was only after he had been a superman that he achieved the final dignity of being human. His humanity, which emerged late in life, ruined him. It was as a human being that Henry suffered the terrible humiliation at Le Mans and Gisors and defeat on the field of Colombières near Tours. It was the human being sick unto death that was carried on its last ride from Colombières to Chinon and thence to the grave whose open jaws devoured him at Fontevrault. None of the world about him understood the reason for his fall; and none, save perhaps wizened old Eleanor watching events from her tower, could realize that his defeat was more spectacular than his success. But when his sons betrayed him, when one after the other they mocked him and made war on him, when they permitted their archers to shoot at him while he stood in military parley with them before the walls of the cities they had stolen from him—when this treasure of affection made him the fool of the world, Henry's life became ashes, and his body returned to the dust.

2

The fat old king was lonely. He sat in his château at Le Mans overlooking the bright river and the clean countryside of Maine while messengers, one after the other, brought word of the approach of his enemies, closer and closer, under the leadership of Philip of France and Henry's troubadour son, Richard the Lion-Heart. He might have done much for Richard had Richard not been his wife's darling and therefore his enemy. . . . Again and again he had made overtures of peace and friendship to Richard. Again and again these overtures had been rejected. The fat old king was lonely. He limped up and down the walls of his castle. A June sunset was upon him. . . .

3

King Henry in his glorious youth, when every castle fell before him and the world trembled at his step, made merry with Thomas à Becket, the young churchman. Becket had taken orders, but only the first orders. He was still a free man, free as a bird in his actions, swift as a hawk in his thought. He became a faithful falcon to the king. Some chroniclers say that Becket's father was Gilbert, a Saxon knight, and that his mother was a Saracen woman whom Gilbert had seduced while on the Crusades. She knew only two words of English; one of them was "London," and the other was "Gilbert." She followed him home from the Crusades and ran through the streets of London calling his name and ultimately found him. Thomas had studied at Bologna and had been a student of a student of Abelard's. He made himself the king's man and became the king's chancellor. With a crowd of poets and pimps and wild women the young king would often descend on Becket in his sumptuous palace in London. He would sit on the table while Becket finished his supper, and together they would plan wild parties.

Then Becket was made archbishop of Canterbury and as such the most powerful lord of England. Henry might subdue his independent barons and bend them to his will, but the primate, richer and more powerful in his own right than any baron, had as his support the great moral force of the church at Rome. The primate could not be subdued. The strife was long and bitter. The king's fury raged more fierce at each new impertinence of the archbishop; the archbishop's obduracy gleamed the brighter with each countermove of the king. Becket was exiled from England. After seven years an apparent reconciliation was effected, and Thomas returned to Canterbury. His first official act was to excommunicate all the prelates, bishops, and clerks who had been friendly to the king. Then he returned to his palace, and since it was Christmas day and Thursday he ate meat like all the rest of the world in great high spirits.

Henry received word of these excommunications when he was at Avranches on December 29. The king cried: "If all my friends have been excommunicated, by God's eyes, I'm excommunicated too! What a pack of fools and cowards I have nourished in my house, that not a one of them will avenge me of this one upstart clerk!" Four of his knights rid him of the upstart clerk, and England had another martyr and Henry a new difficulty. Henry shut himself in his room and for three days refused to eat or see visitors. When the pope heard the news he went into deep mourning. All the barons in England who had been waiting for the king to make a false step suddenly discovered that they were true sons of the church and that Henry was their legitimate enemy. Thomas, the *bon vivant* and the obdurate protector of the church's temporal interests, became a saint. He had sought martyrdom, and he had found it.

4

The old king paced the walls of Le Mans at night waiting for the knot of his enemies to tighten around him and shear from him his earthly power and humiliate him before the world. He thought of many things. He never forgot a friend and never forgave an enemy. Thomas had been both friend and enemy. Henry had been responsible for the death of Thomas; and yet, though he had caused that death, he had not intended it. He had done penance both as a king and as a private person. As a king he took oaths and made promises and gave large gifts of money to Templars. His private penance he performed three years later when he returned to England.

He made a pilgrimage to Canterbury. As he came in sight of the cathedral church he dismounted, and, in bare feet, forbidding all present to do him honor or treat him as though he differed in any way from a private pilgrim, he walked to the church. At the steps where Thomas fell, he dropped to his knees, kissed the spot, and wept. Then he came to the tomb of the saint. Here he lay for a long time weeping and praying. He made formal confession of his sins and restored all its rights to the see of Canterbury. All the churchmen present were invited to punish him. He removed his upper garments, and each priest gave him five blows with the rod and each monk three blows. He fasted all that night, and the next morning before he left for London was given, as a sign of reconciliation, a drink of holy water in which some of the saint's blood had been mixed. That he survived was a miracle of less importance to the medieval mind than the immediate arrival of news that the army of Scotland had been defeated and that the Scottish king, one of Henry's most persistent enemies, had been captured. Henry, the citizen of England, had purged his soul; and Thomas the saint had brought a measure of success to Henry the king.

5

Thomas had gained a sainthood, and Henry had dreamed of an empire rivaling that of Rome. His lands were too vast for him to handle alone, but he had sons. To Richard, who was popularly believed to have the lion's heart, he gave the lion's share, Aquitaine. To John he gave Brittany; and Henry, his oldest son, he made partner in the rule of England. There were two kings: Henry the father, the old king; and Henry the son, the young king. "When I alone had rule of my kingdom," he said, "I let nothing go of my rights; and now that many are joined in the government of my lands, it were a shame that any part of them were lost." The barons, who hated the old king for conquering them, flocked to the court of the young; the wife, who hated her husband for subduing her, spurred the son to revolt; Philip, the king of France, who envied Henry his lands and power, invited the son to share in his pleasures, ate with him at the same table, slept with him in the same bed. . . .

The day came when Richard refused to recognize the rights of his elder brother and when Bertrand de Born rode south breathing hope of death and damnation toward Richard and the old king. A war was fought between the two brothers. The old king watched cynically from London. Then to preserve his kingdom he threw his forces with Richard. Henry and Bertrand the troubadour grew desperate. They robbed monasteries and pillaged nunneries. After burning a castle a few miles south of Bertrand's castle, Hautefort, the young king was seized with dysentery. He sent a message imploring his father to come to his bedside and grant forgiveness. Henry, fearing treachery, as well he might, since he had become now somewhat aware of the temper of his offspring, refused. The young king died in sackcloth on a bed of ashes repenting of his sins. Henry mourned for him as David for Absalom.

Richard was now the heir apparent and with his father marched through Aquitaine and Touraine punishing the rebellious vassals. Hautefort, Bertrand de Born's castle, was taken after stubborn resistance. Bertrand was condemned to death. Dante a hundred years later thought that Bertrand had been the chief cause of the rebellion. He was brought before the king to show cause why the sentence of death should not be imposed upon him.

The king said: "Bertrand, Bertrand, thou hast always boasted that thou hadst never need of more than half of thy intelligence. It seems to me that to-day thou art in great need of all of it."

"Sire," said Bertrand, "what I have boasted is true, and it is still true to-day."

[194]

But the king said to him, "Indeed it seems to me that to-day thou hast lost it all."

"Indeed, Sire," replied the poet, "to-day I have none left."

"And how is that?" asked the king.

"Sire," replied Bertrand, "on the day that the valiant king, thy son, died, I lost my sense, my knowledge, my reason altogether." The king when he heard Bertrand speak thus of his son and when he saw Bertrand in tears, felt his heart contract so powerfully that he fainted.

When he had recovered, he cried weeping: "Bertrand, Bertrand, thou wast right to lose thy reason in the cause of my son, for there was never a man in the world whom he loved more dearly than thee. For love of him, I will not only grant thee thy life and return to thee thy goods and thy castle, I will add my love and my good graces and five hundred marks of silver for the damages which thou hast suffered."

6

The fat king paced the walls of Le Mans at the hour before dawn. The armies from Tours had advanced still further. A village just outside of the town was being burned. He must decide what was to be done, whether he should capitulate with his enemies and betray the city of his birth, or whether with his seven hundred fighting-men he should make a last and desperate stand. Perhaps he must think of moving, of flight. He had spent all of his life in movement. He had seldom stayed a week at a time in one place.

He had traveled over rough paths, through thickets, over hills, through marshland and fen, and always as the king traveled there followed behind him his disorderly court, his army of secretaries, lawyers, knights in mail, barbers, hucksters, barons—each with dozens of retainers; an archbishop or two with their households, bishops and actors, judges, suitors, confectioners, "singers, dicers, gamblers, buffoons, wild women and what not." The court was frequently forced to dine on stale black bread and old beer. It was forced to sleep in the open, in pigsties, in the mud.

If the king has proclaimed that he intends to stop late in any place, you may be sure that he will start early in the morning, and with his sudden haste destroy every one's plans. It often happens that those who have let blood or taken purges are obliged at the hazard of their lives to follow. You will see men running about like mad, urging forward their packhorses, driving their wagons into one another, everything in confusion as if hell had broken loose. Whereas, if the king has given out that he will start early in the morning, he will certainly change his mind and you may be sure he will snore until noon. You will see the packhorses drooping under their loads, wagons waiting, drivers nodding, tradesmen fretting, all grumbling at one another. The men hurry to ask the liquor retailers and loose women who follow the court when the king will start for these are the people who know most of the secrets of the court.

At other times when the camp had composed itself to sleep, a sudden messenger would gallop in with despatches. The king would order the camp to be broken. Messengers would be sent ahead to announce the approach of the king, and the cortège would push forward through the muddy paths, the cart-loads of heavy state papers foundering and overturning, the horses struggling in the mire, the wagoners shouting, the courtiers swearing. . . . Then the king might suddenly change his mind and stop for the night at a cabin in the woods where there was food and lodging for one man only. "And I believe, if I dare to say so, that he took delight in our distresses." The knights, separated from their body-guards, would wander through the thickets in the darkness and fight to the death for the possession of some place of shelter which a dog would have disdained. "O Lord God Almighty," the chronicler concludes, "turn and convert the heart of the king from this pestilent habit, that he may know himself to be but man, and that he may show a royal mercy and human compassion to those that are driven after him not by ambition but by necessity."

My lord, the king [said another chronicler], is sub-rufus or pale red; his harness [armor, which he wore very tight in his youth, for he was vain] hath somewhat changed his color. Of middle stature he is so that among little men he seemeth not much, nor among long men seemeth he over little. His head is round as in token of great wit, and of special high counsel the treasury. His head of curly hair when clipped square in the forehead showeth a lyonous visage, the nostrils even and comely according to all the other features. High vaulted feet, legs able to riding, broad bust, and long champion arms which telleth him to be strong, light, and hardy. In the toe of his foot, the nail groweth into the flesh and in harm to the foot overwaxeth. His hands, through their large size, showeth negligence, for he utterly leaveth the keeping of them; never, but when he beareth hawks, weareth he gloves. Each day at mass and counsel and other open needs of the realm, throughout the whole morning he standeth afoot, and yet when he eateth he never sitteth down. In one day he will if need be ride two or three journeys, and thus he hath oft circumvented the plots of his ene-mies. A huge lover of woods is he so that when he ceaseth war he haunteth places of hunting and hawking. . . . Homely and

[197]

short clothes weareth he. When once he loveth, scarcely will he ever hate; when once he hateth, scarcely ever receiveth he into grace. . . . When he may rest from worldly business, privily he occupieth himself with learning and reading and from his clerks he asketh questions . . . none is more honest than our king in speaking, ne in alms largesse. . . .

Thus he was in his prime, but now he was growing old. The square form had grown fat. The huge paunch had bowed the legs still more; the toe-nail had produced a habitual limp. The face was lined and worn. . . .

7

The situation Henry found himself in as he paced the château at Le Mans was no new situation. It was more critical for him now only because his sons happened to be leading the rebellious barons and because Philip of France was outguessing him and because he was growing old and weary of the struggle. He had dreamed of an empire for himself and his sons. Henry had died in rebellion against him. Geoffrey had said to a peacemaker: "Dost thou not know that it is our proper nature, planted in us by inheritance from our ancestors, that none of us should love other, but that ever brother should strive against brother and son against father? I would not that thou shouldst deprive us of our hereditary right nor vainly seek to rob us of our nature." Richard was now the darling, not only of Henry's spiteful wife Eleanor, but of Philip of France. The empire was broken.

He had had hopes of Richard's friendship after the

young king had died; but Richard soon showed his temper. "Give me my rights," he said, "that I may arrange my kingdom." On formal occasions, Richard, like his elder brother, insisted that Henry offer him the cup of wine. "It is fitting," said Richard, "that the son of a king should be served by the son of a duke." There remained only one son who had not yet declared himself; it was young John Lackland. Henry spared no pains in his attempts to ingratiate himself with this young man. In John, Henry thought he might find an heir who would be loyal to his father's interests and spare no pains in humbling his proud brothers, Richard and Geoffrey. At a conference with Philip of France, Henry proposed to transfer Richard's lordship of Aquitaine to John. When he heard this, Richard was standing near Philip. Without a word he ungirt his sword and stretched out his hands in a dramatic gesture to do homage to the king of France for England's continental possessions. The king's horse reared. The court was in confusion. The knights drew their swords. Henry spurred his horse to the open and calling to two courtiers said: "Why should I revere Christ? Why should I think him worthy of honor who takes from me all honor in my lands and suffers me thus shamefully to be dishonored before that camp-follower Philip?"

His son Geoffrey had treated him as badly as Richard. During one of the frequent filial rebellions, Henry was parleying with Geoffrey in the market-place of Limoges in front of the château. Geoffrey's archers aimed a shower of arrows at the king. One of the arrows pierced the ear of the king's horse. Henry withdrew the arrow and pre-

[199]

sented it to Geoffrey, saying, "Tell me, Geoffrey, what has thy unhapy father done to thee to deserve that thou, his son, shouldst make him a mark for thine archers?"

His lords were in revolt, and a great solitude fell upon him. Tours was in the hands of his enemies; Philip and Richard were approaching from the east; and the fat old king limped up and down the walls of Le Mans undecided whether he should flee northward or offer open battle. At dawn, the enemy set fire to a suburb to the west of Le Mans. With the enemy to the south and east and fire to the west, escape to the north would soon be cut off. Henry summoned his fighting-men and rode out, cut his way through the crowd at the bridge, and rode north. He spurred his horse up the small hill near the village now called La Bazogue and looked back on his burning city. He cursed God, and in his curses there was still the defiance of the superman. "The city which I have loved best on earth," he cried, "the city in which I was born and bred, where my father lies buried, where is the body of St. Julian—this, Thou, O God, to the heaping up of my confusion, and to the increase of my shame, hast taken from me in this base manner! I therefore will requite as best I can: I will assuredly rob Thee too of the thing in me which Thou lovest best!"

The king and his party rode furiously by by-paths, through mud and mire, under the scorching sun. They burned their bridges behind them. Once Richard, spurring ahead of the pursuers, came up with the fleeing king. One of the king's men raised his lance. Richard cried: "God's feet, marshal, do not kill me. I have no hauberk."

The marshal struck his spear into Richard's horse so that it fell dead. "No, I will not kill you. Let the devil kill you," he shouted.

From the hill where Henry, looking back on his burning city, cursed God, I lose the trail. If there be local traditions, I have not been able to collect them. There are a thousand small paths and trails that may or may not have been made when Henry fled through the country. It is a land of gentle undulating hills and low valleys, each with its streamlet and its bit of marshland. The hills are pleasant, and the valleys are rich, but sometimes in the heat of June the mist rises from the marshy places, hot and unpleasant. That night Henry reached La Fresnay. He threw himself on his couch and refused to allow even Geoffrey the Bastard, the result of his adventure with Rosamond Clifford and the only issue of his body that remained faithful to him, to throw a cloak over his shoulders. He despatched messengers into Normandy to summon the remnants of his army, and once again, resolutely and with grave heart, turned his face toward his enemies and marched southward again to the city of Tours, his ancient heritage. All the castles on the route were held by his enemies. He could scarcely find a place to rest for the night.

On June 30, 1189, his army appeared before Tours, where the French king and Richard the Lion-Heart were encamped. But just as his army glimpsed the towers of the château rising beyond the river, Henry was seized with a sudden illness. Unable to meet the French king, he fell back down the river, under the high vine-clad hills where the wine of Touraine grows into beauty and ripens into richness. He was carried to the fortress of Saumur, where Richard his son, seven years earlier, in the first flush of the combat, had summoned a meeting of barons. The French king cried, "God has delivered mine enemy into my hands." He commanded Henry to meet him on July 3 at Colombières, a field south of Tours.

Henry started for the meeting. He traveled back up the river as far as Ballan and the house of the Knights Templar. A terrible agony struck him. He leaned against the wall of the house, trembling in every nerve. His followers brought him a camp-bed. A messenger was despatched to Philip, and even Philip was compassionate. Not so Richard, the true son of his mother, the old woman of the tower, now tasting her revenge. "He feigns sickness," said Richard, "to gain time"; and Philip sent word that Henry must at any cost meet him the next day, July 4, and hear the terms of peace.

Henry's followers wished him to ignore the order, but he insisted on obeying. "Cost what it may," he said, "I will grant whatever they ask to get them to depart. But this I tell you of a surety: if I can but live, I will heal my country from war and win my land back again." On the fourth of July, through the sultry summer heat, he rode to Colombières. On one side of the field, fresh and strong and in bright armor, surrounded by his arrogant lords, with Richard at his side, was the French king. A papal delegate and an English bishop, already suitors to the new rulers, were prominent among the French lords. The world had gathered at Colombières to see the humiliation of fat old Henry, the man who for fifty years had ruled the world.

As he rode across the field, he clung to his horse as though
in a last effort. His huge body was wasted, and the skin
hung round him in folds. Philip, struck with a sudden pity,
called for a cloak to be laid on the field, that Henry might
sit for the conference. Once more Henry burst into a rage.
"I will not sit," he cried; "even as I am, I will hear what
you ask of me and why you cut short my lands."

The heat was intolerable. The sky was liquid brass.
High above the conferring monarchs were insubstantial
fleecy heat-clouds. The poplar-trees along the north end
of the field drooped. The very earth was hot to the touch.
The stench of sweaty men and sweaty horses, of leather and
chain-armor, was thick in the air. Hot bitter dust filled
the nostrils of the men.

Philip read his demands. Of a sudden there was a peal
of thunder from the inscrutable sky. The horses reared,
and the monarchs, hearing the voice of God, fell apart.
They spurred their horses together again to continue the
parley, and again there was thunder, more terrible and more
awful than before. And there were no clouds in the sky,
and there was no rain in the air, and there was no wind
from the north, only the two monarchs in the center of the
field, and the proud scornful army on the one side, and the
small handful of men on the other; and one of the kings
was sick unto death; and an impotent God spoke from a sky
of brass! Henry reeled on his horse, and his friends rushed
forward to prevent him from falling. He made his submission. As he turned to ride away he passed close by
Richard his son, and he whispered in a hoarse voice, "May
God not let me die until I have worthily avenged myself

[203]

on thee!" Richard thought it was a merry jest and told it to his companions at the French court.

Henry rode back to Chinon. Never a town in the world can be lovelier than the town of Chinon. In the center is a small square, crowded to overflowing with plane-trees so that in the hottest afternoon the place is cool and dusky and silent save for the eternal rustling of the leaves. An occasional wedding party crosses the square to the church at the west of the town, and the dress of the bride is white against the black evening-suit of the groom. A cart rattles up the cobbled stones. A bell tolls, and a funeral crosses to the church at the east. *"C'est la mort,"* sighs the *garçon* on the hotel. But now that the wedding party has reached the church at the far end of the village, the bells ring out: *"C'est la vie! C'est la vie."* Henry loved the people of Le Mans, but he loved better the château at Chinon which he had enlarged and rebuilt according to his own plans.

A deputation of monks from Canterbury with a new list of demands was awaiting Henry's arrival at Chinon. They forced their way through swords to the king's bed. They trusted that "in thy afflictions thou mayest pity the afflictions of the church." They forced their way into his presence. "The convent of Canterbury salutes you as their lord. . . ." But Henry interrupted: "Their lord have I been and am still and will be yet, small thanks to you, ye evil traitors. Now go ye out. I will speak with my faithful servants."

As the monks filed out, one of them stopped and laid his curse on the king, who trembled and grew pale at the terrible words: "The omnipotent God, of his ineffable

[204]

mercy, and for the merits of the blessed martyr Thomas, if his life and passion have been well pleasing to Him, will shortly do us justice on thy body." Geoffrey the Bastard sat at the king's head and drove away the flies that were collecting on his shrunken face.

The messenger returned from Philip with a list of those who had conspired against the king, to whom the king had promised forgiveness. The king commanded that the list be read. It was handed to Geoffrey. Geoffrey cried: "Sire, may Jesus Christ help me! The first name which is written here is the name of Count John your son!"

The king sat up in his bed. "Is it true," he said, "that John, my very heart, whom I have loved beyond all my sons, and for whose gain I have brought upon me all this misery, has forsaken me?" Then he turned his face to the wall. "Now hast thou said enough. Let the rest go as it will. I care no more for myself nor for the world." He grew delirious. In his delirium, his invincible spirit broke out in passionate denunciations. He cursed the day he was born. He cursed his sons and the God that made them and the wife that bore them; he cursed the blessed sunshine and the birds and all the creatures that lived or breathed or swam. "Shame," he muttered. "Shame on a conquered king!"

He died.

On his feet were put golden shoes with golden spurs, on his finger a ring of gold, and in his hand a golden scepter, and on his head a golden crown. He was carried to Fontevrault by the little road that follows the river Vienne as far as La Rocherau woods—it is a few yards to the east of the present highway—where it turns west and becomes a country path shaded by huge trees and leads to an ancient château now used as a farm-house. The farmer is very friendly and will give you a glass of his own wine, which, if you take the trail in June, you will find welcome. It is

> Cool'd a long age in the deep delved earth,
> Tasting of Flora and the country green,
> Dance and Provençal song, and sunburnt mirth!

It is full of the warm south, and beaded bubbles rise to the brim. From the farm of the château, the trail turns north and winds back and forth and in and out and around, skirting this wall and that field until it reaches Fontevrault itself. When they carried Henry along this trail there were monks chanting and knights in armor; the peasants in the fields no doubt stopped their work to bow their heads as the procession passed, and irreverent boys ran along ahead and followed behind.

Richard hurried to Fontevrault from Tours, where he had been celebrating his victories. When the king's body was carried into the chapel, it was found shorn of its golden ornaments; and when Richard demanded them back, the treasurer as a special favor sent a ring of little value and an old scepter. As a crown, Henry wore the gold fringe torn from a prostitute's petticoat, and as a robe, the petticoat itself.

Richard prayed before the altar, and as he prayed blood spurted from the mouth and nose of his dead father. It was wiped away, and again he prayed, and again the miracle was wrought. Richard shuddered and ran from the abbey.

Chapter IX

The Trail of a Desperate Lover

BLAYE TO TOULOUSE

Toulouse

Chapter IX

1

THE trail of Jaufre Rudel, who died for love of the incomparably beautiful lady whom he had never seen, leads into the garden of Gascony. The swift trail his romance made through the minds of his contemporaries and successors leads into the aromatic garden of romantic love. One may go into the garden of Gascony by getting on a boat at New York and getting off at Bordeaux, and if one does so, one will pass within a few feet of Jaufre's birthplace, the city of Blaye. To get into the garden of romantic love, however, is another matter. It is now thought to be a dangerous garden, in which grow complexes of various complexions; and Dr. Freud, the great gardner, swears that it is haunted by the ghosts of our mothers and that the sweet maidens we had thought to find are shape-shifting creatures, born in the caverns of our subconscious.

The Middle Ages had no fear of romantic love, and the twelfth century thought it quite a novelty and the latest thing in emotions. The young exquisites about the court of Gerard II, Jaufre's brother and the reigning prince of Blaye, those about the courts of Eleanor of Aquitaine and

Raymond V of Toulouse, exhibited this passion with as much pride as the gilded youth of to-day parade a passion for airplaning or surf-bathing. Now exercise is supposed to be the cure of all human ills; once love was the universal healer. In those days young men were advised to fall in love with as much seriousness as they are now advised to fall out of it. Young ladies in the remoter châteaux looked forward with longing to the day when, securely married, they might take a lover in much the same way as our grand-mothers anticipated the day when they might take a hus-band or as our daughters long for the triumph of their first divorce. Love—and by that was meant secret and romantic love for a mistress who was already married, love which would bring loss of appetite, paleness and a flutter-ing of the heart, a delicious trembling up and down the spine, a fear of I know not what, a nameless hope, love which delighted in secret words, in rendezvous in moonlit gardens—was a new invention of the eleventh and twelfth centuries, which also produced Gothic architecture, the modern state, the romantic novel, lyric poetry, modern commerce, the Crusades, self-government, flush-toilets in the south of France, the woman movement, and other trifles. The beautiful ladies and sweet singers of southern France of the epoch I describe were most decidedly, fla-grantly, proudly, and obviously in love, and being in love was something new in the history of the world.

To write that women before the twelfth century did not love would be to write nonsense; but there is a difference between loving and being in love, and if you do not know that difference there is many a medieval treatise that will enlighten you better than I can; and if you have forgotten that difference, there is many an American high-school girl well read in the popular novel of our own time who with perhaps a touch of scorn in her voice will remind you. Plato thought of love as the yearning for the absolute, the universal desire of man to make himself whole and complete. He made of love a philosophical doctrine without much of a body. Ovid and the sophisticated Romans thought love was essentially a physical passion and a pleasant pastime. The differences between the pagan and the medieval ideals of love are made manifest by a comparison of Ovid's "Art of Love," or Longus's idyl, "Daphnis and Chloe," with the story of Aucassin and Nicolette or the romantic tradition of the passion of Jaufre Rudel, prince of Blaye.

Ovid treats love with lightness and charm. He smiles as he discusses the sorrows of lovers, for love will occupy the attentions of young men but not the meditations of wise men. The twelfth century wrote of love as seriously as Ovid had written lightly. The twelfth-century writers described love as the source of all life, the generator of all activity, the purpose and sanctification of all being. Love became a religion, and ultimately religion became love. Poets expressed their emotions to the Virgin Mary in the same terms· they had used in writing to their mistresses, and love for a woman became love of Woman, and troubadourism decayed, and the thirteenth century came into existence, with Thomas Aquinas its philosopher, and Dante, guided by Beatrice, its interpreter.

I have been unable to determine how the difference be-

[211]

tween loving and being in love was discovered, nor can I
say whether the new woman (now nine hundred years old)
or the troubadours were most responsible in establishing
the cult of love. Both the new woman and the troubadour
had something to do with it. They seem to have been in
alliance, and, having discovered something good, they seem
to have made the best of it. To understand this cult, which
has some importance even to-day when its devotees meet by
the millions in darkened rooms to watch with eager eyes
the shadows of men and women pursuing each other on a
silver screen, a brief examination of both the woman's
movement and troubadourism is necessary.

2

Marriage seven hundred years ago was pungently described by one of its victims, a queen and a charming lady,
as *una podrida*, which may be translated briefly as "a
mess." Youngsters were frequently betrothed before they
were born and were married before they were quite dry behind the ears. Under these conditions, husbands and wives
might have the respect and affection for each other that
brothers and sisters are supposed to have; but a wife who
had seen her husband spanked by a governess could not
easily regard him as a great hero. The object of these
marriages was property. It was easier to win the estates
of a neighbor by paying a priest to pronounce a few words
at the altar than to take the estates by siege or war, which
were frequently dull and sometimes dangerous. But the
wife in whose gift the estate lay was not the entirely sup-

pliant creature of the legend of Griselda. If the story of the patient Griselda was told at all in the twelfth century, it must have been regarded by the women as a merry burlesque. The wife of the twelfth century always had relatives (in this she was not distinguished from the wife of to-day); but the mother who could call in a host of armed sons to avenge slights, real or fancied, done to her daughter was perhaps more to be feared than the mother-in-law of to-day who must be content to call down hosts of angels to be her witness.

The marital relations of the twelfth century were very different from marital relations in the Dark Ages, when marriage by robbery was not infrequent. If the twelfth-century husband had just cause—a bad temper, for example, indigestion or something of the kind—he might without fear of interruption spank his wife and send her to bed without any supper. If the cause were really just, the relatives-in-law would probably say nothing. If he had no cause— and this occurred more frequently than the historians who delight in showing the differences between the twelfth and the twentieth centuries like to admit—the husband was called to account for his actions. If he mistreated his wife he might find a new war on his hands. If his wife had a clever poet as her *ami*, he would be held up to ridicule as a boor, a ridicule which, in the twelfth century, was as much more terrible than it is now, as personal dignity, which was the source of a warrior's power over his followers, was more essential to a civilization of warriors than it is to a nation of shopkeepers.

Moreover the south of France had been the seat of European civilization ever since the youth and beauty of Rome began spending its winters on the western Riviera and brought into that country the civilized vices. In those days, no fashion was so new, no sophistication so subtle, no perversion so perverse, that it had not been tried first by the gentry of that country. That civilization had not been exterminated entirely during the winter of the Dark Ages, and it flowered anew in the springtide of the twelfth century. From here it spread eastward to Florence and Dante and northward to London and Chaucer. Civilization means idleness, and idleness means women, and women mean love. If the women are sophisticated and intelligent they make use of their natural talents and their economic position to make love amusing. If the women are dull, love becomes lust; if they are brilliant, it becomes lustrous with a thousand implications and subtleties.

The poets of the south of France were gentlemen of leisure; the women, the products of a long tradition of civilized living, were intelligent and held an economic position more firm than their ancestors in preceding centuries. When, as has happened occasionally in the long centuries which bridge the gulf between them and us, adolescent girls realized that they did not love their husbands, or, loving them, were not in love with them, the poets came to their assistance. As a result of poetic collaboration, a theory of romantic love was evolved. The disorder and social anarchy of medieval marriage was put into order and law by a theory and code of rules which constituted the theory and code of romantic love.

Troubadourism began with William of Aquitaine, Eleanor's grandfather, who regarded love as a physical passion which was, in its way, pleasant. He was a mighty lover and honored some of the objects of his devotion by writing poems to them in the manner of the poems sung by wandering minstrels and professional entertainers. For him love was essentially a physical passion. The more love there was in the world, the better was William of Aquitaine satisfied. At one time while quarreling with the church he threatened to found a convent of prostitutes. The most beautiful and efficient was to be the "sister superior." In his songs the doctrine of love is not elaborated. The beginnings of it are there, but very faint. His songs are better than the songs of the professional entertainers because his mind happened to be better and his talents were superior. Moreover he was a powerful prince, and whatever he did was, therefore, memorable.

The second stage is the stage represented by Bernard de Ventadour. Bernard regarded love as realistically as William of Aquitaine, but he refined his realism. Love was the most pleasant and delightful passion that he had experienced. For him, to live was to be in love. He said:

> Life without love—what is it worth?
> The man whose heart is never fed
> With love's sweet food indeed is dead;
> He's but a cumbrance on the earth.
>
> Lord, may Thy hatred never move
> So fierce against me that I may
> Survive a month, a single day,
> And have no heart to sing for love.

[215]

This stage of troubadourism is presented again, but with a slight difference, by Jaufre Rudel, prince of Blaye, whose story you will read in a moment. In the third stage, love which had been an absorbing passion became a religion, and the Virgin Mary became the prototype of all womanhood. In her was found the beauty of all women, woman's gay laughter, her dark mystery, her enticement. As the mother of the loving God, she herself became God. I suppose that at this time women were still beautiful and men still loved ardently; but the civilization which produced the women and the men was being rent by a great and terrible civil war. The castles were being razed. A wave of protestantism swept the country, and those who were not destroyed by it transferred their love to an eternal mistress.

The civilized south had achieved tolerance, which is one of the virtues of civilization. The lords of that country said that if a man wanted to be a heretic, that was his business, and since he would burn for it hereafter, there was no good reason to put him on the bonfire now . . . and these burning questions of religion were, after all, not quite so important as some people made out. It was more important to be a gentleman than to be a Christian. Violence was bad form. One day the lords found themselves in opposition to the church. They were called upon either to betray their friends and save their souls or to save their honor and protect their friends. Thus because most of them were not interested in religious matters, they were surprised to find the world attached greater importance to these things than they had thought possible. Although there were many backsliders, many of them fought and died like gentlemen for friends with whose opinions they were not in agreement.

3

Jaufre Rudel, a prince of Blaye, said that he loved the princess of Tripoli, that she was beautiful beyond compare, and that he loved her the more dearly because he had never seen her. His chronicler says that when the time appointed by the fates was ripe, Jaufre set out to seek his mistress and that he perished within a few hours after his arrival at Tripoli. Bald-headed scholars, whose hearts are little artichokes and whose minds are as keen as razors, bend over the poetry of Jaufre and the account of his chronicler and say that both the chronicler and the prince were liars. They say that Jaufre, writing of his mistress, was thinking of the church militant, and whoever heard of a man loving a woman he had never seen, and conclude that he did not know what he was talking about. His chronicler, they say, was a sentimental idiot, and people do not die for love, and there is no mausoleum where the chronicler says there ought to be, and if Jaufre did love the princess of Tripoli as he said he did, which princess of Tripoli did he love? Since I am unable to answer either their questions or their arguments, I present them to you for what they are worth. On the one side was the statement of Jaufre, who was the prince of a reigning house and an honorable gentleman; and against this are the statements of the modern scholars. Jaufre said, "Far away is the château, and in the tower she sleeps peacefully beside her husband"; he says, "My malady is dangerous, but it can be cured by one little kiss from the lips of my lady far away," and the scholars answer that he is talking about the church militant. You have his word against theirs. You may choose.

The account of Jaufre's chronicler contains a few details. It explains that Jaufre, prince of Blaye, became acquainted with Geoffrey of Anjou, one of the brothers of Richard the Lion-Heart and the son of Henry II of England and Eleanor of Aquitaine. Geoffrey was very fond of the poet and kept him in his service. Jaufre heard of the lady of Tripoli from pilgrims returning from the Holy Land and fell in love, and in praise of her composed "many beautiful songs." Love must have entered Jaufre's heart through his ears, which is a very important fact to remember. There are three ways in which love can gain possession of a person: through the ears by hearing praise, through the eyes by seeing beauty, or through the mind by meditating on virtues.

Being strongly taken by the desire of seeing this lady, he bade farewell to his patron, Geoffrey, who did all things possible to dissuade the poet from the journey, took the habit of a pilgrim and embarked. During the voyage he was seized by a malady so grave that those of the boat, thinking he was dead, wished to throw him into the sea. And in this condition, he was brought into the harbor of Tripoli; and his arrival was made known to the lady, who left her friends that she might succor the suffering pilgrim. Being come to the ship she took the poet by the hand, and he, knowing it was his Lady, incontinent in the face of this sweet and gracious reception, recovered his spirit and thanked her that she had restored his life to him and said to her: "Most gracious and illustrious princess, I am no longer in fear of death now that . . ." But he was unable to complete his compliment. His illness grew and augmented, and he gave up the ghost in the arms of his mistress, who had him placed in a rich and honorable sepulcher of porphyry and had engraved upon it in letters of gold several verses in the Arabian tongue.

Jaufre's fate raised the philosophical question for the poets Gérard and Peyronet as to whether one loved best a lady who was present or one who was absent. Other philosophical spirits debated whether love was stronger when it entered through the eyes or when it entered through the ears. Both of these problems were connected with the old problem as to the origin of love, a problem which a poet as late as W. Shakspere raises in the poem:

> Tell me where is fancy bred,
> Or in the heart or in the head?
> How begot? How nourished?
>   Reply, reply.
> It is engender'd in the eyes,
> With gazing fed; and fancy dies
> In the cradle where it lies. . . .

The hero of a story published in a popular American magazine is made to assert: "I dreamed of you before I saw you while I was lying wounded in the trenches, and I came to New York to search for you. . . ."[1] The young

[1] To illustrate the persistence of this tradition, I quote without permission, the following passage from a story by I. A. R. Wylie in the "Saturday Evening Post" for May 8, 1926 (p. 32, col. 3):
"' . . . I loved you before I had set eyes on you. . . . When I saw the reproduction of the Vandyke I thought to myself, "When that little girl grows up I shall marry her—or no one."'
" 'But Roger, the little girl grew up and died hundreds of years ago.'

man on the silver screen refers to his mistress as "My dream woman!" Whether Jaufre actually did participate in this amazing adventure, I do not know. His contemporaries certainly thought that he did and imagined him as I do, a young man of great charm and some beauty—Geoffrey of Anjou was particular in these matters—setting out from Blaye, a few miles north of Bordeaux on the Golfe Gironde, crossing Gascony to Toulouse and beyond to Narbonne, where he took ship for the Holy Land and the lady of his dreams.

4

Jaufre's birthplace, the city of Blaye, is situated on the cross-roads. The pagan tripper traveling south in search of war and booty, the Roman legions traveling north on the same honorable quest, the medieval pilgrim from Normandy or Anjou who eased both his soul and his body by a vacation pilgrimage through the pleasant country of Gascony, as well as the medieval merchant traveling from the supercivilized and sybaritic south north to London, all passed through the city of Blaye.

The road to the north begins at the base of the hill which now bears the citadel which once bore the city. It leads

---

" 'So people think. I knew better. Some instinct stronger than reason sent me in search of her. And when I saw her I knew.'

" 'Knew that I loved you?'

" 'Knew that you were the man I'd been waiting for all my life. . . ' "
etc. The title of the story is "With Their Eyes Open."

These illustrations could be multiplied a thousandfold from all the popular magazines of western Europe. They are embroidered by various kinds of psychological analysis, but they grow from the same rich soil of human vanity and titillate the same emotions as the story of Jaufre Rudel.

north through Saintes, Poitiers, Tours, and Paris or Normandy. Eleanor of Aquitaine, Bernard de Ventadour, Charlemagne, Pepin, Roland, William of Aquitaine—to name only a few of the thousands of illustrious people who followed this trail—all passed Blaye and stopped there for a night or two. For the travelers from the north, Blaye marked one step in a long journey. Here they could take ship and float to the city of Bordeaux. Thus they could avoid crossing three rivers which were troublesome and expensive. From Bordeaux they could turn east to Rome or the Holy Land or south into Spain.

If, therefore, you had a new scheme of salvation to dispose of, or if you had made the acquaintance of a new or potent god or saint, you would take up your abode in this pleasant city. From here your converts would carry the glad tidings into all parts of the civilized world. Thus Romans, Saracens, Franks, Aquitanians, and Christians put their marks on Blaye and built their shrines. The traditions of the potencies of these various saints and gods grew with the passing years and with the enthusiastic exaggerations of the tourists. Although the name and history of a god might be forgotten through the centuries, the tale of his prowess remained and was attributed to a new saint, and Blaye became a city of travelers' traditions, than which there is nothing historically less accurate or philosophically more true.

St. Martin, of Tours and elsewhere, sent St. Romain to Blaye to convert the city. After building himself a hermitage at the bottom of the hill, says his chronicler, the blessed saint preached with so much fire and performed miracles with so much brilliance that he baptized the inhabitants and build a church on the foundations of a temple to the false God. The church was at the end of the road, a few yards from the river, and an ideal situation for the development of a religious cult. St. Romain preserves travelers from danger and sailors from shipwreck, an ideal recommendation for a saint in a travelers' city located on the shores of a broad and stormy gulf. "Never a sailor," says the biographer, "has been drowned if he gazes ardently at the basilica of the saint." "Assure yourself a safe and pleasant passage," say the biographer's modern brethren, "by buying . . . " It amounts to much the same thing.

But the tomb of the saint was important for the dead as well as living. To be buried in soil blessed by the priest and sanctified by the bones of a saint was, it was thought, additional insurance for heaven. Roland and Olivier were buried in the Church of St.-Romain and added luster to their own virtue and fame to the city. Roland and Olivier, the followers of Charlemagne who founded France, were as great heroes to the Frenchman of that time as Washington is to us or Arthur is to the English. They had taken an army south into the Pyrenees—they followed the old trail, via Blaye and Bordeaux—and joined the army of Charlemagne and defeated the Saracens at Roncesvalles. On their return, they were caught in a narrow pass, and their rear-guard was completely destroyed. It was a great fight and is well described in that popular novel of the twelfth century, the "Chanson de Roland." The bodies of Roland and Olivier were brought to Blaye for burial, and the medieval tourist could see not only the tombs but

he sword of Roland, the sword Durendal that had drunk
of the blood of many pagans.

After the death of these heroes, Charlemagne sent word
hat Olivier's sister, who was Roland's betrothed, be
brought to Blaye, but that the news of Roland's death be
kept from her. The authors describe in great detail the
premonitions of the lovely virgin and her terrible grief
when Charlemagne himself told her the sad truth. She
begged permission to watch for one night at Roland's tomb.
As she watched, a miracle occurred. Roland, accompanied
by an angel, appeared to her and said:

> Sweet sister Aude, do not grieve for me;
> Weep not, sweet sister, and shed no tears.
> You see me now in God's company. . . .

La Belle Aude called Charlemagne and all his knights and
old them of the miracle. Then she made confession of her
ins, the little sins of a beautiful woman—surely God must
have treated them gently—and died.

This and the story of Jaufre are the kinds of story that
ould be elaborated by the travelers as they put behind
hem the long weary leagues. Medieval tourists shared
with the modern commercial traveler a love for stories, and
he longer the story the better; but its length must be
ounted in miles, not in words.

5

The gulf of the Gironde is wide, and of an evening when
he tide comes in breasting the strong current, it comes as
a wall of water. On either side of the gulf are low brown

[223]

hills, very low, very brown, and the sun above is very hot
Three or four hours from Blaye the gulf becomes the Garonne River, which makes a broad curve and runs through
the heart of Bordeaux.

The heart of that city is not a medieval heart. It is
brilliant with electric lights and opulent and modern. The
Place des Quinconces with its cafés and trees and lights is a
chastened Paris, and the tourist who loves Paris will find
himself at home there, except that Bordeaux is modern
France, and Paris is cosmopolitan France, which is a difference marked by a great distinction. Except for the
Cathedral of St.-André, which was not quite complete when
Eleanor's marriages were performed there, one will find
scarcely a stone in Bordeaux that had been put in the place
it now occupies when Bordeaux was the medieval metropolis of the southwest, exporting, as it still does, hogshead
upon hogshead of claret to pour down the insatiable British throats.

But Bordeaux, like other cities on the main road, is a
city of traditions. One day Charlemagne came to Bordeaux. He had recently failed in a filial attack on the life
of his father; and his father, somewhat irritated by the
son's attentions, had banished the young man from Gaul.
Charlemagne went south into Spain along the route we
have been following and there took service with the lord
of Toledo. He performed many brave deeds, not the
bravest of which was his marriage with the lord's daughter,
whom he had converted from paganism and brought to
Bordeaux. Here he built for her a magnificent castle which
you may still see if you go to the Palais Gallien, but if you

look at the building with even a cursory glance, you will note that it was not built by Charlemagne, but that it is the remains of a Roman amphitheater built some five hundred years before Charlemagne was born.

The Church of St.-Seurin, not far from the Palais, was built in the eleventh century on the foundations of an older church, which itself was built on the site of a temple to the false gods. About the history of St. Seurin there is a scandal, not suggested by the Allées Damour but associated with these alleys of love which happen to be an ancient cemetery. St. Seurin had been sent out by the famous St. Martial whose relics are at Blaye. Seurin had been delegated by Martial to convert the good people of Bordeaux, whose religious beliefs at that time were in a shocking state. He went to the old temple of the false gods and built himself his own church and after many years of good and pious labor rendered up the ghost. He converted not only the people of Bordeaux, he converted their dead ancestors; and in a short time the graves about the church became known as the graves of Christian saints. Bordeaux was beginning to compete with Blaye. Now Blaye had the graves of Roland and Olivier and Martial; but Bordeaux had only the doubtful palace of Charlemagne, the grave of St. Seurin, and the graves of a few doubtful pagan-Christians. A grave is more important than a palace, for the grave is the enduring while the palace is only the transitory home of the body. Bordeaux did its best. The clerics formed a progressive club and took as their motto, "Wake up, Bordeaux," and discovered the graves of several powerful Christian martyrs in the Gallo-Roman graveyard about their church. But even these were not sufficient. One night the monks left Bordeaux and by stealth stole the authentic wand of Roland which Charlemagne had deposited at his grave in Blaye, and they felt that they were making progress. Their greatest and final achievement, however, was the discovery and proof by such evidence as the twelfth century found necessary that Christ in the company of the chief priests of the region had with His own hands dedicated and consecrated the soil of the graveyard which is now Les Allées Damour. They now felt no fear of competition from Blaye, and satisfied with the results of their labors they were contented, let us hope, to live a long and useful life in the chapter-house of the church. The business of creating legends and writing novels was in the Middle Ages a kind of municipal advertising and was, all things considered, not less veracious—although its veracity was of a different kind—than the municipal advertising of the enlightened twentieth century.

Even in Roman times Bordeaux was a city of wealth and luxury. A Roman princess who loved sea-bathing ordered that a road be built to the sea twenty-five miles away. She laid it out herself, and it ran straight as a string, due west. The cost was defrayed by one of her courtiers, who is reputed to have been handsome, cruel, and wealthy.

At St.-André Eleanor of Aquitaine, who at fifteen had lived more intensely than many a modern woman has lived at fifty, bowed her head while the bishop read her marriage service and her proud sister Petronilla began the seduction of the princely Raoul. Although there were always poets at Bordeaux when the Aquitanian princes lived there, Bor-

deaux is not the chosen home of poets. For many hundreds
of years, Bordeaux was an English city, and the Bordelais
and the English are alike in their love of commerce and their
skill in bargaining. The bourgeois, though he was frequently a mimic of the vices of his master, did not foster
poetry because he did not need poets. His success depended
on the size of his bank-account rather than on the size of his
army, which would be directly proportionate to his fame.
His wife was a thrifty housekeeper and not a high-born
lady. If she wanted amusement she could visit her friends
in the next street, attend her clubs, and gossip. It was
not necessary for her to worship at the shrine of love, and
when she was so indiscreet as to be overcome by love of a
poet—and the poets were always worrying her—her husband was so far from complaisant that he hit the unhappy
lover over the head so hard that he never stopped running
until he reached the kingdom of Aragon.

The Bordelais have forgotten many things in the last
seven hundred years, but they have not forgotten how to
buy and sell claret, and the sweep of the great river into
the city is still as magnificent as it was a thousand years
ago. The quays are broad boulevards lined by huge old
houses of the eighteenth century, spanned by magnificent
bridges, and on them there is eternal activity and the smell
of boxes and claret and dried prunes. From the cathedral
tower one looks out on the low hills of the northeast, shim-
mering with heat and rich color, covered with vineyards
which are absorbing the southern sun to produce a claret
much better than many people will admit claret can possibly be.

6

The trail which Jaufre and his friends followed from Bordeaux the inhospitable to Toulouse, where all poets were made welcome, is the old Roman road. It is a broad road, and in the summer it is thick with the heavy white dust of the south. At times there is the flash of a canal at this side or the other, and that is all as it should be, for a road without a bit of water gleaming through the trees is as dull as a cocktail without ice. In the morning and the evening the air is clear and warm, and sometimes the trees which line the road fall away to disclose the cliffs of the valley rising sheer in the distance, crowned by a church or a château. Sometimes a cold wind from the Pyrenees blows down through the happy fields and transforms the road to a cloud of dust. Then one continues one's conversation in the inner room of the café, where with one or two brave mustachioed Gascons, the descendants no doubt of D'Artagnan himself, one listens to the chronicle of country life, the state of the vineyards, and, "*Parbleu*, those United States! Why do they want poor little France to pay them so much money?" One realizes that these Gascons have a sense of humor peculiar to themselves.

The Roman road leaves Bordeaux not far from the Gare de St.-Jean—saints and railway-stations in France are for some obscure reason, clear no doubt to the logical Latin intelligence, frequently associated—and follows the river south for a considerable distance until it chooses to bend its course southeasterly. This road is supposed to have remained on the left bank of the Garonne, which runs with a wide and gracious curve from Toulouse to Bordeaux. The course of the railway approximates the course of the road as far as Langon, where the railway crosses the river to St.-Macaire. The Roman road is supposed not to have crossed the river but to have continued to Agen, where it turned south to Auch and thence east to Toulouse. Its course is fairly clear as far as Langon, but between Langon and Damazan it has many vicissitudes. All that I can assure you of on this part of the trail is that hundreds of poets and saints and warriors did travel from Bordeaux to Toulouse and that they must have traveled on one side of the river or the other. The country is full of châteaux. Some of them are mentioned in the songs of the poets, more of them are not mentioned, and almost all of them are sadly dilapidated. The troubadour was not a consistent traveler. He was, in every sense of the word, a drifter. He would ride out of his way many a mile for a good dinner, and all I can hope to do in the case of Jaufre and his friends is to indicate the general direction of the drift and a few of the towns they may have seen and stopped in.

The road leads a few kilometers west of the river through the pleasant towns of La Brède, Virelade, and Podensac, which have all at one time or another given heroes to France, and on to Langon, where the modern road crosses to St.-Macaire on a hill with its double row of walls and towers and in its narrow and dirty streets many an old house. The old town sleeps quietly, almost deserted on its hill. At one time the crush and activity of humanity was so great that it was a wonder the walls could hold it all, but to-day a sleepy cat suns itself in the *place* and a donkey blocks the small street so that one cannot pass.

A day's journey by foot beyond St.-Macaire is Marmande, a "new town" built by Richard the Lion-Heart when he came to possession of this country in the twelfth century, a very new town when Jaufre Rudel stopped there for the night. The significance of these new towns in the social history of the time is enormous. All of the south of France from the Atlantic to the Rhone was undergoing the remarkable and pleasant experience of being rich. It had always been prosperous, but the prosperity which came over it in the twelfth century was unlike any prosperity it had known in the past. The country had been in the hands of the English for only a few decades. Bordeaux was an excellent harbor, and the peasants of all that thick neck of land which connects Spain with the continent floated their wine, olives, fruits, and wool down the broad backs of the Garonne and the Dordogne to Bordeaux, where they were transhipped to London. Commerce of this kind and on this scale was new in Europe, and the peasants were reaping a golden harvest. Old towns were repaired, and new towns were built "according to modern scientific plans," with broader, straighter streets and a "logical arrangement" of municipal buildings. Around every mill, every farm, every village, were built high thick walls to keep thieves and robbers out and happiness in.

Agen is a hard day's walk beyond Marmande, and Agen cares little about the world, and the world cares little about Agen. These burly Gascons with their bristling mustaches, their round oaths, and their epic blasphemies are in them-selves a world for themselves. The antiquarians have dug around Agen and discovered that the hill behind the city was a pre-Roman fort (*"Sacré!"* says the Gascon; "what do you think of those Romans building a fort behind our city?"); they have pried stones loose in the churches and have scraped the walls and have published many learned volumes. And all the time, the Gascon peasant sits in his café and curses genially the small things in his world which are the big things in ours, and speaks reverently of the big things in his world which are the small things in ours.

The town sat restlessly on its hill. It shifted from one side to the other and from the hill to the valley. Each time the town shifted, a new and better château was built, and these are all excellently described in the learned volumes which you may read if you have a mind to. Agen was the center of both Roman and medieval roads, and up and down these roads with his black mouth and golden words and loving heart ran St. Bernard, and tried to convert the here-tics who even in his days were infesting the city, and tried in vain to save them from eternal damnation.

Beyond Agen is Moissac, and beyond that is Montauban, and further still is Toulouse. The oldest road turned south at Agen to Lectoure and Auch and thence east to Toulouse, but the medieval road probably followed the river and the châteaux.

7

The cities of the south differ from cities of the north. Commerce and industry have ebbed away from the south, and as they have ebbed they have left the cities much as they were in the days of their prime. In the north one can begin with the bones of the Middle Ages or the Renaissance and find them covered with the flesh and fat of modern industrialism. But in southern cities, where flesh and fat exist, it is the flesh and fat of another period. Toulouse and Montpellier are largely Renaissance. Carcassonne and Aigues-Mortes are essentially thirteenth and twelfth century and are all of a piece. There is hardly a stone in either of these cities that spoils the style, the unity of conception and feeling. Industrialism has passed over them like a cloud. Not even its shadow remains.

Although Toulouse as we find it now is late Renaissance, it was, when Jaufre and his friends lived there, wholly medieval and perhaps the most modern and advanced city in France. Its lords were not only impeccable in their vices, hypercivilized in their taste for women, and assiduous in their cultivation of poets; they were in their ways distinguished political economists, and their citizens enjoyed an independence and freedom which made them envied by the citizens of Carcassonne and Agen. In that great struggle between lord and merchant which preceded our struggle between merchant and laborer, the lords of Toulouse granted privileges which marked them as enlightened if not incendiary revolutionists. When the Albigensian heresy burst into flame, or rather when the church representing the interests of the conservative lords blew it into flame, the tolerance of the lords of Toulouse brought down upon them the wrath of organized society and the "disdain of all right-thinking men." In the struggle which ensued, the civilization of the south was almost entirely destroyed.

Toulouse claims to be the oldest city in France and pretends to be modern; but in its modernity there is a slatternly youthfulness. Its dinginess has not aged sufficiently to become mellow, and the Renaissance buildings that give the town its character are the worst of their kind, which, as any traveler knows, can be very bad indeed. To this Renaissance body, Toulouse has added a bright and forward-looking twentieth-century spirit which makes her somewhat incongruous.

Of the two-hundred-odd troubadours whose names have been preserved, about a score are connected in some way with the history of Toulouse. Many were born there, and others retired to Toulouse or the pleasant monasteries and courts in the neighborhood to enjoy a mellow old age. The Raymonds of Toulouse, despite their follies and frequent immorality, much of which, by the way, is attributable to the malice of their enemies, were gallant gentlemen and made full use of the troubadours in the business of love and politics. The counts of Toulouse were in constant war with the kings of Aragon on the east coast of Spain, and between Toulouse and Barcelona traveled, in both directions, constant streams of poets. A troubadour who disgraced himself at the court of Toulouse was welcomed at the court of Aragon, and when he disgraced himself at Aragon he was welcomed back to Toulouse. Peter of Aragon and Raymond of Toulouse outdid each other in bidding for the services of the best, the most fashionable, and the most skilful of poets.

Hugues Brunet, a gentleman of Rodez, which is a pleasant city across the mountains north of Carcassonne, was an excellent poet, but because he had no voice could not sing his own songs and was constrained to give them to another. He was so well liked that the count of Toulouse and the king of Aragon both offered him many presents if he would enter their service, but he refused, being enamoured of a gentle lady who would have none of him. Disappointed here, he turned his attentions to the wife of his master, the count of Rodez, where he was more successful. "The count perceiving this was constrained to make no sign as if he knew because he took great pleasure in poesie and because he was well assured of the chastity of his wife."

Of Rémond de Mirevaux there is much to be said. Perhaps he was too handsome and too talented to be lucky. Perhaps his artistic gifts were greater than his discretion. Perhaps his misfortunes were due to an evil thing he did in his youth. At his father's death, Rémond inherited a bare fourth of the château of Mirevaux, whose picturesque ruins are a few miles north of Carcassonne. "He knew more about love and courtesy and the other sciences that were fashionable at his time than any other who has written; he was loved by Count Raymond of Toulouse, and the intimacy between these two became so great that they called each other by the secret names of lovers. The count gave him arms and horses and everything that he needed. He was also loved by Pedro, king of Aragon, and the viscount of Béziers and Carcassonne, and by Rémond de Saissac, and all the lords and gentlemen of the country. There was not

a lady or demoyselle in any castle of the Provence but
wanted Rémond in her company. They all desired to see
him, to enjoy him, to hear him sing, and to have his friendship and familiarity because he knew very well how to
honor them and pass the time sweetly with them, and no
lady of that country thought she had succeeded socially
unless she had at least one song dedicated to her by Rémond
de Mirevaux. But there was never a scandal about them
or about him . . . and he never received a single lover's
favor from them, and they deceived him shamefully one
and all." This account errs on two points, as you shall see.

Once Rémond de Mirevaux, Peire Vidal, Hugues Brunet,
and other troubadours found themselves at the court of
Loba de Perrautier. (She was, I think, then holding court
at the château of her uncle at Cabanet, but that is unimportant.) They were all dying for love of her, and she kept
them all at a distance. She would pretend not to understand that the songs sung in the great hall were intended
for her; and when an *aubade* was chanted at dawn in the
garden, she would send one of her ladies in waiting to the
window, and the lady would smile and blush and bow and
pretend that the serenade was intended for her instead of
for her mistress. Below in the garden the poets would
gnash their teeth and rattle their swords and call upon the
"Putaine de Dieu." She pretended that she preferred
Rémond de Mirevaux to her other suitors, for she realized
"that he was a good poet and would make her famous among
all the noble lords of the country, but all the time she was
deceiving him cruelly for she was receiving secret favors
from a knight"; and while the others were breaking their

[235]

hearts for her in the garden she was receiving into her room another whom she seemed to treat with indifference when others were near. Love, according to the romantic code, should be kept secret, but there was a limit to secrecy. Loba's method of procedure made the best poets in France look like fools and feel worse.

Nothing in the Middle Ages could be kept secret for long, and one day the entire court knew of her deception, and the entire court was furious. Rémond's friends, who were also his rivals, turned upon the lady and insisted that she had acted dishonorably and wrote bitter satires against her and her lover, who, for shame, was forced to leave the court. Rémond alone pretended to be faithful. "My love for you is so great," he said, "that I can endure dishonor itself for your sake. The evil speakers slander you. I believe no word of it." When no one in the court would sing to her any more, Rémond sang to her; and when none would walk with her in the shady gardens, Rémond was at her side. This faithfulness was at last rewarded by true love, of which she made no secret; and while all the court was marveling that Rémond should have succeeded at last, he treated her shamefully and in a manner that laid her open to worse scorn than she had received hitherto. He left her and paid open and obvious court to an obscure woman in Narbonne and wrote a poem explaining the reasons for his revenge.

All of Rémond's great passions turned to dust and ashes, and his cleverness was never so great as the cleverness of his mistresses. One time he was paying court to Adalasia, the wife of Bernard de Boisseson of the Château

Lomber. She did all in her power to inspire him to write for her better songs than he had written for the others. She would display her knowledge of the art of poetry by ridiculing the poems of Rémond's rivals. "Am I not beautiful?" she would ask as they walked up and down the garden. Rémond would assent. "My ankle," she would say meditatively, "you think it is not well turned." And she would raise her skirts ever so little so that the smallest of feet and the most dainty of ankles would appear for a moment. Rémond would protest that by . . . "My figure," she would say and run down a small path to pick a blossom. "My figure is ugly." Rémond insisted that none could withstand her and that Peter of Aragon himself, who was taking all the châteaux of the country, would have to acknowledge himself her vassal. She said it was a pretty compliment, and she said he should make a poem about it, and she said he should send it to Peter in the form of a challenge, for she thought Peter would be amused. He did and announced in his poem further that if Peter came, he would "be treated according to his degree." Peter came and was treated according to his degree, and the next morning the entire court knew that Rémond had been deceived again and that he had been used only as a decoy for the Aragonais.

Rémond married Guidairença, a poetess, in the way of business, and she too was unfaithful to him. He paid court to Ermengarde de Castras and wanted to divorce his wife and marry her. She consented. While he was at his castle arranging the details—he gave the castle as a free gift to Guidairença and her lover—his affianced bride married

Olivier de Saissac. In despair and humiliation Rémond retired to a monastery, from which he emerged just before the Albigensian crusade.

In all of these passionate comings and goings, Rémond and his friends stopped at Toulouse. Sometimes they would spend a season or two at the court of the powerful Count Raymond, or at the court of his rival; sometimes they would make up week-end parties in the numerous castles of Raymond's powerful vassals.

Peire Rémond lo Proux of Toulouse is famous among poets for having been faithful to one lady for an entire year, and he wrote a poem lamenting that love would not let him be faithless to her who treated him with unprecedented cruelty. He mentioned the tragedy of Jaufre Rudel in his great history of tragic love, which has since been lost. William of Aquitaine, the first troubadour, held the city of Toulouse for two years until Raymond came back from the Crusades and drove him out. Bernard de Ventadour, Bertrand de Born, Guilhem de Cabestanh, Gaucelm Faidit, Folquet de Marseille, and many others lived in and about Toulouse and made the thick nights musical with their tinkling songs.

The tradition of troubadourism still flickers in Toulouse, a feeble flame, in the Consistoire du Gai Savoir, an organization founded in the fourteenth century when troubadourism had died completely. The founders of the society, who were "learned, subtle, and discreet," wished to serve "that excellent and virtuous Lady Science so that she might furnish and give them the gay art of writing in verse and teach them to make good poems so that they might speak and recite good and remarkable words . . . in praise and honor of God, our Lord, and His glorious Mother and all the saints of Paradise for the instruction of the ignorant, for the restraint of foolish lovers, and in order that all might live in joy and happiness and dispel boredom and sadness, the enemies of the Gay Science." They mastered the technique of troubadourism without the troubadour's felicity. They mastered the body of poetry, but missed its soul; for that soul had fled more than a hundred years earlier when the great families were destroyed by the plague of puritanism which descended on the south of France.

Modern Toulouse is Renaissance and nineteenth-century, all but the cathedral church of St.-Saturnin. In the early morning or evening it is a splash of rose against dark violet mists. Its many-storied bell-tower is an intransigent challenge to the passing of time and the mutation of fashions, whatever those fashions may be.

Chapter X

The Trail of a Vagabond Poet—I

LES BAUX TO AIGUES MORTES

Marseilles

Chapter X

1

The fashion of troubadourism lasted for two hundred years. It began between 1050 and 1100 in Aquitaine in the west of France. It flourished between 1100 and 1200 throughout the south of France. Between 1200 and 1300 it died in eastern France and western Italy and dying transformed itself into the world poetry of Dante and Petrarch. Between Aquitaine and Avignon, through the southernmost part of France, cut a great highway, the Via Tolosa of the chronicles and the itineraries. It united the great congregations of poets, the western with the eastern. It was a garden path, and on each side of it blossomed in yellow stone and ivied walls amid black cypress and silver olive-trees the châteaux of the lords and ladies who were patrons to the poets, and the châteaux of the poets themselves. It was a highway of intrigue and passion and romance. The poets in their gay clothes, the gifts of complacent patrons, pranced back and forth beneath the ineffable sky, followed by a pretty boy singer or two, meditating new subtleties, new compliments, and pretty graces.

At the western source of the trail were Bordeaux, Toulouse, and Blaye, and thence were other paths, cutting into the north, Poitiers, Limoges, Tours. At the eastern head of the path were a cluster of great cities: Avignon, Arles, the capital of a kingdom, Tarascon, the home of the ferocious dragon, and Beaucaire, whence Aucassin and the lovely Nicolette started out on their wanderings. Of a spring morning the dew is fresh here, and the flowers of the field still are so white beside a lady's bare foot that one cannot distinguish the flowers from the foot or the foot from the flowers, and the figs, in late summer, cold and fresh, drop into your mouth. But the châteaux are hidden behind high walls of black cypress, and if you labor the dead white trail on a summer evening, they will whisper to you of secret things.

Directly east of the head of this trail, a few miles after you cross the Rhone at Beaucaire and Tarascon, perched on a small range known as the Alpines, is the deserted city of Les Baux, the sometime capital of all this broad country. One of the barons of Les Baux was the king of the Provence, and another was the emperor of Constantinople. The ladies of Les Baux were married by the emperors of the world and loved by the poets of the south. Azalaïs des Baux was a great lady and the wife of a baron; but Azalaïs would have been forgotten, as many another great lady has been forgotten, were it not for the kiss which Peire Vidal stole from her lips while she slept, or for the songs which Folquet of Marseilles made in her honor before he turned to the more profitable business of killing heretics. Few would remember Berengaria save for the love which Guilhem de Cabestanh dedicated to her before he transferred it to the lovely Tricline, who finally ate his heart.

[244]

The ruins of Les Baux are on the top of a hill. There are only two roads to this city, one on the north through St.-Remy and Tarascon, and one on the south through Paradou and Arles. For four hundred years there has been no lord of Les Baux, and the great castles are falling back into the rocks from which they grew. The small mountains on which the town is built are of smooth white sandstone. Centuries of quarrying outside the city have made long deep tunnels into the sides of the hills. The city still retains the whiteness of this beautiful stone and, when the sun comes from the right direction, can be dazzling in its brilliance. The windows gape at the summer night, and lizards and rock-rats rustle the small stones as one sits perched on a broken arch looking over the valley.

I do not know what the ruins of Les Baux looked like when Les Baux was a flourishing capital; but the ruins of Les Baux are square ruins, and in the palaces where the dead and imperturbable doors gape at the gaping tourists the windows are pointed and Gothic. When the mistral blows from the northwest, the city seems to shrink together and become compact, as though it would present a solid front to its adversary; but in the midday sun, it sprawls over the top of the hill, its square stones in slatternly, unhappy balance against other square stones, its windows empty.

For five hundred years Les Baux was the center of affairs. When crusading and poetry were the fashion, Les Baux cultivated crusaders and poets; when asceticism was the fashion, it cultivated ascetics. The lords of Les Baux were sufficiently removed from the old Roman road between

[245]

Marseilles and Lyons—that great artery of medieval and
ancient France which transported the infirmities of civilization from Marseilles to Lyons and thence by other great
roads northeast to Coblenz, northwest to Cherbourg, and
west to Tours—that they could cultivate their aristocracy,
and with little fear of interruption by the vulgar middle
classes could practise the aristocratic vices with the impec-
cability of kings and the precision of poets. The ladies of
Les Baux were beautiful, and one of them, according to
tradition, was chaste.

The traditions of Les Baux are brilliant. Here troubadourism reached its highest, if not its greatest development.
The poems became so subtle that none but the initiated
could understand them, and the poets prided themselves on
this subtlety, for, said they, poetry is an aristocratic art to
be practised by ladies and gentlemen who have the leisure
for study. It is not an art of the people. The populace
has its jongleurs and its minstrels who tell silly stories in
a silly way. We can write poems of fifty lines on two
rimes. We can say a dozen things in a phrase if you are
learned enough to understand what we say. Ours is a
beauty of the intellect; theirs is a beauty of mere passion.
There is much to be said for their point of view, but this
is not the place to say it.

The sestina was a kind of poem particularly popular.
It contained six stanzas, and each stanza contained six lines.
The words which concluded each line of the first stanza concluded each line of every other stanza, and their arrangement followed a definite order. The difficulties of this
form are obvious. The poet was required to write a poem

[246]

of thirty-six lines. Each line must end with one of six words, and the position of each of these words was rigidly determined. Moreover the music for the song must follow these permutations, and the whole must be harmonious. Evidently the poets who cultivated this form of poetry were more concerned with saying things well than with saying them profoundly. Poetry was good form and good manners, and to good form and good manners these poets and their audiences attached an importance inconceivable to a race like our own which is concerned with "results."

The exquisites who practised this art foregathered at Les Baux, and here the adept were sifted from the bunglers. Behold the poor troubadour, laboring at some obscure château, at Mirevaux, at Vaquières, or elsewhere, to perfect his poetry. He has learned all the songs of all the poets who have wandered through his part of the country on business or love. From them he has learned a few of the difficult rules of his art. Finally his poems are done. He slings a bag of them across his shoulder and departs for the great capital of Les Baux or Toulouse. Here he will be certain of finding an audience, and here, if he have grace of person or charm of manner, one will give him a hearing. Azalaïs and her daughter Berengaria des Baux have a weakness for troubadours, and perhaps their kindness will inspire him to improvise another canzone. Perhaps they will permit him to dedicate one to them. If he be competent, he will be praised; if he be incompetent, he will be ridiculed. The good will be sorted from the bad. He will find a patron and fall in love, and his wanderings will continue.

The sorting at Les Baux was done perhaps in the pavilion

[247]

of love in the garden which lay a few feet below the ruined city on the hill. On many a summer morning as the city cast its shadow over the garden the officers of the court assembled: the Lords of the High Privileges of Love, the Provost of the Hawthorn, the Seneschal of the Eglantine, the Marshal of Mourning, the Bailiff of Delight, and presiding over the court was the Queen of Love. The air of a summer morning can be hot and heavy. The roses drooped in the shade, and thinly clad the ladies reclined on their couches, conversing in undertones while the boy singers chanted sirventes and debates as to the nature of love and its beauty. The atmosphere was charged with passion and sensuousness and rich perfumes.

2

One of the poets of Les Baux was Guilhem de Cabestanh, who, partly perhaps because of his charming manner and honeyed words, and partly too perhaps because the Château de Cabestanh was somewhat isolated and dull, had captured the heart of his master's wife and for reasons best known to himself found it necessary to travel. He came into Les Baux one spring evening and within a short time had won the love and the, as usual, undying devotion of pretty Berengaria des Baux, the daughter of the lord of the city. Berengaria was a sweet young thing and very serious, a firm believer in the proverbs, "Look before you cross the Rubicon," and, "When you've captured your man, put salt on his tail," and, "A bird in the hand will fly away unless you hold him tight," and other bits of popular wisdom. She knew that she loved Guilhem, and apparently he loved her, but appearances are deceptive. Marriage was excluded, both because of the difference in their positions and by the fact that they loved each other, which latter fact our wise ancestors of the twelfth century regarded as an inevitable obstacle to marriage. Berengaria consulted a wise woman.

The wise women of old dwelt in huts, were shape-shifters appearing sometimes as toads and sometimes as women, were called witches, had intercourse with the devil, and gave bad advice. The wise women of to-day live who knows where, are shape-shifters—expert in transformations and cosmetics, conduct columns in the newspapers, have spiritual intercourse with "higher things," and give salutary though frequently futile advice to maidens like Berengaria. The old woman commanded Berengaria to pluck "several stocks of the verayre with your own hands, my dear, when the moon is full and bring them to me." The woman made of these an infusion, and of the infusion she made a wine. The next time Guilhem blotted the moonlight of Berengaria's window, she gave him some of this wine to drink. The effects were immediate. Guilhem's face was contorted as though he were laughing at a terrible and unutterable jest. He writhed on the floor in his silent mirth. He was thought to be at the point of death. When he recovered his composure sometime later, he discovered that his love for Berengaria had been a mistake, and he left Les Baux to fall in love with Tricline Carbonelle.

Triciline, a lady full "of science and good virtues, was the wife of Rémond de Seilhans. Guilhem sent her one of his songs, which, by way of precaution, he addressed to Rémond, her husband, a rude and unpleasant man whose only pleasure was in the hunt and in murder. The lady thus apprised of his love felt a reciprocal passion pierce her heart, which, her husband observing, awakened in him the vulgar passion of jealousy." He invited Guilhem to visit them as a guest and confronted the two several times but without success. With Tricline's permission he pretended to love Tricline's sister, and when the sister was invited to the château he seemed to pay ardent court to her. So crude and vulgar was this man Rémond that he spied upon the lovers and found proof positive. He kept his information to himself. One day he and Guilhem went hunting. They became separated from their comrades, and he treacherously struck Guilhem to the earth and with great satisfaction buried his sword in Guilhem's body up to the hilt. He cut off the head and put it in his hunting-bag. He cut out the heart and gave it to his cook.

There must have been an interesting dinner at the Château de Seilhans that day: excuses for Guilhem who had been "called away on urgent business"; obsequious smirks from the host of poor relatives that battened on the lord of every castle; Tricline distracted and absent-minded because Guilhem had not said good-by, and villainous Rémond for once in his life affecting the manners of the cultivated lords and pretending concern for the health of his wife.

"You're not feeling very well to-day, my love," he said.

"I never felt better," she answered, looking up at the raftered ceiling of the hall that she might not meet his eyes.

"You are pale, my love," he said. "You should be more in the open."

[250]

"My bower is so pleasant," she answered, "that I should wish never to leave it." But her face was turned toward the window, and her eyes followed the white ribbon of the trail which led into the valley to the hermitage where she had met Guilhem the day before.

"But you are not eating, my dear," he said. "I fear you don't care for the game I bagged to-day."

"Indeed, my lord, it is the best I have ever tasted," and she forced a bite down past the lump that rose in her throat.

"Quite so," snarled Rémond. "That which you have just eaten is the heart of your paramour." Reaching down under the table he drew from his hunting-bag the head of Guilhem, which he held up by the hair close to her face.

"My lord," said Tricline, who was a lady always and retained her composure even at this difficult moment, "what I told you was the truth. I have never eaten better meat and . . ." here she faltered for just a moment . . . "by God, I shall never eat worse." She drew a steel poignard from her belt and with it pierced her tender bosom and died.

3

Azalaïs, the mistress of Les Baux, was celebrated for her chastity, and if any poet won favors from her the secret lies buried discreetly with his bones. Once, either before or after Folquet entered the service of Richard of England, he was severely smitten by the charms of Azalaïs and spent several seasons at Les Baux paying unsuccessful court to her. When she died he wrote, according to one chronicler, an "elegant poem" in her memory.

Peire Vidal, the tempestuous ne'er-do-well of the troubadours, was less patient. She refused him all favors. When
he made a song to "Pretty Eyes," so phrased that it could
apply only to her and so written that it could come only
from Peire, she affected not to understand. She would not
give him the public kiss on the cheek which would make
him her eternal servant and vassal, and had Peire not been
the bosom crony of Hugues des Baux, Azalaïs's husband,
Peire would probably have given over the combat. But
the more he praised Azalaïs, the more Hugues liked and
petted him; and the more Hugues liked him, the safer was
Peire. Les Baux was a strong city and Hugues a powerful
lord, and there were divers husbands in the surrounding
cities who would have liked to meet Peire on a dark night,
and Azalaïs *was* charming, though unfortunately chaste,
and one had to keep in practice. . . .

One night when Hugues was elsewhere, Peire stole into
Azalaïs's bedroom and implanted upon her ruby lips a kiss,
which was in violation not only of civil and divine law
but also of the law of romantic love, which stated explicitly
and in so many words that the lover must be glad to accept
what his mistress offers him and he must not take from her
anything which she wishes to keep for herself. Azalaïs
thought that the kiss was from her husband, or so she said,
and awakened smiling. When she discovered her mistake,
she proceeded to make a tremendous scene. She wanted
Peire killed immediately, but Hugues said it was only a joke
and was very much amused by it. Peire was banished from
Les Baux for a time.

In Peire Vidal's life good and bad luck were mixed in

somewhat equal proportions. Whatever he did was dramatic. He was "the son of a furrier of Toulouse and he sang very well and was a sovereign musician. Whatever he saw pleased him, and whatever pleased him, he thought ought to be given him. He could write and compose more quickly than any of his contemporaries and he was a great boaster. He sang of his follies in love and in arms and lied about both. A lord of St.-Gilles had Peire's tongue cut out because Peire had slandered one of the lord's relatives. Fearful of more punishment to follow, he retired to Hugues of Baux and lived merrily and carefully there for some time."

When he left Les Baux he took the road that leads down the steep side of the mountain, through the Val d'Enfer which Dante is supposed to have described in his Inferno, until he came to Paradou and the larger trail which led to the abbey of Mont Major in the suburbs of Arles.

A century and a half later, when troubadourism was all but dead, an apostate monk left the abbey and made himself the "scourge of poets." He wrote the lives of all the troubadours, both those whose works he had read and those of whose works he was ignorant, and then, repenting, he wrote a long poem in which he admitted that he had left the abbey to follow a life of good food and voluptuousness and that all he had said about the poets was untrue, which makes things somewhat difficult for modern students.

The monastery seems to be a part of the rocks on which it is built. In the center of it is the church of Our Lady, and in the center of that the cell which St. Trophimus is supposed to have occupied while converting the country.

[253]

After he had succeeded, more or less, he went to Arles and built the great church which still bears his name. The Arlesians are somewhat boastful and swear that Trophimus was a friend of St. Paul. Since the Arlesian women are said to be the most beautiful women in France, one must be content to take their word about things which happened long ago.

4

The Arlesian women admit that they are beautiful, but they insist that their beauty has a tragic origin and explain it by a tale which illustrates something of the imaginative heritage of the provençal poets. Once upon a time, many, many years ago, the Greek hero Herakles . . . (*"C'était un bon saint, Herakle,"* said the mother of the house, interrupting her daughter who was telling the story. *"Ecoute, maman, ce n'était pas un saint; c'était un païen."* *"Quoi donc!"* grumbled the woman, and asked what I expected nowadays, and didn't the young people always know best, and she guessed she knew the difference between a Greek and a saint, she did. . . .) After this interruption the Arlesienne proceeded to explain that many, many years ago Herakles was driving his wild white oxen along the great highway between Toulouse and Arles. The Rhone was in flood, and each small river spread into a thousand streams over the wide plain of the Camargue. At every ford there was a stampede, and at every stampede the herd became smaller. There was no food. Herakles labored day and night, and when the cattle were too weary to go further he sat on a rock and rested his head on his bare brown arms.

Finally he came to Arles on a green hill with plenty of pasturage, and there he met Galatea, the lovely Ligurian princess who added to her other accomplishments that of chief shepherdess to her father's flocks. For a long time they watched their flocks together, living on garlic, onions, and love.

The time came when Herakles, the divinely ordained righter of human wrongs ("He was a saint, as I told you," said the old woman), remembered his mission. An inexorable fate, as demoniac and compelling as that which drives dipsomaniacs to the bottle or Calvinists to heaven, forced this unhappy man to do one kind act a day, and now forced him to do it elsewhere. Galatea the lovely was sleeping in the moonlight, one bare arm under her head, and her sweet breath redolent with garlic. He left her, collecting his herd with the herdsman's melancholy "Hooho . . . Hooho . . ." and drove them into Greece. When Galatea awoke she was very unhappy but evidently not inconsolable, for she was later married to a chief of her own tribe. She never forgot the divine Herakles, however, and in her eyes and the eyes of her daughters one may still see the sadness of a woman who has loved a God.

Arles is a city on the cross-roads, and since the time of Herakles it has been a city for tourists. In Roman times, the road between Marseilles and Lyons joined the great road to Toulouse at Arles. The Romans made Arles a free city in an attempt to lessen the importance of Marseilles, dominated by Phenician traditions. They built here a huge arena and a beautiful Greek theater. Arles was the last city in the Western Empire to stand before the bar-

[255]

barian invasions, and when the Romans had finally been exterminated the barbarians built their town within the arena. The town expanded and grew rich. The Arlesians converted the dead in their Gallo-Roman burial-ground and discovered that Christ had consecrated this one too with his own hands. The arena, the theater, and the church are, each in its own way, magnificent, and around them is a net of narow cobbled streets, the streets of the troubadours.

I have records of no less than thirteen poets who, at one time or another, partook of the hospitality of the Arlesian lords or made love to the Arlesian women. Since the Arlesian women combined pride with beauty, this love was in many cases tragic. Hugues de St.-Cyr, a gentleman, loved a gentle lady of the Provence called Clermonde de Quideram of the city of Arles, who was so accomplished and brilliant among the women of the country that she compared with none, not only in beauty but also in good sense and kindliness, in whose praise he made many good songs in the Provençal tongue. In one of these he said that he had three great enemies who tortured him to the point of death every night: his eyes forced him to love a woman whose station was far higher than his; love held him in durance and forced him to be faithful to his lady; the third and most cruel of all was his lady herself, to whom he dared not confess his passion. What could he do? These cruel enemies would not permit him to die, but preferred to see him languish in despair. He sought wild and desolate places. He wept and sighed and made songs of his distress, and always, as an accompaniment to his sorrow, he heard the murmur of the impetuous stream . . . "Sweet Thames,

[256]

run softly till I end my song . . ." And Hugues de St.-Cyr hit upon this device some three hundred years before Spenser.

Gaubert or Gasbert de Puycibot was the son of a gentleman of Limoges. At an early age he entered the monastery of St. Leonard, where he learned how to sing and how to write poetry and music. In all of these arts he achieved great proficiency. He had a cousin, and when, under cover of devotion, she visited the monastery, he would sing his poems to her very softly so that his brethren might not hear them, and she, with head bowed, would say to him that it was a sin and a shame for him to waste his life in this prison when he might win for himself great glory and fame as a poet.

He believed her and joined the suite of Savaric de Mauléon and with him visited many famous courts along the Via Tolosa. At one of these he met a beautiful demoiselle with whom he fell in love, and for whom, as was proper, he made many beautiful songs. But she would have nothing to do with the impecunious clerk. Gaubert told his patron Savaric about his difficulty, and "Savaric, who loved learned persons and good poets granted him the favor and had him passed knight and gave him revenue and horses and married him to the young lady." Now this marriage was accursed, as some marriages are, and as these young people should have known had they paid proper attention to the rules of chivalric love. But they lived in the beginning of the thirteenth century when the old customs were breaking down and France was already trembling with the first agonies of the Albigensian Wars.

[257]

Some time after they had been married, Savaric and his knights undertook a small war with Raymond of Toulouse against Aragon. While she was living alone, awaiting the return of her husband, Madame la Châtelaine de Puycibot met an English knight—probably a tourist with a Cook's ticket, a thermos bottle, and a Murray doing southern France on his way to the Riviera—and he made violent love to her in the manner of these gentlemen when they become aroused. They came to an understanding and fled to the city of Arles, where they lived for many months in happiness and contentment. When Gaubert returned from the war he too stopped at Arles and by chance took a room across the road from the room his former wife was occupying.

She looked out of her window and saw him. Her former love for him returned, and she was filled with loathing for the English knight. In the twilight she slipped into Gaubert's room, and they sat there together for a long time looking at each other, saying nothing, and letting Love do its work in their hearts. . . . The next morning they departed for Avignon and in repentance of their sins entered the severest religious houses they could find. Gaubert never sang another song as long as he lived; and his wife, more beautiful than ever in her nun's costume, turned her eyes resolutely away when she saw an English knight with a Cook's ticket and a guide-book striding down from the Rocher du Dôme.

Bertrand de Marseille was related to the viscounts of Marseille. In his youth he was fat and indolent and remained so until he came to Arles and saw one of the ladies of that city of the house of Porcellet, when, by the sovereign power of love, his fatness and indolence vanished and he began writing poems to her, which is nothing less than a miracle, for the writing of Provençal poems is extraordinarily difficult. Despite Bertrand de Marseille's entreaties, Porcellette de Porcellet remained cold. Later, she married a gentleman of the Eyguières and within a few years bore him twelve beautiful sons. This, however, is not surprising, because the Porcellets are a prolific race.

They were originally of Les Baux. An early mother of the family was once walking on the hill outside the city of Les Baux when she met an old woman who asked for alms. The lady was impatient and made some slighting comment on beggars. The old woman cursed her with a widow's curse and, pointing to a sow in the middle of the road, said: "May you have as many sons at one birth as that sow has at every litter!" Shortly afterward the lady was brought to bed of nine sons.

When Peire Vidal visited Arles, the church of St.-Trophimus was being repaired with stones taken from the theater and the arena. An unknown sculptor was chiseling these stones into the hyperbolical symbols of Christianity. In the figures of the Christ on the porch and the hypersexual beasts in the cloister, the stones have bared their souls and the tortured spirit of history still lives. The stones have echoed to the screams of gladiatorial combat; they have absorbed the great cadences of pagan combat. Now they glare confusedly at the pretty Arlesian women who perform their morning devotions.

[259]

5

Arles sits in the center of a tangle of roads like a beautiful spider in her net. One line of the old Roman road is followed by the modern railway due east to Aix-en-Provence and on to Fréjus. A spur drops down to Marseilles. Another leads northeast to the Cottian Alps and Milan. A third continued up the right bank of the river to Avignon and Lyons, the Roman capital. Another went northwest to Nîmes, where it joined the true Via Tolosa, which curved beside the Rhone to a point just opposite Avignon, where it crossed and joined the road on the left bank. This is the trail that Petrarch followed when he went to college at Montpellier. From Nîmes he, and perhaps Peire Vidal before him, went southwest to Lunel and thence to Montpellier.

But the trip Arles-Nîmes-Lunel, if it followed the Roman road, covered two sides of a triangle. St.-Gilles, directly west of Arles, was an important city during the Middle Ages and carried on a considerable commerce. There must have been a trail between these two cities. Directly west of St.-Gilles is Vauvert, and there was certainly a trail between Vauvert and Lunel as early as the fourteenth century, and in all probability much earlier. The present road which connects these two towns hugs the bases of very low hills which rise directly out of the marshes of the western Camargue and, if my assumptions are correct, follows the old trail which ran along the head of the Camargue, due west to join the Via Tolosa at Lunel.

Flat and marshy as an old pancake, the plain of the

Camargue stretches south from Arles to the Mediterranean. Hardly any tree breaks the force of the mistral, the winter wind which sweeps down from the northwest. Hardly any leaves give shade and comfort to the traveler under the summer sun. It is a desert plain, the Camargue, and the mother of legends. Scattered at great distances are large farm-houses. Huge walls have been built around them for protection, and at times a line of black cypresses. The werwolf haunts the Camargue and the fairy fox; and whether these spirits lead you to great wealth or to sudden death, they will lead you finally to madness. At the southern end, built on the sands is the city of the three St. Marys, Les Saintes Maries. In the spring the Gipsies from all over Europe gather here to do homage to their patron saint and every year there are miracles performed in the high fortified church. St.-Gilles is at the northern extremity of the plain, a bare four leagues from Arles. It was here that Peire Vidal lost his tongue for slandering a gentlewoman, and it was probably not by this road that he traveled from Arles to Lunel.

6

The paths on the Camargue are tortuous and lead between quicksands, and the poets whose names are connected with these paths led tortuous lives. One of these was the gentle knight Cadenet, whose castle is now in ruins a dozen leagues north of Aix-en-Provence. He had a remarkable passion for a certain Marguerite de Ries and a remarkable run of bad luck. Unlike many of his fellow-troubadours

[261]

he was unable to salve his disappointment when she refused to have him, and, though he tried nobly, was unable to fall in love with another mistress.

When Marguerite refused to grant him any favors, he took service with the marquise de Montferrat, but to his sorrow, he found himself constantly singing the praises of the gentle Marguerite, and instead of recovering from his malady of love, it grew worse each day until, unable to bear so much suffering, he returned again to the court of his first love. She granted him certain minor liberties. He might see her for a few moments each day. On meeting her in public, he might touch his lips to her hand. He might not, under any condition, imagine that she accepted his homage. He might not refer to her as the lady of his dreams. He might . . . He might not . . . And all the time that she was exulting in her power over him, she was laughing at him behind his back. Fashions were changing. Poetry was on the decline. Young ladies amused themselves by arts which were less gracious and less difficult.

Cadenet discovered Marguerite's ill usage and in his chagrin married a gentle lady who was beautiful and virtuous, but she died within a year. Not only was he unfortunate in love and in domestic arrangements, but now he had to suffer the attacks of the Galliardes, the speakers of evil, who said that he deserved to lose his wife because he had only married her in spite, and that he was really faithful to Marguerite. This angered him so much that he wrote a very polite song thanking the gossips for attributing such faithfulness as he had not deserved. He next turned his attentions to a novice of the convent at Arles, who deceived him cruelly. This last deception was too much. He joined the Templars at St.-Gilles and turned his love to the Mother of God, "in whose honor he made many pretty songs which pleased his brethren exceedingly." He died fighting the Saracens.

Rostand de Berenguier had the misfortune to fall in love with a very old woman and a witch, "and she was the most expert in sorcery that any one has ever seen, whether in mixing drugs, in observing days of good omen, or in administering love potions." For some obscure reason, she experimented on her lover and gave him a potion which transported him beyond sense, and he would have remained that way forever had not a gentle demoiselle— who was acquainted with him because of a song he had made in her honor—taken pity on him. She was a daughter of the house of Cybo and lived not far from Marseilles. "He was restored to his reason and understanding by means of a drink which she gave him containing a sovereign drug and antidote, which favor the poet recognized, and he immortalized her in a goodly number of songs and became amorous of her, leaving the witch and retaining the Genoese, who was a very proper demoiselle, beautiful, virtuous, and well learned in poetry." She seems to have regretted her kindness to him or to have thought him more attractive as a madman than as a poet, for as soon as he was cured of his illness she cast him off. In his anger he wrote a satire against her, which was an ill natured thing to do and not in the least courteous. Berenguier then tried to join the Templars at St.-Gilles, but the Templars, perhaps because of his notorious conduct with the witch but more likely because of his discourteous conduct toward the Genoese, refused to admit him to their order. He took revenge upon them by writing an improper poem called "Concerning the False Lives of the Templars," as a result of which, by divine punishment, he died.

7

Peire Vidal had every reason in the world to regard St.-Gilles, where he had lost his tongue, with suspicion. When he went from Les Baux to Toulouse he must have traveled by the Roman road northwest to Nîmes. The small city of Bellegarde, the first stop on this route, rises out of the plain on a small hill which seems twice its height in comparison with the flatness of the surrounding country. There is something of magic in Arles, and whenever I leave it its influence stays with me until, with a kind of shock, I realize that I am in another town, where life, though it may have been lived just as intensely, has left for us fewer records. Thus, as I remember it, the town of Bellegarde is shabby, and its tower is a poor thing, and though its position on a hill is dramatic and picturesque, it is too far from Arles to share its grandeur and too different to be quite a part of it.

The hills which begin at Bellegarde continue to Nîmes and beyond to the uttermost limits of the Provence. They are seldom high hills, but they are pleasant, and sometimes their ruggedness suggests very, very small mountains. They are covered with grape-vines. The peasants speak Provençal, a very old language, as different from French as Spanish or Italian. When they speak French, it is with the accent of the Midi, of which the most notable characteristic is the pronunciation of the final "e." This gives their speech softness and languor.

At Nîmes the road joins the Via Tolosa, which Peire Vidal probably and Petrarch and many others certainly followed southwest to Lunel.

Modern Lunel has forgotten all about the twelfth century and is no longer aware that it was once an important city. It occupies itself to-day with its dull and pretty municipal park and spends as much time as possible in the café and as little as necessary on the wide, hot, and dusty streets. When the Saracens retreated through southern France, they left at Lunel, Montpellier, and Narbonne a large number of learned Jews whose fame spread throughout Europe.

About the time of Peire Vidal or a little earlier, Jausserande de Lunel, the daughter of a noble prince and his exemplary wife, was receiving with complaisance the moralistic love-poems of Guilhelm de Agoult, who, because he was possessed of a large personal fortune, was described by his contemporaries as benign, modest, virtuous, and excellent in knowledge and judgment. Guilhelm disapproved of the madness of the youth of his day, and he pointed out their errors to them with an air of gentle reproach. The true lover, he said, can do nothing that will bring dishonor upon himself and his mistress; he will not win her by trickery; he will not take from his mistress anything which she does not give him freely, nor will he do any dishonorable thing for her. One must always remember that the sex is frail, he concluded, and we must forgive women many of their smaller vices. He wrote a treatise telling all about it under the title, "La Maniera d'Amar dal Temps Passat."

8

Directly south of Lunel is Aigues-Mortes, a city which Peire Vidal certainly did not visit, for it was built some seventy years after he died; but I mention it here because it is more entirely in the style and manner of thirteenth-century architecture than any other town in France. Aigues-Mortes is a fortified city built by St. Louis as a seaport in the midst of the dead waters. Its gray brown walls rise straight above a brown gray plain. At places the smooth dead waters of the *étang* reach to the bases of the walls. At other places, the plain itself, covered with rough marshgrass and dotted with pools invisible except when they flash the sunlight back into your eyes, stretches out as far as one can see. It is a dead city in dead waters. The streets are narrow and white. There is no life in it.

The tide of life has passed and carried with it the boasting Crusaders and the saintly king. The peasants do a little trading in salt and a little trading in fish. If you shiver in the cold wind of a winter afternoon, they say pleasantly, "*Il fait froid.*" If you perspire on a summer morning, they say, "*Il fait chaud.*" They ask you whence you came and tell them, and they answer, "That's very far from here." Whatever they say is pleasant and quiet and a little dead. The *aigue* comes in from the marshes around Aigues-Mortes and shakes them. Most of them die young, but those who survive are very old indeed. . . .

Chapter XI

The Trail of a Vagabond Poet—II

MONTPELLIER TO CARCASSONNE

Carcassonne

Chapter XI

1

In travail and agony, the city of Maguelone bore the city of Montpellier. All that is left of Maguelone, built on the sands of the Mediterranean, is a ruined cathedral, a caretaker, the whisper of the waves on the sands, and the cry of wild birds flying over the reeds. When the inhabitants of southern France were less civilized than the Indians who greeted Columbus after his long voyage, Maguelone was founded as a trading-post by the mysterious Phocæans, whose civilization has disappeared and taken almost all records along with it. In Roman times the great cities along the Via Tolosa were Nîmes, Maguelone, Narbonne. The Roman power decayed, and Maguelone became Christian and barbarian. The Saracens occupied the city. Some of the inhabitants remained, but others fled north to the village of Montpellier. The Saracens were driven out, but Maguelone was destroyed in the attempt, and again there was a migration northward. Maguelone recovered only to be destroyed once more, and once more Montpellier profited. With each destruction Maguelone became older and more feeble, as though a curse had been put on her; and Montpellier grew in power and pride.

The road to Maguelone leads over orange sands. At
the left is the blue Mediterranean and at the right the
leaden *étang*. The road leads through low pines. Except
for the cathedral all vestiges of the old city have disappeared. On each side of the cathedral portal are saints
chiseled in relief, and above the portal is another saint, or
perhaps God himself, with a lion and a little angel. These
three look out over the foam-flecked ocean to remember,
perhaps, the glories of their dedication by the bishops of the
eleventh century and the vagaries of their decline.

2

When Peire Vidal trod the Via Tolosa, Maguelone had
lost its power. He came into Montpellier over a route now
called the Boulevard de Nîmes, which led him to the foot
of a small cliff surmounted by a château, which has since
been destroyed and replaced by a quiet Esplanade, which
leads directly to the Place de la Comédie in the center of the
town. In the center of this *place* are three naked ladies
in bronze, which represent, however inadequately, the good
Montpellierite's notion of the Graces. At one end of the
place is the inevitable municipal theater, where, in the
winter, French and Italian opera is sung very badly; and
around the edge of the *place* are crowded café after café
in friendly competition as to which can be the most jovial,
the most pleasant, the most expansive. Peire Vidal found
the city surrounded by walls. It was a city of tortuous
streets and was more or less loyal to his friend and patron
Peter of Aragon. At intervals on the spacious boulevards
that have replaced the old walls and in the narrow by-

streets one finds vestiges of the town visited: two towers at opposite ends of the town, a bit of wall which forms the back of a livery-stable, the cathedral with its curious porch. . . .

But Montpellier was more than a great city in the Middle Ages, it was a center of learning, a university town. Thousands of students gathered here to listen while their masters talked to them about medicine and Roman law. Since a stranger in a strange town had no civil rights, the students incorporated, formed a city within a city, made their own laws, tried their own cases, and established complete student self-government. The knowledge of medicine they gained came largely from the Saracen physicians who had lived in the city and left much of their wisdom behind them. The knowledge of law was the result of the experiences of the Montpellierites themselves, who even then were making difficult and complicated experiments in democratic government. The city thus became a center for cultivated people and pedants and, since the lords were generous, a gathering-place for poets.

Roolet de Gassin met Rixende de Montauban at Montpellier when troubadourism was at its height; and many years later, when troubadourism was no more than a memory of a pleasant perfume, Peire Bonifaciis paid assiduous court to a lady of the house of Andrea de Montpellier, "whom he wooed both by poems in the Provençal tongue and by the arts of magic. Seeing that nothing would advance his suit he gave himself to the study of alchemy and searched until he found a stone that had the virtue of converting all metals into gold. He made a song in which he described the magic powers of the Oriental gems, and he put the diamond at the head of his list, saying that it had the virtue of making men invincible. He said the Cretan agate made a man pleasant of speech, amiable, prudent, agreeable; that the amethyst preserved from drunkenness; that the cornaline will appease the anger of a judge; that the 'jacynth' provokes sleep; that the pearl brings heart's-ease; that the cameo when graven in images is efficacious against hydropsy; that the azure stone when hung on the necks of children makes them strong; that the Indian ruby if worn while sleeping preserves against bad dreams. One cannot experience the virtues of the sapphire unless one is chaste. The emerald is good for the memory; the topaz restrains anger and luxury; the turquoise brings luck, and the beryl increases love. . . ." He was a wise and learned man, and I would not like to believe that the doctors of medicine in the present university, who administer glandular extract to preserve youth and psychoanalysis to prevent bad dreams, are more learned than Peire Bonifaciis.

Wherever Peire Vidal went he wrote songs to Azalaïs des Baux and sent them back to her, either by boy singers in his employ, or by troubadours traveling east along the Via Tolosa, or in manuscript addressed to his friend Folquet de Marseille, who was at the same time his rival. At Montpellier his funds seem to have run low, and he wrote a song ostensibly addressed to Azalaïs but obviously intended for a protector whom he calls Dragoman. He sang:

Seigneur Dragoman, if I had a good charger our enemies would be in a bad way. . . .

[272]

When I put on the strong double hauberk and hold in my hand the sword which Sire Gui gave me a short time ago, the earth trembles at my step. . . .

For bravery I am equal to Roland and Olivier; for gallantry to Montdidier. . . .

In all things I am a true knight. I have mastered the art of love. Never will you see a knight who can be as charming as I in the hall, or as terrible as I when my sword had left its sheath. . . .

And if I had a horse the king of Aragon could sleep sweetly and happily, for I would preserve the peace for him at Montpellier. . . .

Lady Vierna, thanks from Montpellier. . . .

Says Peire's biographer, "He sang of his follies in love and war and boasted about both."

Of the stolen kiss, Vidal sang:

Delicate body, gently molded, have compassion on me. Pity! Counsel her to pity me for I am distressed and afflicted. Helas! Lady, do not kill me for it were a shame and a great sin to let me die in despair. . . .

I would be more happy than any other creature, if the stolen kiss had been granted freely. Sometimes covetise is the ruin of the wisest. . . .

Beauty turns wisdom into folly. . . . I would be no coward if I turned my eyes away from your beauty . . . but when you speak I am unable to leave your side. . . .

3

The Via Tolosa runs southwest from Montpellier to Mèze, thence northwest to Montagnac, and then southwest again to Béziers and Narbonne. A medieval itinerary suggests that there may have been a short cut between Mèze and Béziers via St.-Thybery, which the author spells St.-Hybery, for which reason and others I suspect that the author did not make the trip himself but gathered his information from others. Misinformation found in guide-books and due to ignorance is not, by the way, the only difficulty in tracing the trails of the troubadours. Guide-books in those days were written like railway travel folders of the present time, for the purpose of attracting tourists to important or ambitious monasteries; that is to say, for the purpose of advertising. Thus if you were going from Avignon, for example, to Compostella along the Via Tolosa, every conceivable inducement would be offered to persuade you to leave the highway for a day's excursion to monasteries which lay just off the beaten track. Both your soul and the monks' bodies would prosper as a result of your visit. The authors of these books probably thought that any fool can follow the broad highway, but even the wisest will need friendly help and advice if he is to discover the retreats of his spiritual fathers.

Béziers is the third great city on the route, and Peire Vidal undoubtedly stopped here for a time. He was a friend of Beatrice de Béziers, whom all the troubadours praised, and of the Viscountess Agnes de Montpellier. At one time in her career, and it was an unhappy time for her, Beatrice became the wife of the much-married Raymond of Toulouse, who for a time held the record in large-scale divorces. His enemies have suggested that he kept a harem in addition to his various wives. I have no doubt that the clerks who wrote the histories and were largely in the employ of the dominant power, the church, have maligned him.

The flat tidal plain of the Mediterranean stretches from Béziers to the sea, and this city, like Bellegarde, achieves a vicarious dignity by contrast between the flatness of the plain and the apparent height of its walls. It seems to reach up, precipice upon precipice, above the road; and upon the very summit, above the city ramparts and well fortified against the attacks of the heretics, is the church of St.-Nazaire.

During the Middle Ages life in Béziers was agitated. Like Montpellier, Narbonne, and Toulouse, it was a commercial city. The lords who owned the land were of less importance than the merchants who carried on the trade. The inevitable results of a commercial civilization are democracy and protestantism. Other civilizations are, for other reasons, sometimes democratic and sometimes protestant, but commercial civilizations are so inevitably. Raymond de Trencavel, lord of Béziers, showed hesitation in granting the bourgeois all they demanded and was suspected of treachery toward them. The angry merchants demanded their rights, and when Raymond fled to a church, hoping to find sanctuary there, they fell upon him and murdered him. His son wisely sought safety in flight from the city but reappeared some time later with an army. The consuls of the people negotiated with him and agreed to permit him to enter if he would grant a general amnesty and not seek to avenge his father's death. The young man consented, but as soon as he was established he locked the gates and ordered a general massacre and a looting.

This dastardly action was wiped out by a later Viscount Raymond de Trencavel, who, a good son of the church

himself, sacrificed everything he had, even his life, in protecting the merchants whose religious opinions he condemned. On July 21, 1209, Simon de Montfort, the bishop
of Béziers, and St. Dominic, all bent on the extirpation of
heresy, appeared before the walls of the city with an army.
They commanded the city to yield. It refused and after
a short scuffle was taken. The bishop had a list of those
who were to be burned for their heresy, but in the confusion
there was no time to sort the sheep from the goats. When
asked for advice, he shouted: "Kill them all. God will
recognize his own!"

The massacre was memorable. Everybody rushed for
the cathedral of St.-Nazaire, which offered the protection
of a place that was both holy and well fortified. They
were packed so tightly in the church that they could not
move. Then the soldiers of the crusaders arrived and
guarded every door but one, which they broke down. First
five abreast until they got into the church, and then ten,
twenty, thirty abreast, they worked their way down the
church, systematically killing every one there, men, women,
and children. And all the time the butchery was in progress,
the priests rang the bells as though for a marriage service.
All were killed here, as well as in the other churches and
in the streets. Only a handful escaped to Narbonne. Later
the bishop of Béziers apologized to the pope very mod-
estly for having killed only forty thousand people. The
city was burned, pillaged, ruined. . . .

To-day Béziers is peaceful. The bourgeois spend their
Sunday afternoons parading up and down in the pleasant
parks or on the small square in front of the church over-

looking the broad plain. They gaze with blank eyes toward the sea. *"C'est bien tranquille ici,"* they murmur, and again, as though to make quite certain, *"C'est bien tranquille. . . ."*

4

Beyond Béziers is Narbonne, famous to those who know, for its excellent honey, its fine church, and its distinguished past. This is the city where Ermengarde de Narbonne lived whenever she was not visiting the country houses of her friends; it is the city where Peire Rogier lost his heart to little Hugette des Baux, and where Peire Vidal wrote a poem which illustrates the astonishing virtuosity, the passion for compliment, and the raciness of diction of the troubadours. The fifty-six lines of this poem are all written on one rime, "-ana" and "-ona" (pronounced "-ana" and "-awna"), with clever variations in the consonantal accompaniment. Peire sang:

Dear friend, sweet and sincere, amiable, gracious and good, my heart spreads itself before you and before you alone. I love you with a love which is sincere and humble, and I treasure your love more than the wealth of Lombardy and France.

You are the tree and the branch where the fruit of love ripens. Your sincere love comforts me. I fear no evil. It takes from me sadness and sorrow and blesses me with perfect happiness.

With red and white, beauty has fashioned you to bear the crown of the imperial throne. You are so sweet and so human that the whole world grants you sovereignty in joy and perfection, in valor and honor.

She has perfect feet and body, the sweet Lady Guilhelmona. She deceives not. She betrays not. And she wears no shoes or stockings.

I know no gentle citizen sweet as lovely Guilhelmona, not even Yolanda, daughter of the Lady Constance who taught young men the art of dancing. [Some kind of a satire is evidently intended here, but the reference is lost upon me.]

Not the army of the viscount now could drive me out of Narbonne. Of all the ladies under heaven, not a blonde or a brunette, not a Christian, Jew or pagan lady can compare with you in beauty.

Rich old hags are nothing to me, if their riches grant no favor or their invitations are ungracious. But from the gentle Guilhelmona, I esteem more dear the promise of a lovely laughing body than the wealth of rancid witches . . .

In the last stanza, which is offensive to twentieth-century taste and therefore not to be translated, Peire expresses himself somewhat fully and picturesquely as to the fate deserved by one who had done the lovely Guilhelmona a wrong.

In the twelfth century, Narbonne was the great seaport of the south and the rival of Marseilles. The Romans who took over the city when it was still a Greek colony deflected an arm of the river to run through Narbonne and keep its harbor from silting up. The dike they built lasted until the fourteenth century, when it broke. Since then the Narbonnese have watched the sea recede farther and farther from its docks. At the time when the troubadours were making the court gay with their songs, Narbonne was divided into three towns. One part was governed by the lords bishops of the church, who naturally hated the heretics. A second portion was governed by the viscounts, closely related to the Trencavels. A third section was the Jewry. In the Jewry, Moise Khimbki, a learned rabbi, wrote long commentaries and became so famous that Narbonne was a center of Hebrew learning, and in the château Peire and his friends sang about love.

The merchants made treaties with Italy and the Levant. Jaufre Rudel probably took ship here for Tripoli. The narrow streets were crowded. Pretty bourgeoises and pretty Jewesses, gallant and fastidious young men whose fathers were merchants but who felt themselves destined for better things, a yellow roof at the end of the street gleaming in the sunlight, shadowy figures seen through an open window, human beings in a dusky room, laughter and ribald song in the inns, exquisites fingering their diminutive swords, a crowd of dirty students in eager disputation, the smell of garlic, the sound of wooden shoes tapping on the cobbled pavement. . . . Then came Simon de Montfort and barefooted St. Dominic who begged his bread, both of them men in whom fanaticism and opportunism were curiously mingled, and behind them the rabble of puritan crusaders.

Simon de Montfort, one of the mad de Montforts, was the grandson of the earl of Leicester and the father of the rebel Montfort in England. Raymond of Toulouse, whom Simon ruined, is said to have wept at his death and to have admitted that Simon was possessed of the qualities of a great soldier and an excellent prince. He was utterly fanatic and possessed of an energy which is difficult to comprehend even to-day, when energetic fanaticisms of other kinds are being exhibited in various parts of the world. He was besieging the Château de Termes, a stronghold of heresy. When the château capitulated and several of the heretics offered to join the church, Simon ordered them all burned. "If they are honest," he said, "the fire will cleanse them of their sins. If they are liars, they deserve to be burned."

When he overcame Raymond of Toulouse, he insisted that Raymond promise among other things that he and all his nobles and all his peasants should wear no clothes of value and should put on their heads the black cap of serfdom; that he demolish all his châteaux and fortifications, to the very foundations; that none of the nobles should live in a town or even in a house, but that they should sleep in the open fields like villeins; that Montfort and his officers be permitted to take anything they pleased from any individual in the former domain of the count of Toulouse, and that none should offer resistance no matter what the officers wished to take. After Raymond had promised all this, he was to make war on the infidels until Simon, at his pleasure, should recall him. At this time, Folquet de Marseille, whom we have met before in different company, was bishop of Toulouse and a lieutenant of Simon's.

All the lords of the Provence declared themselves on the side of Raymond. A priest said to Simon:

"Your army is small in comparison with the army of your adversaries, which includes the king of Aragon, who is skilful and experienced in war. He is followed by many counts and a numerous army. The battle will not be equal if fought between a small army like yours and a great army like his."

At these words Simon drew a letter from his pocket. "Read that," he said.

It was a letter from the king of Aragon to the wife of a Toulousan nobleman. The king wrote that he was driving the crusaders from Toulouse for her sake and paid her many compliments and expressed the hope of an early assignation.

"What of it?" said the priest, who seems to have been something of a realist.

"What of it?" cried Simon in a voice of thunder. "Let me tell you that God will not desert me when I fight a heretic who tries to circumvent God's designs for love of a woman!"

In 1115 he took a title, and the pope confirmed it, making him, "By the grace of God, Count of Toulouse, Viscount of Béziers and Carcassonne, and Duke of Narbonne." It was fortunate that this title came by God's grace, for it certainly did not come by the grace of popular opinion in these cities which he had ruined so that they never fully recovered. He died two years later.

After the massacre at Béziers, the few survivors rushed to Narbonne and with the heretics of that city crowded into a château just outside the city gates. The place was small and badly provided with food so that the refugees had to send to Narbonne for supplies. The bishops of Narbonne preferred the heretics to Simon and his crusading army, but when they saw he intended to visit them, they helped him. The massacre at Béziers had been terrible enough to awaken popular feeling, and Simon was persuaded to offer amnesty to any who would recant. "Do not fear," he said to his friends; "we shan't lose a one of them." He was right. Not a man or woman recanted. When the gates opened every man and woman in the fortress ran upon the knives of their adversaries like sheep to the slaughter.

No civilization could stand spectacles of this kind.

Whether the church was right or wrong in its pretensions, and whether civilization is a blessed or cursed thing, the fact remains that after the Albigensian Crusade troubadourism died, and troubadourism was merely one aspect of a broad, rich, and cultivated attitude toward life. Not only was the economic basis of the civilization of the south destroyed, but the spectacle of wholesale butchery dehumanizes. Even before these crusades, men were, as they are to-day, sufficiently brutal; but their brutality, like ours, was controlled by a set of social sanctions which were rigidly observed. The throwing off of these sanctions—and again the throwing of them off is a symptom rather than a cause—set civilization back for a hundred years. Man progresses by means of his conventions and not despite them. He goes forward by trying very hard to stay just where he is. The best way to go backward is to try to go forward.

Before the crusades, fanaticism had not been characteristic of the cultivated worldliness of the south. More characteristic and less unpleasant is the pretty scandal the chronicler suggests in his account of the life of Peire Rogier, the poet. "Peyre Rogier was a canon at Clermont, though some say he was canon at Arles and at Nîmes. Having quitted his position, and realizing that he was young, handsome, and of good family, and being assured that he would profit more in the world than in the church, where he saw nothing but envy, jealousy, and quarrels among the clergy, having, as I say left his monastery for the reasons I have told you, he gave himself to poetry in our vulgar Provençal tongue and made himself comedian and invented pretty and ingenious comedies which he played with great success at the courts of the lords and princes." He was received favorably wherever he went, but particularly well, it seems, by the viscountess of Narbonne, who gave him many rich gifts.

"He fell in love with one of the demoiselles of the countess called Hugette des Baux, but by her friends, little Baussette. She was the daughter of Hugues des Baux," Vidal's patron, " and married . . . who was the son of . . . who later became . . ." and so on with local gossip. "Peire Rogier sang for her many good songs, and some say that he received from her the last favors in love, which scandal one should not believe, for she says to him in a song which she sent him that he is mistaken in his suit and that she finds nothing that he does is pleasant or agreeable. But others say that this song means nothing and that she only sent it to him to cover up the love and affection she felt for him. But this I take to be slander and a great pity. . . ."

5

As one emerges from Narbonne, the horizon to the south is clouded by the Corbières Mountains, whence emerges (according to Professor Bédier, for I was not able to see it) a solitary rock bearing on its summit the Château de Termes, which was cruelly besieged by Montfort during the crusades. The Via Tolosa follows the river to Lézig-nan, a little town surrounded by a swarm of châteaux and dependent in the twelfth century on the abbey of La Grasse to the south, where Peire Rogier, the lover of Baussette, retired in his old age.

The road, redolent with traditions, winds wearily to Carcassonne. On either side are little round hills which at midday seem to lie on their backs panting beneath the brilliance of the sun, a brilliance which seems to wipe the world clean of color except the white of the road and the grayish brown of the grass. But when the brilliance of the sun fades, other colors appear. A startling black piles itself about the bases of the hills. The white and radiant sky becomes a pale blue; this deepens into mauve, into intense red, into indigo. These colors catch the dolmens and the châteaux on the hills. They float above a sea of misty color. A peasant with white bullocks silhouetted against the sky becomes a symbol too profound for analysis. He is Man himself, heritor of the past, victor and victim of his own traditions, clinging to the final and immutable reality, the earth which with unmoral fecundity gives him his daily bread. At this hour, if one has planned one's walk judiciously, one should come in sight of the walls and towers of Carcassonne, placid on a hill.

It is more or less as the troubadours left it in the twelfth and thirteenth centuries; a château and a town and a cathedral curtained from the rest of the world by several walls. The earliest stones in these walls were placed by Roman captives. Later the walls were repaired and enlarged by the Visigoths, the Saracens, the Trencavels, who were also the owners of Béziers, and, in the late thirteenth century, by St. Louis himself, who built the outer girdle of walls, made Carcassonne into a fortress, and forced the citizens to build a new town in the valley.

Roger Trencavel with his wife Agnes de Montpellier

awaited the approach of Simon de Montfort and his crusaders at Carcassonne. He had done his best at Béziers;
he had fortified it and prepared it for a siege and had then
retired, before the approaching army, to Carcassonne, the
seat of his county. From his towers, which commanded a
good view of the approaches to the town, he saw pouring
over the hills by every available road, and even across the
fields, the armies of the crusading hosts, experienced warriors clad in pilgrims' cloaks, some of them sincere, some
of them merely avaricious, and all of them eager for blood.
He saw them encamp, and he saw the mushroom-like tents
of the leaders erected at safe distances from the walls. In
the center of Carcassonne, under an elm-tree, were gathered
Roger's dependents, the heretics, whose lives God had confided to his care when He made him suzerain of the country.

Simon de Montfort demanded that Carcassonne capitulate. Simon de Montfort boasted of the massacres at Narbonne and Béziers. Simon de Montfort threatened a worse
fate to Carcassonne. He was greeted with derisive shouts
from the walls. The town had no water. A subterranean
passage was dug from within the walls to the river some
three hundred yards away at the base of the hill. Burning
oil and burning lead were poured on the machines of the
crusading hosts. Huge stones were catapulted from the
walls. There were deeds of gallantry on both sides. Simon
de Montfort, at the risk of his own life, rescued a common
soldier who had fallen into the moat and was being covered by a rain of small stones.

Montfort sent an embassy headed by one of Roger's
relatives. Roger and twelve of his men were offered safe-

conduct if they would deliver the rest of the city into the hands of the enemy.

"You may tell these priests," he shouted, "that I will let them tear the hair from my chin and head, the nails from my feet and hands, the teeth from my mouth, my eyes from my sockets, that I will be skinned alive or burned at the stake, before I will deliver up to these butchers one of my people, he be serf, heretic, or felon, which God confided to my charge when he made me suzerain of these countries."

According to Mrs. Gostling's quotation of Frederick Soulie, who writes as though he had been a witness[1] of these events, Roger crossed the courtyard of the castle and arrived at the Place of the Elm-tree, where all who were not guarding the walls had gathered.

"Do you know what the legates of that demon Innocent III have dared to offer me, your sovereign and defender? That I should leave the city, I, the thirteenth, and give the rest of you over to their mercy."

"And what would that mercy be?" asked some of the serfs and women.

"The mercy our brothers of Béziers have obtained," cried Roger, pale and trembling with rage so he could scarcely find breath to utter the words, " the butchery of all the men to the last, of all the women to the last, of the old people, the children, Catholics, Protestants, laymen and clerics. For at Béziers, our city of Béziers, in Béziers, the rich, the noble sister of Carcassonne, not a foot is left above the soil to come and bear us news, not a hand remains to sound the alarm. Dead! Dead! To the very last! That is the mercy of the Legates. . . ."

[1] Frances M. Gostling, "Rambles around French Chateaus" (London, 1911), p. 255.

Of course they got him in the end. They offered him safe-conduct outside the city walls when the capture of the city was imminent, in order that he might discuss terms. Roger knew that they were lying and sent his citizens out by the water-gate. As soon as his enemies had him in their power, they forgot their offer for safe-conduct, fell on him, put him in chains, and threw him into one of his own dungeons, where, not long after, he died a natural death as the result of having eaten poisoned food.

The troubadours regarded all these changes in the fortunes of their patrons at first with chagrin and later with dismay. Peire Vidal, who spent several seasons in Carcassonne and the châteaux near it in pursuit of his mistress, the Wolf, Loba de Perrautier, sang, when these troubles were just beginning:

Evil has conquered the world.

At Rome the pope and the false doctors have thrown the church into distress and have irritated God. They are fools and so sinful that the heretics have become bold. Since they commenced the trouble, it is difficult that it should be different than it is. But I will not take sides.

The king of France is insincere with regard to the honor of Our Lord. He has abandoned the Holy Sepulcher. He buys, sells, and engages in commerce like a serf or a bourgeois.

Yesterday we knew that the world was bad; to-day we see that it is worse.

But I am not sad. A pure joy guides me and permits me to remain in the perfect friendship of her whom I love best. If you wish to learn her name, inquire in the country of Carcassonne. . . .

Peire's friends sometimes teased him because his father had been a furrier, and when Loba de Perrautier (Loba,

[287]

from *loupa*, wolf) referred to it, he said, "You are my wolf; permit that I be yours." He dressed himself in wolf-skins, and the lords and ladies pursued him over the grounds of the château. Unfortunately an envious enemy loosed the hounds, and Peire, unable to free himself from his disguise, was almost killed before the hounds were pulled away. Loba herself nursed him back to health. This is the same Loba who was involved in the unpleasant affair with Rémond de Mirevaux, and Rémond may have been one of the hunting-party.

Carcassonne is almost too medieval to be true. The restorations leave nothing to be desired; "wherever possible the original stones have been used in the walls"; but there is in Carcassonne something of the theatrical, a sense of life arrested, that one does not feel in the remoter untouched villages, where life continues to be lived on the classic scale, where churches become stables, and where the stones from the walls are built into the peasants' bedrooms. The people of these villages are like the people of the Middle Ages; scornful of their past and skeptical of their future, trusting in *le bon Dieu* to send them rain for their crops and to bring them safely through another year. The people of Carcassonne are chiefly interested in their past and hurl dates and architectural terms at you with the rapidity of a high-power machine-gun and the composure of an Oxford don.

The postern-gate is still there through which the troubadours slipped trembling at the proximity of their mistresses; the church where the lovely ladies heard mass and made assignations still stands as it was enlarged in the fourteenth century; and one can still walk around the walls of the town in thirty minutes or so to catch a view of the Pyrenees gleaming in the west and the suggestion of the sea in the east. The walls rise like a curtain of masonry at the summit of the hill, and one feels that they, like the true church, will never fail.

6

Sometimes when Peire Vidal traveled this road he would go on to Toulouse to pay his respects to Count Raymond. At other times he would turn south at Carcassonne to visit the counts of Foix or Peter of Aragon beyond them in Spain. More than fifty of his poems have been preserved, and of his life many traditions are current.

He is said to have gone on a crusade with Richard the Lion-Heart and to have stopped off at Cyprus, where he met a peasant girl who said she was the daughter of the emperor of Constantinople. He married her forthwith and announced to all the lords of Christendom that he claimed the title of his father-in-law. He returned to France, was received again at Les Baux, and wandered again, with or without his wife, over the Via Tolosa. He penetrated Hungary, and wherever he went he carried with him the art of song, and wherever he went he made love to the ladies, and taught his friends how to make poems, and paid compliments, and was the wonder of the provincial courts, and committed great follies.

He was alive in 1205, but the date of his death is unknown.

Chapter XII

The Trail of a Poet Laureate

ABOUT AVIGNON

Avignon

Chapter XII

1

PETRACCO, Francesco de Petracco's father, was banished from Florence on the same day as Dante who wrote the "Divine Comedy," and on the day that Dante and Petracco stormed the gate of Florence on the south side of the city and were repulsed, Francesco was born, which was July 20, 1304. Between the years 1300 and 1400 two Italians were writing rich and fluent poetry, and one of these men was Dante and the other was Petrarch, and both of these men made use of the pleasant devices which the troubadours had discovered; but since they were ignorant of the way in which the troubadours sang their poems, they wrote their words to be read as literature and not to be sung. Mr. Ezra Pound, who has written many good songs in the manner of the troubadours, though his understanding is sometimes clouded by his friendship for one of them, has said that the poems of Campion who lived in England at the time of Shakspere are the half of the troubadour's art preserved by Dante and Petrarch, and that the musical sonata represents the other half of their art. The troubadours wrote both words and music and intended their songs to be sung. For this reason they were very careful of the words they used in their songs, that each should be fitting

[293]

to the note at which it was to be uttered. Their music was more philosophical and abstract than any music we know to-day and was written for learned people, for which reason it cannot be played on the phonograph, as the melodies are not suited to the Charleston in which people to-day take great delight.

Dante learned the manner of writing poems from Guido Cavalcanti and was well learned in the Provençal tongue. But the manner he learned was no more than the mold into which he poured his thoughts, which were melted by the divine fire of his passions and poured from his lips like liquid gold. Such was the heat of his nature that his words still glow and retain much of the inner light which he communicated to them, as in the poem beginning,

> All ye that pass along Love's trodden way
> Pause ye a while and say
> If there be any grief like unto mine,

or that other beginning,

> Ladies that have intelligence in love,
> Of mine own lady I would speak with you,

or that other,

> A very pitiful lady, very young,
> Exceeding rich in human sympathies
> Stood by, what time I clamored upon death,

or indeed any poem which he wrote in honor of his lady, Beatrice, known to her friends and companions as Bice Portinari.

Dante's companions who taught him how to write in the Provençal tongue lived a hundred years after the greatest troubadours had died, and they no longer remembered the meanings which these troubadours, Bertrand de Born, Bernard de Ventadour, and Arnaut Daniel, attached to their words nor how these poets thought about love. Thus they separated love of the spirit, which they called Love, from fleshly love which they ignored or called "irregularities of youth," and love of one's wife which they did not describe at all but took for granted. Although the troubadours frequently committed "irregularities" and did not think about them much more than Petrarch or Dante, in their connection of Love the body and the spirit participated. Thus Dante and Petrarch misunderstood the nature of the poetry of the troubadours. This is not to be regretted, for from this misunderstanding grew Dante's "Vita Nuova"; and we cannot imagine whether his poems would have been better or worse had he written of love as the troubadours wrote, for had he done so, he would not have been Dante but would have been some one else.

Petrarch was born when Dante was forty-three years old, and as Dante's vision was of the heavenly paradise, so Petrarch's vision was of the earthly paradise. The time in which Petrarch lived was like the time in which Bernard de Ventadour lived, but with this difference, that whereas Bernard saw the earth and its beauty and looked beyond to catch a glimpse of heaven, Petrarch saw heaven and its beauty and looked beyond to catch a glimpse of earth. Petrarch was brought to Carpentras, a city near Avignon, when he was very young, and he spent much of his life between Avignon, Carpentras, and Vaucluse, where he had a summer house. On several occasions he traveled along the Via Tolosa.

2

The country about Avignon has to-day much the same appearance that it had when Petrarch lived there. In the very far distance are the foot-hills of the Alps. Closer and separated from them by many miles of rich rolling land is Mont Ventoux, which Petrarch climbed; and some scholars think that Petrarch was the first man in many hundreds of years to climb a mountain in order to appreciate nature; others think that these are wrong, for as soon as Petrarch reached the top of the mountain, which he did with much difficulty and much wondering of why he had set out, he turned his back upon the view to think about himself and read the Confessions of St. Augustine.

Most of the villages in the district are walled villages, but the walls are very much broken, and the owners of the châteaux have gone away and left them to the peasants and cows and horses and chickens which have taken possession of them or of those parts that seem useful. The villages of the Middle Ages were small, but these villages are smaller, and one may wander about in many a deserted house of the fourteenth century and look out over the walls of the town to the green fields beyond. The houses are tall and flat on the roof and narrow, and there are not enough people left to make it worth while to use the top stories.

Carpentras is one of these towns, only larger than most.

It has electric lights in some parts, but in others it has none and no running water. It is on a very high hill. The room where we stayed at Carpentras was at the top of a high narrow house, and the wind howled about the corner, and the moonlight threw into silhouette the jagged roof-line of the town and the crenelated tower of the Porte d'Orange. One cannot make a tour of the walls from the inside of the town, for houses have been built up against them and over them so that at night the lights of the houses smile down on the traveler. Building a house against the wall of a city is a good idea, because it saves putting up one side of the house, and sometimes you can dig back into the city wall and make an extra room or a cellar to keep the butter fresh.

When Petrarch was in Carpentras he was a little boy and no doubt played about in the square in front of the cathedral, but he did not run away from his lessons. He was such a good boy that instead of trying to get out of studying his lessons, he even read the books his teachers were using and was so assiduous that his father was well pleased and predicted a brilliant future for him. This, I suppose, is a very unusual thing for a father to do, for Petrarch has recorded it and commented about it. Petrarch and his admirers agree that he was not vain, and Petrarch says he does not know why the world thought so highly of him. He spent his life writing a large number of letters to important people and was an adept in the art of making rich men feel comfortable after having done things they never should have done.

Petrarch's father was modest too. One day at the age

of forty-five, Petracco looked in the glass and discovered
that there was one white hair on his head. He began
shouting and making such an uproar that everybody in the
house and street thought he was being murdered and called
the watch.

In the courtyard of the bishop's palace is a Roman tri-
umphal arch, but the palace was built in the seventeenth
century, and I am unable to determine whether the arch
stood in the open when Petrarch was a child in the streets.
Wherever it was, Petrarch must have seen it and dreamed
about it, for he was an Italian and hated France and Carpentras and Avignon, and he thought always of Rome.
Whenever he wrote anything that he thought it was important for posterity to remember, he wrote in Latin. For
many years he wrote two or three of these Latin letters a
day and made copies of them and later edited them very
carefully. They were lengthy Latin essays about important
abstract subjects such as the nature of literature, the good
points in his rich friend's character, and his own experiences. The personal notes were on a separate sheet of paper
and were all destroyed, yet for three or four of these personal notes, if they were the right ones, I would almost
forgive him the several volumes of his Latin epistles. His
love for Laura, which he considered neither grave enough
nor dignified enough for the language of Cicero, he described in Italian poems, yet strangely enough the sonnets
have a dozen readers where the epistles have one.

The papacy was at Avignon only sixteen miles away,
and noble Italian families were living in all of the towns of
the district. A bishop seems to have lived in every ham-

let, and frequently the popes themselves made excursions into the surrounding country, or some important committee would hold conference at Carpentras or at Nîmes. On these occasions life would be interesting. The clerics would come in holiday attire, in silk and satin and many ornaments, and the official business of the church would be postponed while they took great dinners in the episcopal palace; and Petracco, who was a successful lawyer, would be very busy, and Signora Petracco would be flushed perhaps and excited. . . .

But the charm of Carpentras is not particularly in the church of St.-Suffren, nor in the Roman arch, nor even in the little boy that played in the streets—a boy of good family with a round fat face and good eyes who admitted when he had grown up that he had been handsome in his youth—but rather in the arrogance of a town that is so old that it refuses to grow old, of a small city that is larger than many an American metropolis. The population of Carpentras is not of this generation only; it is of the ages and counts in its number the six thousand who live there now and their ancestors back to the first man who built the first stone hut on the hill in the stone age. These built the town, have put themselves in it, and live in it still. They will explain to you about it if your room is on the top floor of a tall house on a windy moonlit night.

3

At the age of fifteen Petrarch was sent to study at the University of Montpellier, and since he was a young man and was not to succumb to his passion for Laura until he was twenty-seven, he might have enjoyed himself were it not for the fact that he was going to study canon law, which he detested, and were he not journeying even farther away from his beloved Italy.

He traveled southwest on the road to Avignon and passed Entraigues, where an old tower built by the Templars still stands, and crossed the river by the newly repaired bridge of St.-Bénézet. This bridge, where *On danse, on danse, sur la pont d'Avignon*, was built, you must know, by a little shepherd boy. One day he was tending his flocks, and a man clothed in nothing but light appeared to him and told him to go to Avignon. The little boy said, "But who will take care of my flocks when I am gone?" The man answered that he was not to worry and that they would be looked after but that the little boy must come with him.

Bénézet started out bravely, and in one hand he held his shepherd's staff and in the other a bit of moldy bread which formed his daily fare. When he reached the Rhone there was no bridge over it and he had to be ferried across. At first the ferryman, a big black man with a wicked mouth and sores on his face, refused to take him because he thought the little boy didn't have any money. But the boy said, "You must take me because I'm going to build a bridge here." This threat of competition made the ferryman so angry that in midstream he fell upon the boy and tried to kill him, but he didn't succeed, for had he killed him little Bénézet could not have built the bridge of which a part is still standing to-day, so you see that the boy did get across somehow.

[300]

When he arrived at the cathedral they were saying mass, but he did not care. He walked right up to the front of the church and said, "See here, I'm going to build a bridge across the Rhone." The priests and the people and the bishop were terribly angry and tried to put him out, but he said: "No, you can't put me out. M. Jesus Christ all clothed in light came to me and told me to come here and build a bridge, and here I am." Then they said he was a wicked boy to leave his flocks, and please to go away until they had finished mass. But he said no, he would not go away, and was going to build a bridge.

Then they said: "So you are going to build a bridge, are you? So you think you can come in here and interrupt our services with that kind of cock and bull story, do you? Well!" And the people around the bishop nodded and shook their heads and said that the boy was getting a little of his own back, and that little boys thought they knew too much these days anyway.

Then the bishop pointed to a big stone in the courtyard of the church. It was thirty feet long and seven feet broad. "Take that," said the bishop, "and carry it to the river if you can."

And the boy picked it up as though it were a shepherd's staff and carried it to the river. "Here," he said, "is the foundation at least."

The bishop said he would not have believed it if he had not seen it with his own eyes, but the people in the church began shouting and singing hymns because a miracle had been performed and said to each other: "Yes, sir, he put it over his shoulder and carried it right straight to the river and said, 'Here's the first stone,' or something like that. I saw him.'' Then they went to the river and tried to push the stone to be certain it was as heavy as they thought it was. And that is the way the bridge came to be built.

The tower of Philippe le Bel, which is across the river from Avignon at the head of the Via Tolosa, had not yet been built when Petrarch crossed. Philip, the king of France, built it later in order to keep a good eye on Avignon, which was not part of his kingdom, so that he might know what the popes and the Templars were about and be prepared, to welcome them if they ever wanted to invade France. Not many years later, the popes built the walls around the city, which are still in excellent repair and are nine feet thick and have thirty-four towers—although I never counted them—in order to keep an eye on the king and be prepared in case he ever decided to invade Avignon. Thus mutually protected, neither was much afraid of the other, and the king and the popes lived together in mutual distrust.

A little to the north of the tower is an old Carthusian monastery and the Fort St.-André, now deserted but very new in Petrarch's time, if indeed they had yet been built when he crossed the river on his way to school in 1319.

Petrarch traveled almost due west along the Via Tolosa until he came to Remoulins, a walled city with an old square tower, whence it was but a step to the Pont du Gard, a Roman aqueduct which, bridging a wide valley, is some nine hundred feet long and five hundred feet high. It is made of three tiers of arches, each one narrower than the one below, and is made of large rocks without cement. It is supposed to have been built by the son-in-law of Augustus, which must have pleased Petrarch immensely. Despite the fact that it is visited yearly by thousands of tourists who go because they are told to go, its lines have great grace and much power.

At Nîmes, Petrarch found a Roman city in the midst of France. In the center of the town is a large arena, smaller but better preserved than the Colosseum at Rome or the arena at Arles. Not far from the arena is a former Roman temple, the Maison Carrée, still in excellent condition despite the profane uses to which it has been put, as a church, a warehouse, and a stable. It stood perhaps on the Roman Forum, and around it are other ruins. Farther away are Roman baths and a temple to Diana, restored and fiddled up by the eighteenth century. Here the fifteen-year-old Petrarch may have felt again the varied life of imperial Rome, its brutal power, its compactness, and its sensuality. Yet I think he felt none of these. The civilization of Rome was to him essentially a civilization of the intellect, and he was more attracted by the vision of virtue which his Roman masters defined but never attained than in the life of blood and bone which they lived.

The Nîmes Petrarch visited was a walled city, triangular in shape, with the arena at the apex. Two of the gates are still standing, hidden behind the mass of new houses, but the walls have been transformed into pleasant boulevards. Nîmes was taken in the Middle Ages many times at war, by siege, and by strategem. The most amusing of these strategems is recounted in the adventurous novel called "Le Charroi de Nîmes," which is too long to be re-counted here.

Uzès, a city which Petrarch probably never saw, is a few miles north of Nîmes. It has a beautiful château and was once the home of the three brothers Uzès, or, to preserve the older spelling, Uzèz. "Although Guy d'Uzèz was the sole lord of the château, which he inherited from his father, the revenue was so small that he and his brothers were unable to subsist on it. Ebles, one of the brothers, who was an astute man, remonstrated to Guy and Pierre on the small income they had, which was not enough to keep them alive, and said that because they knew how to sing and write poems he thought it would be better for them to follow the courts of the princes than to stay at home and starve to death in idleness. His brothers thought this was a good idea, so they wrote their cousin Hellyas, a gentleman of the neighborhood who was a good singer, and begged him to go with them, and he did not refuse at all. Before they left they decided that the songs which Guy invented and the sirventes which Ebles created should be sung by Pierre who was a very good musician, that they would always stay together, and that Guy would take care of the money and divide it between them." They got along very well and prospered until Ebles began writing about the lives of the tyrants and attacked the misdeeds of the lords of the country and the bishops of the church. Then the legate of the pope made them promise not to sing songs like that any more; "so they refused to sing at all but retired to their castle, rich and full of goods which they had acquired by means of their poesy. . . ."

From Nîmes, the Via Tolosa runs southwest to Lunel and thence to Montpellier, Béziers, and the other cities you have read about.

4

Petrarch seems not to have prospered at Montpellier, for after four years his father removed him to the University of Bologna in the hope that the Italian atmosphere might encourage the study of law. When he had been there for three years, he heard of the death of his father, gave up the study of law, and returned to Avignon. The next year he fell in love with Laura.

The only trustworthy accounts of this love are by Petrarch himself, and they are the poems and songs he made about it in the vulgar tongue, a few references in his Latin letters, and the following modest entry on the fly-leaf of his Virgil:

Laura, who was distinguished by her own virtues and widely celebrated by my songs, first appeared to my eyes in my early manhood, in the year of Our Lord 1327, upon the sixth day of April, at the first hour, in the Church of Santa Clara at Avignon; in the same city, in the same month of April, and on the same sixth day and at the same first hour, in the year 1348, the light was taken from our day, while I was by chance, at Verona, ignorant, alas! of my fate. The unhappy news reached me at Parma in a letter from my unhappy friend Ludovico, on the morning of the nineteenth of May of the same year. Her chaste and lovely form was laid in the Church of the Franciscans, on the evening of the day upon which she died. I am persuaded that her soul returned to the heaven whence it came. I have experienced a certain satisfaction in writing this bitter record of a cruel event, especially in this place, where it will often come under my eye, for so I can be led to reflect that life can afford me no further pleasures, and the most serious of my temptations being removed, I may be admonished by frequent study of these lines . . . that it is high time to flee from Babylon [Avignon]. This, with God's grace, will be easy. . . .

Little is known for certain of this mysterious and famous woman. She is supposed to have been married to a certain de Sade, a man of irascible temper. She was a good wife. Her conduct toward Petrarch seems to have been exemplary, for as soon as he declared his passion she tried to evade him, kept her face veiled in his presence, and treated him with honest rigor.

Her position must have been most trying, for Petrarch was a handsome and rising young man and the friend of the most powerful families of Avignon. His poems were excellent and were published as soon as written (that is, passed around among friends to become common property). The kind of thing to which Laura was subjected may be seen by reading the subtitles to several of the poems: "He hopes that time will render her more merciful"; "He invites his eyes to feast themselves upon Laura"; "His heart rejected by Laura will perish unless she relent"; "Night brings him no rest"; "Love makes him silent"; "All that he is is due to her . . . " etc. All of these themes, elaborated and varied with innumerable additions in some ninety sonnets and eight canzoni, were not calculated to bring ease and comfort to the chaste heart of a wife or the jealous heart of a husband. Petrarch was a young man, sufficiently well known so that whatever he did was news. If he met Laura walking in the afternoon, he would stop whatever he was saying, bite his lip, turn pale, become morose, walk as if he were in a trance, and conduct himself generally as young men who are obviously in love and like to have it known have conducted themselves ever since. Then he would write a poem about what he had done, and write it so well that even those people who had not been present to see how love had affected him would learn of it in the poem and would repeat the poem over and over again to all their friends and acquaintances. Ballad mongers learned the poems and recited them on the streets. Laura's husband must have been made glad by them whenever he left the house! Laura, who according to Petrarch's own admission never gave him any encouragement, must have been an angel to submit to this sort of thing for twenty-one years until death relieved her of her persecutions.

During this time Petrarch became the father of two children by a woman whose name is unknown. This intrigue was not called love, and it bothered the poet's conscience not at all, whereas his love he regarded not only as a great fault in his character but also as a great sin. Thus, in the fourteenth century, love must have meant something entirely different from what it had meant to the poets in the early stages of troubadourism. The physical basis of love had been entirely spiritualized. Love, which had originally been a coöperative passion in which the poet and his mistress both contributed, became an introspective passion for the man only. Woman had been apotheosized. Petrarch took Woman out of heaven and made her into woman again. He translated her from a symbol into a human being; but his translation was imperfect, and the human being still had about her some remnants of godliness. If Laura could for a moment have been less chaste and virtuous than she was, one cannot imagine Petrarch as anything but irritated with her for spoiling his pretty picture.

But there is one more thing to note. Although Petrarch's conception of love was entirely different, it was taken directly from the poetry of the troubadours, and Petrarch and his friends thought it was the same. Thus it fell under the ban of the church. Now the church fathers had condemned lust and had condemned adultery—although they were discreetly silent during the twelfth century—and it never occurred to them that a man and a woman could conduct a platonic friendship, or that a man could feel the emotions which Petrarch says he felt for Laura, or that woman could be made the symbol of complete theological beauty which Dante made of Beatrice. Yet Petrarch's thought was dominated by the doctrines of the church fathers, and he regretted his love bitterly and determined to hate the object of it. Woman was still too divine to be quite human, she was already too human to be quite divine. Love becomes the symbol of earthly beauty, and Laura, the beautiful woman, becomes—at the same time that she is a woman, very real and very alive in his poems —the symbol of earthly beauty, the earthly beauty which the puritanical thirteenth century tried to hate but never could hate. Petrarch, looking at the world through the eyes of his teachers, who were bred in that century, re-

garded the beauty of the blue sky as a snare and the thrill
of the senses as a delusion of the devil.

Finally, and this is not emphasized frequently enough,
many of Petrarch's poems about Laura are mere literary
exercises. They were pleasant to write, they made him
talked about as a young man of talent, they were a gesture.
They are inferior to the gestures of the troubadours because Petrarch's virtuosity was inferior. They have a more
lasting hold upon us than the poems of the troubadours
because they represent more nearly the dilemma of the
modern man, for whom love of the spirit and love of the
senses are supposed to be separate for ever and ever and
for all time.

5

One time when Petrarch was thirty-three years old he
decided to climb Mont Ventoux, and although he apolo-
gizes for his ambition, because he thinks that people may
say he is addicted to worldly vanities, he tells us about his
trip at some length because he derived from it a moral
lesson. He had been reading about Philip of Macedon,
who ascended the Hæmus Mountains, in Thessaly, and
said, "It seems to me that a young man in private life may
well be excused for attempting what an aged king could
undertake without arousing criticism."

He had great difficulty in finding a suitable companion
for his excursion, a difficulty not unknown in modern
times. In running over the list of possible friends, he rejected first those who would take no interest in the trip and

whose coldness would dampen his spirits, and then he rejected those whose enthusiasm would be irritating. He
finally decided that his brother was the best companion
he could find, and the brother was "delighted and gratified
beyond measure" at Petrarch's choice.

They left the house in the morning and by evening had
arrived at Malaucène, which lies on the foot of the mountain
at the north, according to Petrarch, but really at the northwest. Malaucène is about eleven miles from Carpentras,
and from Malaucène to the top of the mountain is another
eleven miles, although the second eleven is more difficult
than the first. Malaucène is a delightful little town with
a ruined château, which stands bravely on a rock and
faces the mountains on the one side and the plain on the
other.

Petrarch said: "We found an old shepherd, in one of
the mountain dales, who tried, at great length, to dissuade
us from the ascent, saying that some fifty years before, he
had, in the same ardor of youth, reached the summit, but
had got for his pains nothing but fatigue and regret, and
clothes and body torn by rocks and briers. No one, so far
as he or his companions knew, had ever tried the ascent
before him. But his counsels increased rather than dimin-
ished our desire to proceed, since youth is suspicious of
warnings." They started out with good-will, and the
shepherd followed some distance behind, begging and imploring them not to undertake so rash and foolhardy an
adventure.

"We soon came to a halt at the top of a certain cliff.
Upon starting out again, we went more slowly, and I

especially advanced along the rocky path with a more deliberate step. While my brother chose a direct path, straight up a cliff, I weakly took an easier one which really descended." When he was called back by his companions, he said he had been trying to find an easier path, and did not mind walking farther if he did not need to walk so hard. He became disgusted with himself when he found that he was walking twice as far as his brother, and that while his brother waited for him to come up he could rest, whereas Petrarch grew constantly more weary and irritated. Many times he made good resolutions, and many times he broke them, and always he found that his brother was ahead of him and was resting and fresh. Finally he sat down and said to himself: "What thou hast so frequently experienced to-day in the ascent of this mountain, happens to thee as to many in the journey towards the blessed life. . . . But nevertheless in the end, after long wanderings, thou must perforce either climb the steeper path, under the burden of tasks foolishly deferred, to its blessed culmination, or lie down in the valley of thy sins and (I shudder to think of it) if the shadow of death overtake thee spend an eternal night amid constant torments."

" . . . On the peak of the mountain is a little level space where we could at last rest our tired feet and bodies." To-day at the peak of the mountain there is an observatory, a hotel, and a church, and the automobile road from Carpentras which winds up the gentler slopes on the south and east. The summit of Mont Ventoux is 6254.96 feet high, and this is what Petrarch thought as he looked over the country:

At first, because of the unaccustomed quality of the air and the effect of the great sweep of view spread out before me, I stood like one dazed. I beheld the clouds under our feet, and what I had read of Athos and Olympus seemed less incredible as I myself witnessed the same things from a mountain of less fame. I turned my eyes toward Italy whither my heart most inclined. The Alps, rugged and snow-capped, seemed to rise close by, although they were really at a great distance; the same Alps through which that fierce enemy of the Roman name once made his way, bursting the rocks, if we may believe the report, by the application of vinegar. I sighed, I must confess, for the skies of Italy. . . . An inexpressible longing came over me to see once more my friend and my country. . . . At the same time I reproached myself for the double weakness, springing as it did from a soul not yet steeled to manly resistance.

He thought of Laura. Did the noble eminence on which he stood recall to him the nobility of his love or of her character? Did the pleasant and soft landscape at his feet suggest thoughts of the softness and sweetness of his friendship with her? Did he write a poem about her beginning, "I love to think that sometime we may be . . ." or, "When I am dead . . . "? They did not. He did not. He thought: "I still love but with shame and heaviness of heart. I love, but love what I would not love, and what I would that I might hate. Though loath to do so, though constrained, though sad and sorrowing, still I do love and I feel in my miserable self the truth of the well known words, 'I will hate if I can; if not, I will love against my will.'" Love is a perverse and wicked passion. The world has evidently changed since the days of the troubadours.

He had almost forgotten where he was, but at last he determined to dismiss his anxieties and look about him and see what he could see. "The sinking sun and the lengthening shadows of the mountain were already warning us that the time was near at hand when we must go. As if suddenly wakened from sleep, I turned about and gazed toward the west. I was unable to discern the summits of the Pyrenees . . . not because of any intervening obstacle that I know of, but simply on account of the insufficiency of our mortal vision. But I could see with utmost clearness, off to the right, the mountains about Lyons, and to the left, the Bay of Marseilles and the waters that lash the shores of Aigues-Mortes. . . . Under our very eyes flowed the Rhone."

It occurred to him to open his St. Augustine. "My brother, waiting to hear something of St. Augustine's from my lips, stood attentively by. I call him, and God too, to witness that where I first fixed my eyes it was written: 'And men go about to wonder at the heights of the mountains, and the mighty waves of the sea, and the wide sweep of the rivers, and the circuit of the ocean, and the revolution of the stars, but themselves they consider not.' I was abashed, and, asking my brother, who was anxious to hear more, not to annoy me, I closed the book, angry with myself that I should still be admiring earthly things who might long ago have learned . . . that nothing is wonderful but the soul, which, when great in itself, finds nothing great outside itself." He had seen enough and did not speak a word until he had reached the bottom of the mountain.

6

Petrarch and his brother Gherardo were young men about town in Avignon in 1326. They were nice young men who belonged to the best clubs, dressed in the height of fashion, and were always to be found in the house of the wealthy Colonna family. Petrarch's hair was curled by the "piratical curling-iron," his boots were of the tightest, and his clothes were worn so fastidiously that the slightest puff of wind would disarrange the neat folds. Avignon was at that time very fashionable, and the popes and their nephew-cardinals, the poets and ambassadors and pretty women, must have made it a pleasant spot to spend a season or two.

The social center that year was the house of the Colonna, an important Roman family in exile which Petrarch was very careful to cultivate, with the fortunate result that the next year he went with one of the Colonna boys, who had been granted a bishopric, to Lombez, a few leagues the other side of Toulouse. Although he had ample opportunity to become acquainted with classic troubadourism at Avignon, where the tradition was still being kept alive by a few sweet singers, his opportunities at Toulouse were greatly increased. There can be little doubt that he knew the troubadours fairly well, and in "The Triumph of Love" he presents a list of those who may be taken as his favorites. First he speaks of the Italian troubadours, and then

> another tribe of manners strange
> And uncouth dialect was seen. . . .

In this band were Arnaut Daniel, Folquet de Marseille, Rambaut d'Orange, Rambaut de Vaquières, Peire Vidal, and

> tuneful Rudel who, in moonstruck mood,
> O'er the ocean by a flying image led,
> In the fantastic chase his canvas spread;
> And where he thought his amorous vows to breathe
> From Cupid's bow received the shaft of death.

He had studied carefully the works of several of the troubadours, and whether he took from them merely their ideas, or whether he took their poems too, is still a matter of debate.

Lombez, Petrarch thought, was even less pleasant than the other French cities. The speech of the peasants was crude, and their manners were cruder than their speech. "The bishop, however," he said in effect in the letters which he sent back to friends at home, "is bearing his exile from the wealth and luxury to which he is accustomed with great affability of manner and much charm." Indeed the bishop might well bear his exile with good grace. It was his first bishopric, he was required to stay there for less than a year, the income was considerable, and he would forever after have the rank of at least a lord of the church. But for the Colonna this was merely a beginning. Petrarch's task was to make it as pleasant a beginning as possible. Obviously the poet is still the publicity agent; but instead of advertising his master's proficiency in arms, which is a fair advertisement, since it can be tested easily, or advertising his generosity and largess—for without this largess the poet would starve—instead of paying pretty compliments to a master's wife and cursing his master's character when he feels like it, the poet now devotes his attentions entirely to flattery, which is the more perverse because it was supposed to be taken seriously. When a troubadour says a lady is beautiful, the statement stands because it is bad form to think of any lady as anything but beautiful; but when Petrarch calls the king of Naples wise and says that the king's poetry is immortal and that he is the greatest man of the age, he is telling not only bald-faced lies, but he is telling servile lies, which are, if possible, worse.

The fruits of servility are rich and ripe. A year later the Colonnas furnished Petrarch with the means to travel to Paris and Germany. Later he traveled in Italy and took ship for England. When he saw the shores of that island, however, he had a change of heart. He suddenly felt that his passion for Laura had died and that he might return to Avignon and devote himself again to his studies. He did, and shortly thereafter became the father of a son by the unknown woman. Immediately after this event —that there was a scandal as has been suggested is most improbable, for that kind of error was too frequent in those days to be worthy of notice—he retired to his country house in Vaucluse.

7

The road leads due east from Avignon past Château-neuf, a ruined town on a hill, past Thor, a walled town in the valley, and past L'Isle-sur-Sorgue to a village which is so small that if one could get past the cliffs which sur-round it one would not notice it at all. This is Vaucluse. On the top of the cliff which faces the town is the ruined château of the bishops of Cavaillon, a small town not far south. The stream skirts the feet of the cliff; and if one follows the river path, worn deep by thousands of honeymoon couples—the grotto of Vaucluse is to southern France what Niagara Falls is to us—one comes finally to the deep and quiet pool hidden in the heart of the mountain which is the source of the Sorgue River.

It is a quiet and a romantic spot, but even before Petrarch came here to live, it was a tourist center. When Petrarch was a small boy his father brought him here on an excursion from Avignon. "The little Francesco had no sooner arrived than he was struck by the beauties of the landscape and cried, 'Here, now, is a retirement suited to my taste and preferable in my eyes to the greatest and most splendid cities.' " If this story is true Petrarch was evidently born a prig and was not made one by the circumstances of his education.

He had two gardens, one secluded on the side of a hill and the other on an island in midstream. The island garden contained a grotto where Petrarch retired to read during the midday heat. In this garden, he says, he tried to establish the Muses and thus incurred the displeasure of the nymphs of the stream who had for many centuries considered the island as their own. They refused to understand why Petrarch should have preferred nine old maids, ugly, arid, and shriveled, to their lovely selves and their eternal youth. Hidden in the stream, their bright eyes peering through the water-weeds, they watched him set his

garden in order. Then with musical laughter and splash-
ing of water, they descended on the garden, their naked
bodies brilliant in the sunshine, and destroyed all his
work. Petrarch tried again, and again he failed, and
finally he gave over the attempt.

Occasionally his fine friends would pay him a visit from
Avignon, King Robert of Naples, the Colonna, and others.
One time on his return from a walk he met a group of
people on the road. "The fashion of France has so con-
founded the dress of the sexes that I could not tell which
was which, for all were decked with ribbons and neck-
laces, pearls and rich head-dresses, rings, jeweled caps, and
coats embroidered in purple. We bowed to one another; then—what a pleasant surprise, my dear Guillaume!—I recognized the fair one who causes your heart
to beat. . . . "

While Petrarch was living thus in roots and herbs—
he was at times a vegetarian—and was completely withdrawn from the world he was surprised one day at receiving two letters each begging him to be crowned poet
laureate. One of these letters was from Paris, and the
other was from Rome. These were other fruits of servility. No one to this day has advanced a satisfactory
reason why this young man, who was known only by some
charming and very popular poems in the vulgar tongue,
should have been crowned poet laureate. This honor, one
imagines, should have been offered only to men who have
achieved and have produced some great work, a "Divine
Comedy," for example; and certainly the fourteenth century did not think well enough of love-lyrics, no matter

how perfect and charming they might have been, to make their author laureate of Rome. The fact is, of course, that the invitations came because of Petrarch's skill in making friends rather than because of his skill in making poems. His great Latin epic had hardly been begun.

With the laurel crown—and you may be sure he was not slow in punning on it with the name of Laura, which was unworthy of him and of her—Petrarch arrived at last at the eminence which he still holds. He was not the last of the troubadours, not the greatest of them, but he served to make popular the code of romantic love which still controls our actions and our thoughts, a code which had been perfected by gallant poets and lovely ladies a hundred years before Petrarch was born.

8

I would not have included the trail of Petrarch among the trails of those poets who died so long before he was born, were it not that Petrarch covered the same ground as they, though with a difference, and were he not one of the men who make them visible to us, though indistinctly and through their own temperament. I wish I might have included Dante and his trails, but they would have led us too far away from France. Dante really understood the troubadours much better than did Petrarch, for Dante was a better poet than Petrarch, which Petrarch knew, and for which he was jealous and is said never to have read "The Divine Comedy."

But since Petrarch acted like a troubadour in some things, I have tried to show how his manner and comprehension differed from theirs, and that he was neither so gallant as they nor so sharp. Because he took poetry more seriously than they, his discourses sound sometimes like papers read before literary clubs, filled with good morality and pleasant big words about a subject which the author does not understand. But our gratitude is due to Petrarch for his enthusiasm about Latin literature, and had he been equally enthusiastic about Greek literature we should be even more grateful to him. These, however, are matters that concern the school-teacher and therefore do not belong here.

The things which I thought did belong here are the result of a vision of men with golden voices singing pretty songs to ladies at the hour of dawn, standing in the gardens of châteaux and making of life an exquisite thing according to their own ideas of exquisiteness, a vision of butterflies in an orchard on a rich summer day, of hummingbirds in a garden. I hope I have caught a faint murmur of their song and a very little of the glamour of their civilization.[1]

[1] Several statements in the preceding pages are based on historical tradition only, in the belief that an unproved tradition represents the point of view of the makers of the tradition better than the unproved historical fact. Since both the tradition and the fact were, in several cases, hypothetical, I chose the tradition.

The routes over which people of the twelfth century traveled in France are a subject which has been somewhat neglected by scholars. It is inevitable, theerfore, that others will improve on the itineraries I have suggested. I venture to hope that that improvement will come soon.